BRONX HEROES IN TRUMPLAND

COVER CREDITS
Concept & Layout Pencils
Tom Sciacca
Pencil Finishes & Inks
Ray Felix

INTERIOR CREDITS
Pencils
Tom Ahearn
Ray Felix
Tom Sciacca
Guest Artists
Chris Duckett (p. 87)
Barry Southworth (p. 107)
Chris Pepo (p. 110)
Cover Lettering "Trumpland"
Dan Nakrosis
Interior Lettering
Ray Felix
Color Layouts on *Bronx Heroes in Trumpland*
Ken Cotrona (pp. 52–65)
John Riddle (pp. 43–50)
Dan Nakrosis (pp. 91–95)
Colors and Color Finishes
Ray Felix (pp. 1–99, 102, 110–111)
Writer
Ray Felix
Plot
Tom Sciacca

BRONX HEROES
IN TRUMPLAND

Ray Felix, Tom Sciacca & Tom Ahearn

ARSENAL PULP PRESS
VANCOUVER

ARSENAL PULP PRESS
Suite 202—211 East Georgia St.
Vancouver, BC V6A 1Z6
Canada
arsenalpulp.com

Arsenal Pulp Press acknowledges the xʷməθkʷəy̓əm (Musqueam), Sḵwx̱wú7mesh
(Squamish), and səl̓ilwətaʔɬ (Tsleil-Waututh) Nations, speakers of Hul'q'umi'num'/
Halq'eméylem/hən̓q̓əmin̓əm̓ and custodians of the traditional, ancestral, and unceded
territories where our office is located. We pay respect to their histories, traditions,
and continuous living cultures and commit to accountability, respectful relations,
and friendship.

Proofread by Alison Strobel

This is a work of fiction. Names, characters, businesses, places, events, locales, and
incidents are either the products of the authors' imagination or used in a fictitious manner.

Printed and bound in Canada

Library and Archives Canada Cataloguing in Publication

Title: Bronx heroes in Trumpland / Ray Felix, Tom Sciacca & Tom Ahern.
Names: Felix, Ray, 1973– author. | Sciacca, Tom, 1954– author.
Identifiers: Canadiana (print) 20190222727 | Canadiana (ebook) 20190222735 | ISBN
9781551528052 (softcover) | ISBN 9781551528069 (HTML)
Subjects: LCSH: Trump, Donald, 1946-—Comic books, strips, etc. | LCGFT: Comics
(Graphic works) | LCGFT: Superhero comics.
Classification: LCC PN6727.F45 B76 2020 | DDC 741.5/973—dc23

Dedicated to George Pérez, Jack Kirby, Steve Ditko,
Stan Lee, Neal Adams, Rich Buckler, Will Eisner, Irwin Hasen,
Wally Wood, Howard Chaykin, Walt Simonson, Jim Steranko,
Sal and John Buscema, Joe Sinnott and Vince Colletta,
without their inspiring work we would not be here today!

CONTENTS

SATIRE IS SO NOT DEAD

Humor is subjective. Something that we find funny might simply not be funny to you, and that's okay, because—interestingly enough—we are all allowed to have our own (informed) opinions, be they about humor, comic books or politics, which is good, because this book just so happens to be about all three. There are those of us who passionately believe that the person currently squatting inside the Oval Office is the clown prince of chaos, a monstrous infestation intent on corrupting our political landscape for his own personal profit and destroying our fragile democratic process.

Yet there are somehow those who seem to believe that this individual has been anointed by G-d to be our imperial ruler—needless to say, those folks are both wrong *and* stupid, but you know, whatever. (Remember what I said earlier about having an *informed* opinion.)

Well, if you've gotten this far in the foreword for this book, you either agree with the satirical premise—that trump is both a scourge on our country as well as an evil clown—or you are still (somehow) of the (mistaken) belief that this Mob-connected, crooked real estate developer, multiple business failure, serial spousal cheater, sexual predator and bully, who has repeatedly admitted on camera to breaking the law, and who has on numerous occasions since assuming the office of president violated the Constitution, is our best president ever. All y'all who think the latter probably need your collective heads examined. (Yeah, we know you disagree, but again, only informed opinions actually matter.)

You can call us libtards, snowflakes or whatever your favorite slur-of-the-week is, but know this: trump's presidency isn't funny anymore.

Sure, sure, for those of us growing up in and around NYC during the 1980s and '90s, trump was a clown of epic proportions—popping up on Howard Stern's radio show and claiming that dating during the '70s was his "Vietnam" (arrogantly diminishing the struggle and sacrifice of those who fought over there, especially considering his five deferments for fake bone spurs). Yes, yes, it was funny when he would call up the various newspapers pretending to be his own publicist (making no attempt to disguise his voice) and endlessly extol the brilliance and flamboyant ways of his "boss."

Yeah, you're a fuckin' laugh riot, you ignorant POS.

You know what was really funny? When you announced your candidacy for president. That's right, when you came down that gleaming escalator, telling us that Mexicans were drug-dealing rapists—that was hilarious. It was also funny when you mocked a disabled journalist and when you (wink wink, nudge nudge) encouraged your raving acolytes to lynch journalists (the supposed enemy of the people and reporters of fake news), shoot immigrants and punch liberals and Democrats. But you know what was the funniest part of your run for the White House? The time you told everyone that you were a serial sexual predator with your infamous "Grab them by the p***y" announcement into an open mic.

Good times.

But you know when it stopped being funny ha-ha? On November 9, 2016. That's when it all went to shit.

That was when we all discovered that having a reality show host become the president of the United States perhaps wasn't the smartest thing that we as a country could have ever done. Yeah, we know you said the government should be run like a business, but last we heard, most of your businesses had been run into the ground, costing everyone around you (except you, oddly enough) everything they had.

But we knew all that (or, at the very least, we should have). We knew you and your businesses had been sued some 4,000 times—dating back to the 1970s, with at least 1,300 trump-related lawsuits since 2000 alone. We knew about the fake university, the blowhard antics, the macho posturing, the faux Mob boss persona. It was funny when the late-night talk show hosts bashed you about your inability to close an umbrella, the piece of toilet paper stuck to your shoe, your many twitter-eroes (Twitter typos, trademark pending), Melania slapping your hand away—oh, that was cute *and* funny—and your admission to giving military intelligence to the Russians. That was hilarious when you cozied up to Putin and Kim Jong-un and the tin-pot dictators in the Philippines and Venezuela. Then we read Michael Wolff's book and Chris Christie's book and Bob Woodward's book, and learned that you not only clearly had absolutely no idea how government worked but also never intended to win and were simply running for office in order to renegotiate your deal with NBC for a bigger salary. Yes, we knew all these things, and you know what? It was funny. Well, it was funny 'til it wasn't. And then it really wasn't very funny at all.

It also wasn't funny to see you bash President Obama, calling into question his faith, his birthplace, his patriotism, his ability to lead and every single aspect of his presidency, then turn around and demand that we all "take a knee" and idolize everything that you do. You, the son of a Klan member, don't get to dis the first Black president of the U.S. in racist, white supremacist code phrases while attempting to dismantle his every achievement.

You know what else isn't funny? You, pretending to be president. Want to know why? Because you are so obviously interested not so much in governing as you are in ruling. Only that's simply not the way our democracy works.

The three branches of our government are meant to be equal. You are not CEO, king or emperor. You are supposed to be the president. You and your gop lackeys aren't our leaders so much as you have been elected to be our servants. You were elected (well, not you. You were put into place by Putin and his flunkies) to serve the will of the people, and yes, we know that many (if not most) of the folks who did actually vote for you are just as racist, ill-informed and deranged as you are—but that's not funny either.

The U.S. is not your plaything, so the gop stacking the courts with lifetime appointments of racist, anti-LGBTQ, fake Christian judges is not only not funny, it is wicked-bad as hell. Yes, we know that there are those who believe that the U.S. should be run more like a business, but you see, that is a really bad idea. Government's job is to protect its citizens, whereas business's job is to turn a profit. Cutting programs that feed the elderly, care for the poor and help the needy because they cost money with no clear return on investment is not how you run a country.

This is *our* country, not your private bank. You are here to serve *us*, not the other way around. Your job is to make *our* lives better, not yours.

We see you, and we know who you are. You are a lying, cheating con man who has surrounded himself with other lying, cheating con men. And the thing that is (sort of) funny is that you think you're getting away with it, you think you're untouchable. You aren't. We are coming for you.

We know what is fun, and what is funny, and although it is fun mocking you, you are not funny, which—of course—makes mocking you all the more delicious. And that is the point of this book—to mock you for the fool you are and to remind the world what a total and complete jackass, absolute horrible president and complete disgrace of a human you are. We hope you will soon be impeached, discarded and consigned to the dustbin of history, while the forward-thinking and progressive elements will raise and advance this country's spirit.

Finally (because I need to talk about the book itself), *Bronx Heroes in Trumpland* is brought to you courtesy of the outstanding talents and amazing persistence of both Ray Felix and Tom Sciacca. Ray is the publisher of Bronx Heroes Comics and once took both Marvel and DC to court over the use of the word "superhero" and won. Tom is a former assistant art director at DC Comics, as well as the publisher and editor-in-chief of Astral Comics. We'd also like to thank the fine folks at Arsenal Pulp Press, who agreed that, yes, not only are we funny, but you, Mr Not-Our-President, are fully deserving of our ire and disrespect, and endless mockery. Lastly, your trumpiness, we'd call you a tool, but tools work.

Robert J. Sodaro | October 31, 2019

Robert ("Bob") J. Sodaro is a proud Democrat who served for a decade as the deputy registrar of voters in his hometown. He is also a storyteller who has been writing professionally for more than thirty years. He's written everything from radio ad copy to marketing and promotional material to technical and training manuals. He has worked as a journalist, and yes, he's also written comic books.

BLACK POWER: THE PEOPLE'S HERO

The idea behind the superhero Black Power came from the civil rights movement of the 1950s and '60s and, later, the Black Power movement of the 1960s and '70s. More so, I was influenced by the life of Muhammad Ali, a pivotal figure who inadvertently started a movement simply by giving his honest opinion: "No Viet Cong ever called me a nigger." This statement sparked anti-war protests and condemned racial discrimination in America.

From the 1950s through the late 1980s, America experienced a second civil war, in which human rights united people of all backgrounds to the same rallying call for justice and equality for all. Eventually, this movement expanded beyond the United States, to other colonial governments around the globe.

Some would say that the Cold War was an unofficial World War III, but few ever called it that because the enemy were the working class and the poor—it was a war of the people versus empire. The Cultural Revolution in China and the rise of Communism in Eastern Europe lit a match that ignited countries like Cuba, Bolivia, Vietnam and Africa to fight for their freedom against their white oppressors: the British, the French and the Americans. Colonies around the globe were crumbling, and the right to self-government began to take root and grow in the minds of everyday people.

Political war games led the Afghans to go to war from 1979 to 1989 to oust the Russians, and later form the Taliban. In the United States, several militias and revolutionary groups emerged after the assassinations of John F. Kennedy, Malcolm X, Martin Luther King Jr. and Robert F. Kennedy in the 1960s. People were losing faith and trust in their government, a sense of disillusionment that culminated in the Watergate scandal.

So when Tom Sciacca approached me about doing a crossover comic about fighting Donald Trump with his character Astron Star Soldier, I thought: *Of course!*

Trump is the new Richard Nixon. The title *Bronx Heroes in Trumpland* was conceived as a play on *Alice in Wonderland*—Trump took the American people down the rabbit hole when he ran for president and then shocked everyone by winning the election. It was a sad day in the United States that many people compared to the 9/11 attacks. That's pretty fucking horrible.

With Trump as our leader, our world as we knew it became a never-ending episode of *The Twilight Zone*, with parallels being drawn between the Kent State shootings in 1970 and the killing of Heather Heyer at the Charlottesville alt-right rally in 2017. History is repeating itself as America enters its third civil war—a race war. Yet there is only one human race. Skin color does not divide us on a genetic level but on an economic one. At its core, inequality is the source of the problems in America.

Wake up, stay woke.

Ray Felix | November 4, 2019

WHEN PARODY IS ALL WE HAVE

On June 16, 2015, everything changed. As it did on September 11, 2001, life as we knew it would never be the same. But unlike 9/11, this would be a slow, agonizing road to disaster. On that fateful day, Donald J. Trump—real estate magnate, television personality and media blowhard—famously rode down the escalator at Trump Tower in New York City, accompanied by his wife, Melania, and announced his candidacy for the presidency of the United States before an enthusiastic crowd of supporters, some of whom were paid actors (I know one of them). And thus began Trump's campaign of hate and divisiveness, vilifying Mexicans, Muslims and immigrants alike, to the incongruous cheers of his supporters.

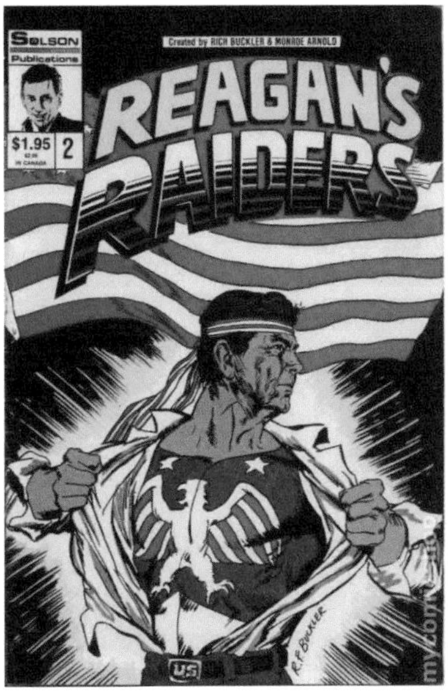
SOLSON
Publications
Created by RICH BUCKLER & MONROE ARNOLD
$1.95
2
REAGAN'S
RAIDERS
US

Of course, those of us who were New Yorkers had seen this many times before. As a self-absorbed business leader, Trump had a legacy of making one outrageous pronouncement after another, whether it was a call for the execution of the Central Park Five or his own plan, never completed, to rebuild the World Trade Center.

So naturally, after a few weeks of his bluster, we all expected Trump's presidential campaign to fizzle out and die a natural death.

It did not.

Instead, Trump ramped up his campaign of inflammatory rhetoric as his popularity rose in the polls and then the primaries, ultimately wiping out his Republican opponents one by one until he snared the Republican nomination.

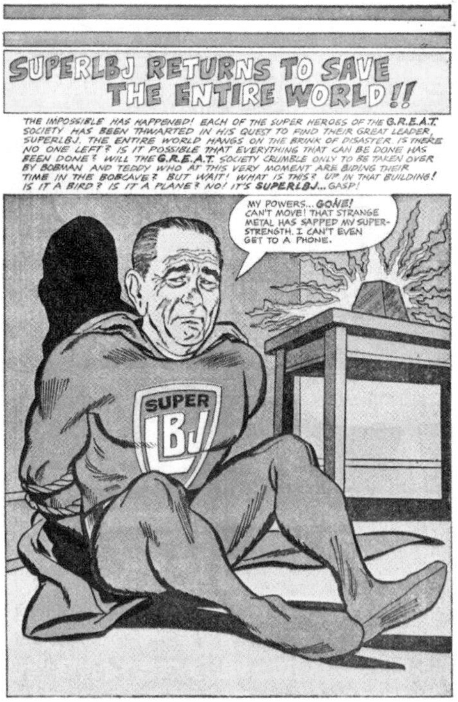
SUPERLBJ RETURNS TO SAVE THE ENTIRE WORLD!!
THE IMPOSSIBLE HAS HAPPENED! EACH OF THE SUPER HEROES OF THE G.R.E.A.T. SOCIETY HAS BEEN THWARTED IN HIS QUEST TO FIND THEIR GREAT LEADER, SUPERLBJ. THE ENTIRE WORLD HANGS ON THE BRINK OF DISASTER. IS THERE NO ONE LEFT? IS IT POSSIBLE THAT EVERYTHING THAT CAN BE DONE HAS BEEN DONE? WILL THE G.R.E.A.T. SOCIETY CRUMBLE ONLY TO BE TAKEN OVER BY BOBMAN AND TEDDY WHO AT THIS VERY MOMENT ARE BIDING THEIR TIME IN THE BOBCAVE? BUT WAIT! WHAT IS THIS? UP IN THAT BUILDING! IS IT A BIRD? IS IT A PLANE? NO! IT'S SUPERLBJ...GASP!
MY POWERS...GONE! CAN'T MOVE! THAT STRANGE METAL HAS SAPPED MY SUPER-STRENGTH. I CAN'T EVEN GET TO A PHONE.
SUPER LBJ

We were still unconvinced, especially when his former mistresses came forward to denounce him, and then the infamous "Grab them by the p***y" comments to *Access Hollywood* were leaked. This was conduct unbecoming of a presidential candidate, let alone a president.

But then, to the shock of the nation, and against all odds, on November 9, 2016, Donald Trump was elected president over the presumptive winner, Hillary Clinton (though his win was probably aided and abetted by Vladimir Putin and a few other shady characters).

But let me digress.

Back in October 2015, when Trump announced his candidacy, he was still a source of amusement for me.

As I gazed at a blank sheet of paper, I wondered: *What would happen if Trump actually won?* Would he become a ruthless and power-hungry dictator of the world? Would he make Gotham City (aka New York) safe for billionaires by turning its inhabitants into robotic slaves? And what if the freedom fighters of the Bronx were the only ones left to fight him?

I started to sketch out a few pages and showed it to my partner, Ray Felix. We had a good laugh, and then promptly forgot about it, knowing that Trump's day in the sun would never come.

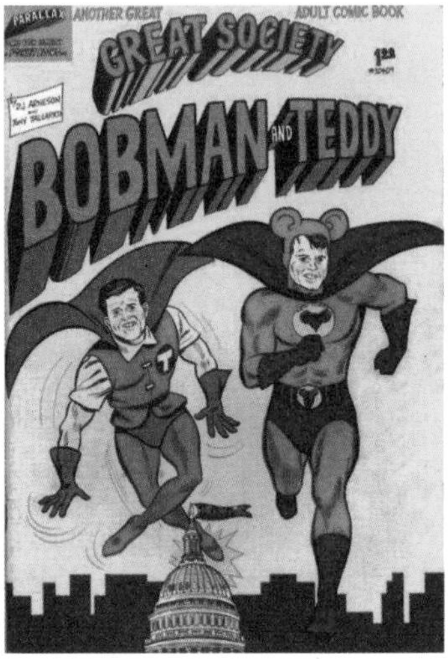
PARALLAX
ANOTHER GREAT
ADULT COMIC BOOK
GREAT SOCIETY
BOBMAN AND TEDDY

Wrong.

After the election, and after a few days to recover from the shock, Ray and I knew we had to bring our project to fruition. And thus began *Bronx Heroes in Trumpland*.

This is a parody. Just so you know. Parodies in comic book form were once all the rage in America, as featured in the late, lamented magazines *Mad*, *National Lampoon* and *Spy*. For some godforsaken reason, parody has all but vanished, save for television's *Saturday Night Live* and the magazines *Private Eye* in the U.K. and *Charlie Hebdo* in France. We wrote *Bronx Heroes in Trumpland* in the tradition of spoofs from days gone by. For me, it hearkens back

$1.95
1
REAGAN'S RAIDERS
THE ULTIMATE PATRIOTIC SUPER HEROES BOOK!!!
mycomicshop

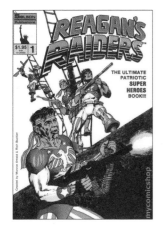

to 1966's political comic book spoof *The Great Society* and 1986's *Reagan's Raiders* by my late pals Rich Buckler and Monroe Arnold.

There was a time in the U.S. when parody was understood and appreciated. But now, we are living in a world where the political reality appears to be a parody of itself. When *The Great Society* was published, the president of the United States could be a subject of satire, but Lyndon B. Johnson was no monster or psycho; he had signed bills creating Medicare and the Civil Rights Act. We could make fun of him and other political figures, such as Ted and Robert Kennedy. We felt safe.

AND SO AS ANOTHER AVERAGE DAY IN THE WORK OF THE G.R.E.A.T. SOCIETY DRAWS TO A CLOSE, THE ENTIRE WORLD SLEEPS CONTENT AND SECURE IN THE KNOWLEDGE THAT IT IS SAFE FROM SUPERVILLAINS SO LONG AS OUR HERO, THE MAN WITH THE SUPERPOWERS, IS ON THE JOB!
BUT WHAT OF TOMORROW? IS THE THREAT OF BOBMAN AND TEDDY REALLY ENDED? WILL THEY CONTINUE THEIR SECRET PLANS TO TAKE OVER THE G.R.E.A.T. SOCIETY. AND WHAT OF THE MANY SUPERVILLAINS IN THE WORLD? WATCH FOR THE NEXT EXCITING ADVENTURE OF SUPERLBJ IN THE SECOND G.R.E.A.T. SOCIETY COMIC BOOK! COMING SOON!

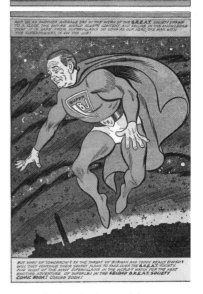

Then, in 1968, Martin Luther King Jr. was assassinated in Memphis, followed a few months later by Robert Kennedy's murder in a Los Angeles hotel. Our dreams, it appeared, were dead.

Then Nixon was elected. The Vietnam War continued. Then Watergate happened. The idealism of the sixties was now long gone, and we found ourselves in the midst of an American nightmare.

PARALLAX
THE GREAT SOCIETY
COMIC BOOK
SALE PRICE
WHY....THAT, THAT COULD BE A GREAT SOCIETY!
BY D.J. ARNESON AND TONY TALLARICO

And still it continued, through Reagan, George H.W. Bush and Desert Storm, 9/11, the Iraq War and the final descent into hell: Donald J. Trump.

As I write this, the spectacle of Trump's presidency is still playing out. How will it end? Will hope triumph over evil?

In the end, what do we have left but parody?

Tom Sciacca | October 1, 2019

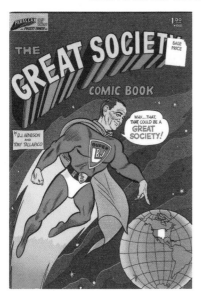

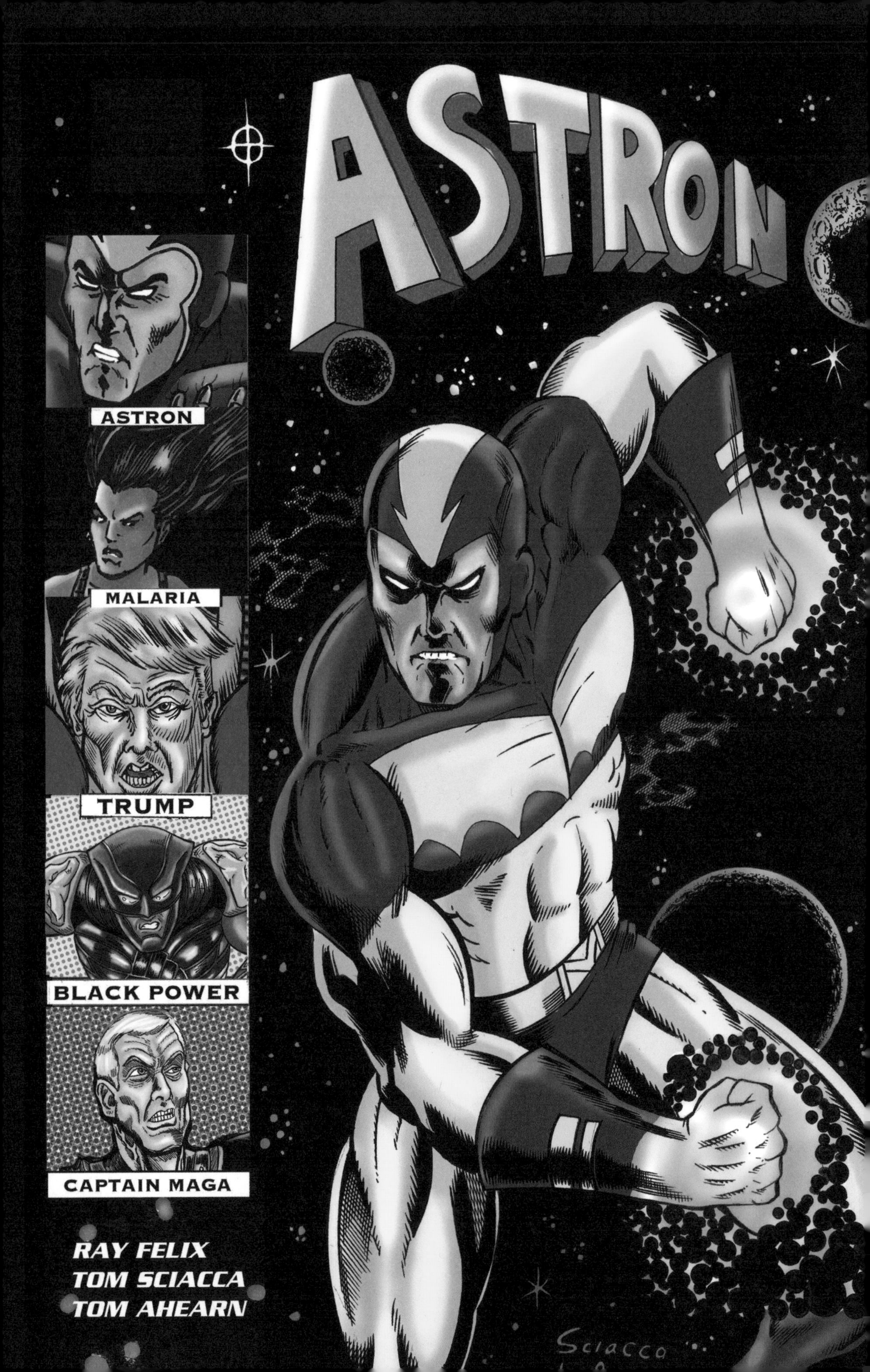
ASTRON
ASTRON
MALARIA
TRUMP
BLACK POWER
CAPTAIN MAGA
RAY FELIX
TOM SCIACCA
TOM AHEARN
Sciacco

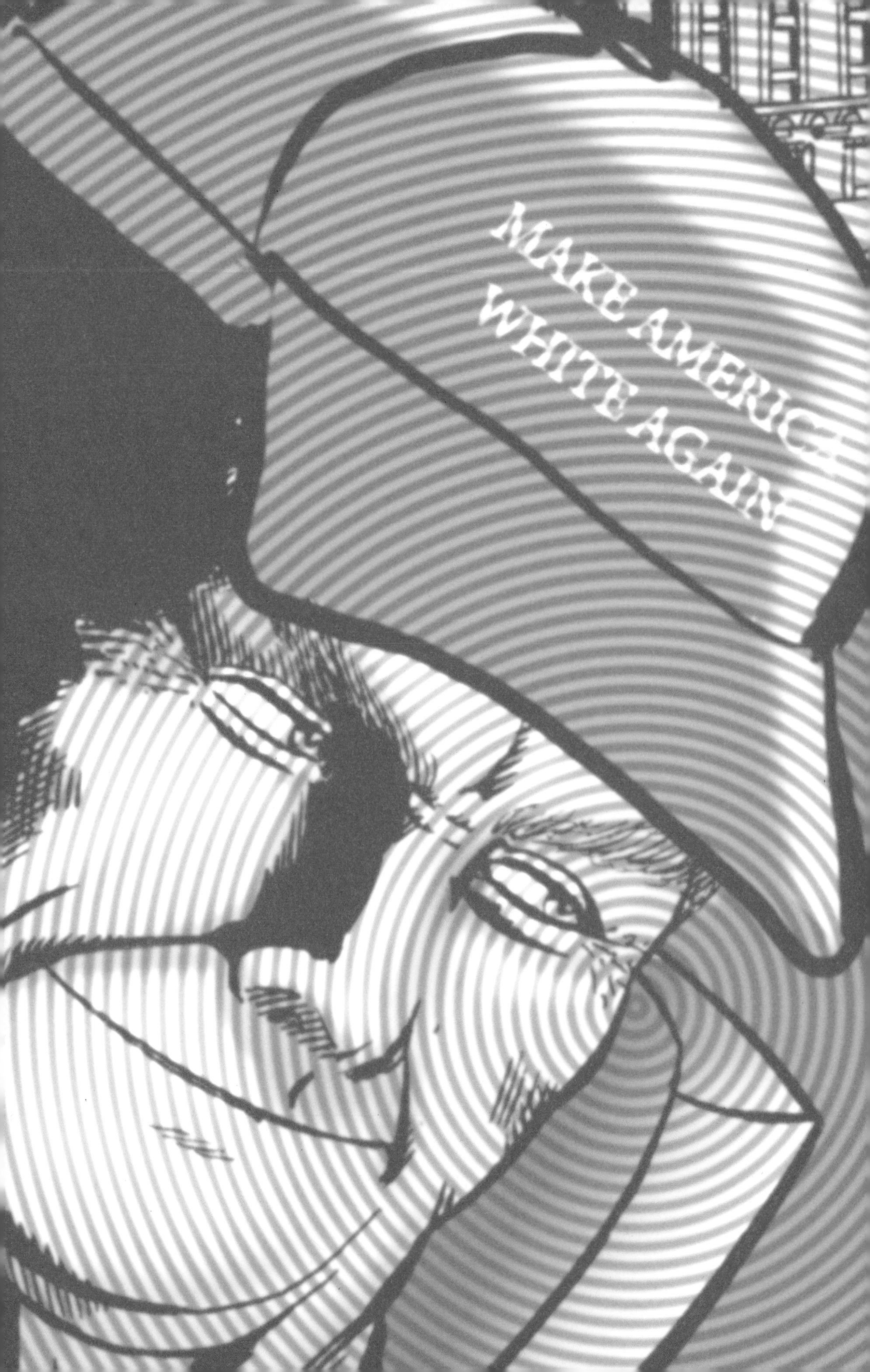
MAKE AMERICA
WHITE AGAIN

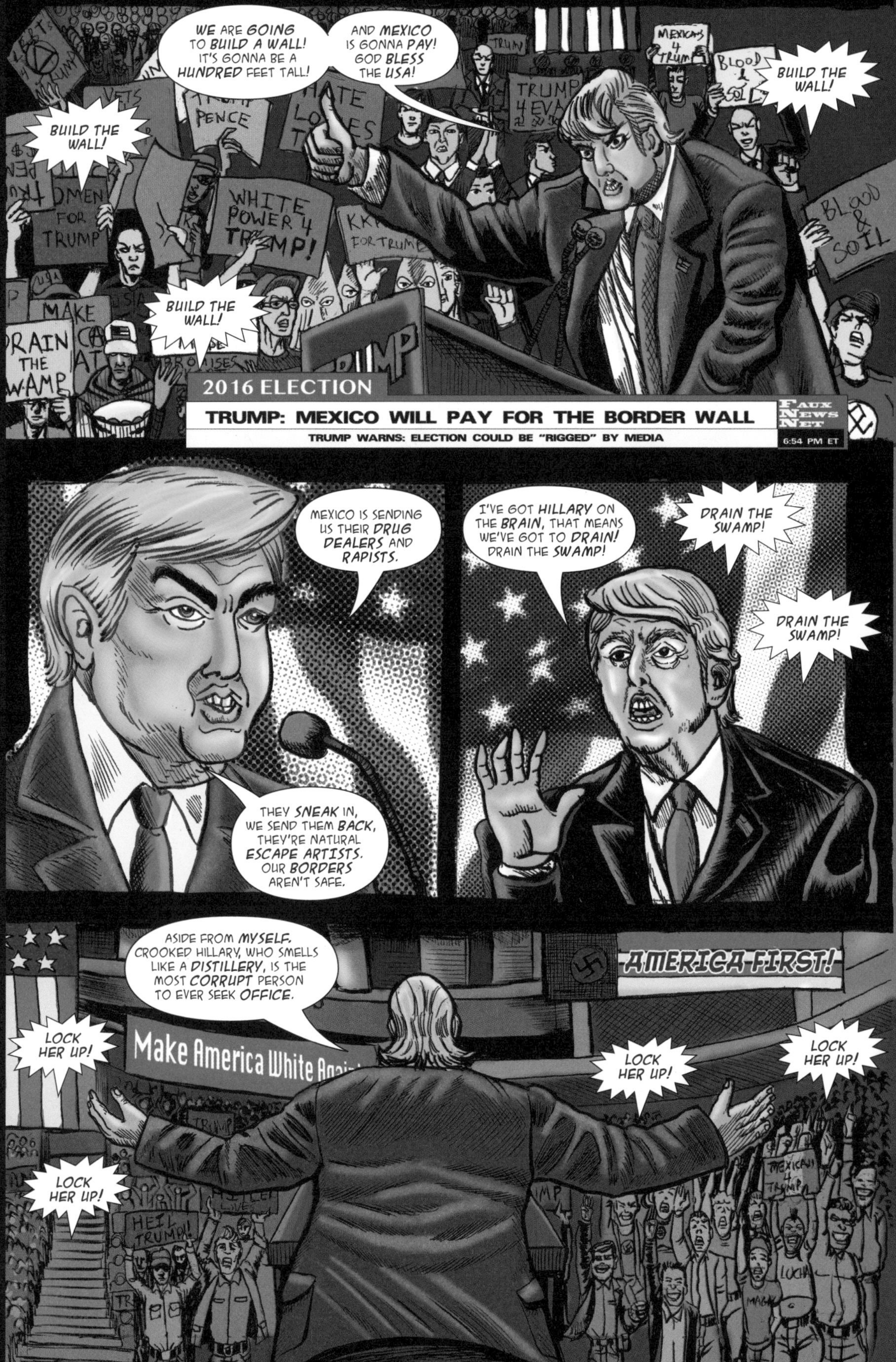
WE ARE GOING TO BUILD A WALL! IT'S GONNA BE A HUNDRED FEET TALL!
AND MEXICO IS GONNA PAY! GOD BLESS THE USA!
BUILD THE WALL!
BUILD THE WALL!
BUILD THE WALL!
2016 ELECTION
TRUMP: MEXICO WILL PAY FOR THE BORDER WALL
TRUMP WARNS: ELECTION COULD BE "RIGGED" BY MEDIA
FAUX NEWS NET
6:54 PM ET
MEXICO IS SENDING US THEIR DRUG DEALERS AND RAPISTS.
THEY SNEAK IN, WE SEND THEM BACK, THEY'RE NATURAL ESCAPE ARTISTS. OUR BORDERS AREN'T SAFE.
I'VE GOT HILLARY ON THE BRAIN, THAT MEANS WE'VE GOT TO DRAIN! DRAIN THE SWAMP!
DRAIN THE SWAMP!
DRAIN THE SWAMP!
ASIDE FROM MYSELF, CROOKED HILLARY, WHO SMELLS LIKE A DISTILLERY, IS THE MOST CORRUPT PERSON TO EVER SEEK OFFICE.
AMERICA FIRST!
Make America White Again
LOCK HER UP!
LOCK HER UP!
LOCK HER UP!
LOCK HER UP!

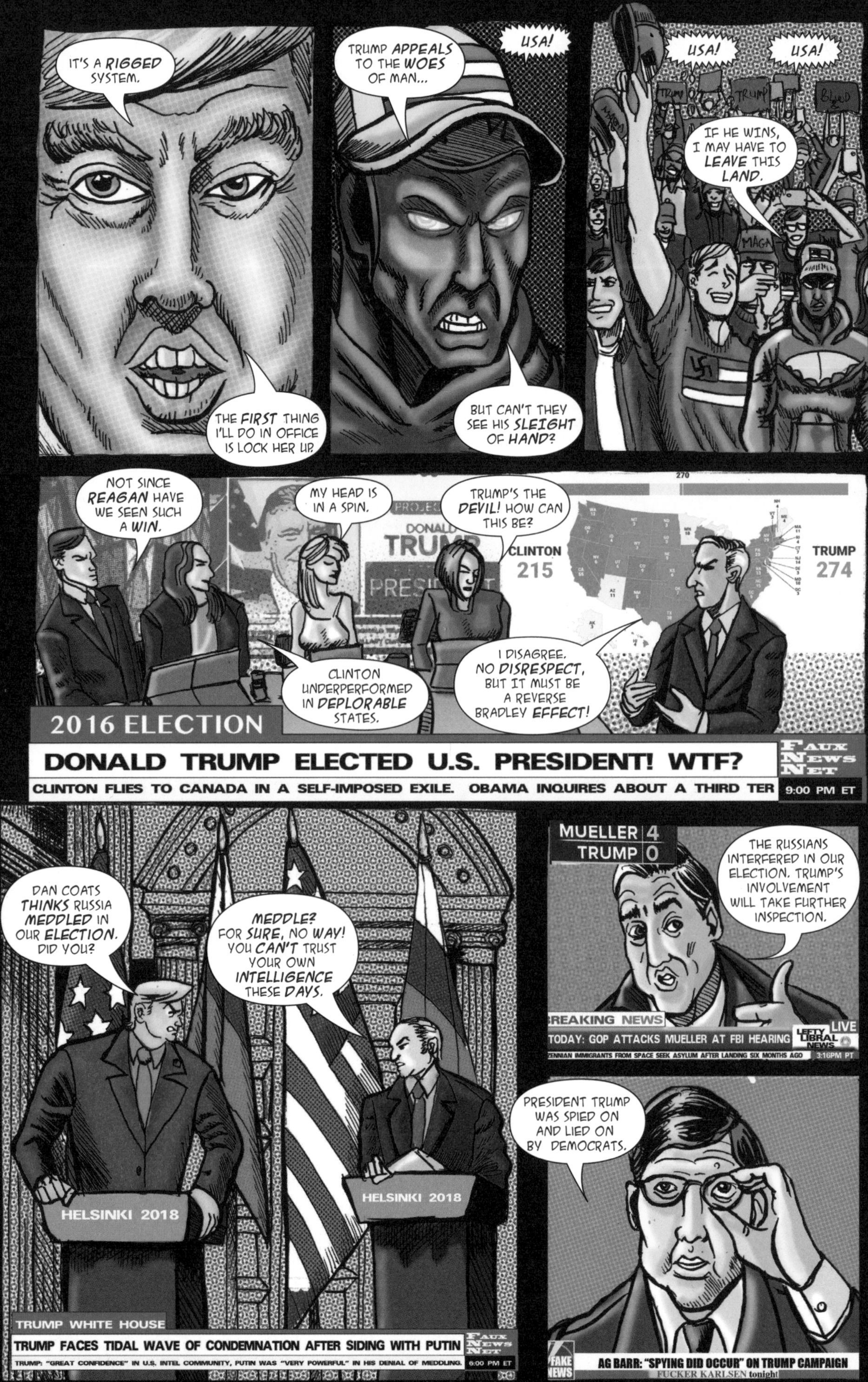
IT'S A RIGGED SYSTEM.
THE FIRST THING I'LL DO IN OFFICE IS LOCK HER UP.
TRUMP APPEALS TO THE WOES OF MAN...
USA!
BUT CAN'T THEY SEE HIS SLEIGHT OF HAND?
USA!
USA!
TRUMP
TRUMP
MAGA
IF HE WINS, I MAY HAVE TO LEAVE THIS LAND.
MAGA
270
NOT SINCE REAGAN HAVE WE SEEN SUCH A WIN.
MY HEAD IS IN A SPIN.
TRUMP'S THE DEVIL! HOW CAN THIS BE?
DONALD TRUMP
CLINTON 215
TRUMP 274
CLINTON UNDERPERFORMED IN DEPLORABLE STATES.
I DISAGREE. NO DISRESPECT, BUT IT MUST BE A REVERSE BRADLEY EFFECT!
2016 ELECTION
DONALD TRUMP ELECTED U.S. PRESIDENT! WTF?
FAUX NEWS NET
CLINTON FLIES TO CANADA IN A SELF-IMPOSED EXILE. OBAMA INQUIRES ABOUT A THIRD TER
9:00 PM ET
DAN COATS THINKS RUSSIA MEDDLED IN OUR ELECTION. DID YOU?
MEDDLE? FOR SURE, NO WAY! YOU CAN'T TRUST YOUR OWN INTELLIGENCE THESE DAYS.
HELSINKI 2018
HELSINKI 2018
TRUMP WHITE HOUSE
TRUMP FACES TIDAL WAVE OF CONDEMNATION AFTER SIDING WITH PUTIN
FAUX NEWS NET
TRUMP: "GREAT CONFIDENCE" IN U.S. INTEL COMMUNITY, PUTIN WAS "VERY POWERFUL" IN HIS DENIAL OF MEDDLING.
6:00 PM ET
MUELLER 4
TRUMP 0
THE RUSSIANS INTERFERED IN OUR ELECTION. TRUMP'S INVOLVEMENT WILL TAKE FURTHER INSPECTION.
BREAKING NEWS
TODAY: GOP ATTACKS MUELLER AT FBI HEARING
LEFTY LIBRAL NEWS
LIVE
ZENNIAN IMMIGRANTS FROM SPACE SEEK ASYLUM AFTER LANDING SIX MONTHS AGO
3:16PM PT
PRESIDENT TRUMP WAS SPIED ON AND LIED ON BY DEMOCRATS.
FAKE NEWS
AG BARR: "SPYING DID OCCUR" ON TRUMP CAMPAIGN
FUCKER KARLSEN tonight

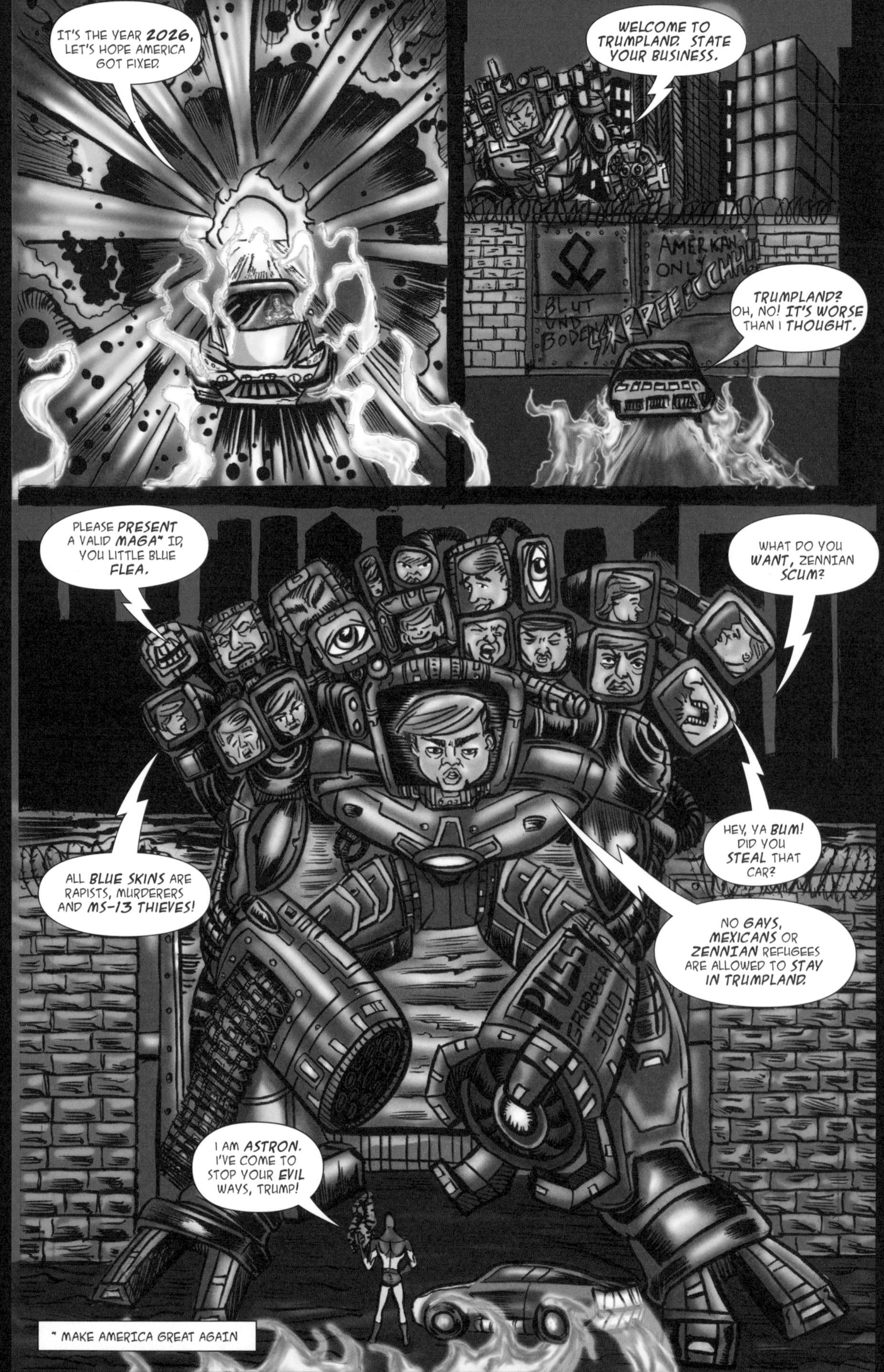
IT'S THE YEAR 2026, LET'S HOPE AMERICA GOT FIXED.
WELCOME TO TRUMPLAND. STATE YOUR BUSINESS.
AMERKAN ONLY
BLUT UND BODEN
SKRREEECCHH!
TRUMPLAND? OH, NO! IT'S WORSE THAN I THOUGHT.
PLEASE PRESENT A VALID MAGA* ID, YOU LITTLE BLUE FLEA.
WHAT DO YOU WANT, ZENNIAN SCUM?
HEY, YA BUM! DID YOU STEAL THAT CAR?
ALL BLUE SKINS ARE RAPISTS, MURDERERS AND MS-13 THIEVES!
NO GAYS, MEXICANS OR ZENNIAN REFUGEES ARE ALLOWED TO STAY IN TRUMPLAND.
I AM ASTRON. I'VE COME TO STOP YOUR EVIL WAYS, TRUMP!
* MAKE AMERICA GREAT AGAIN

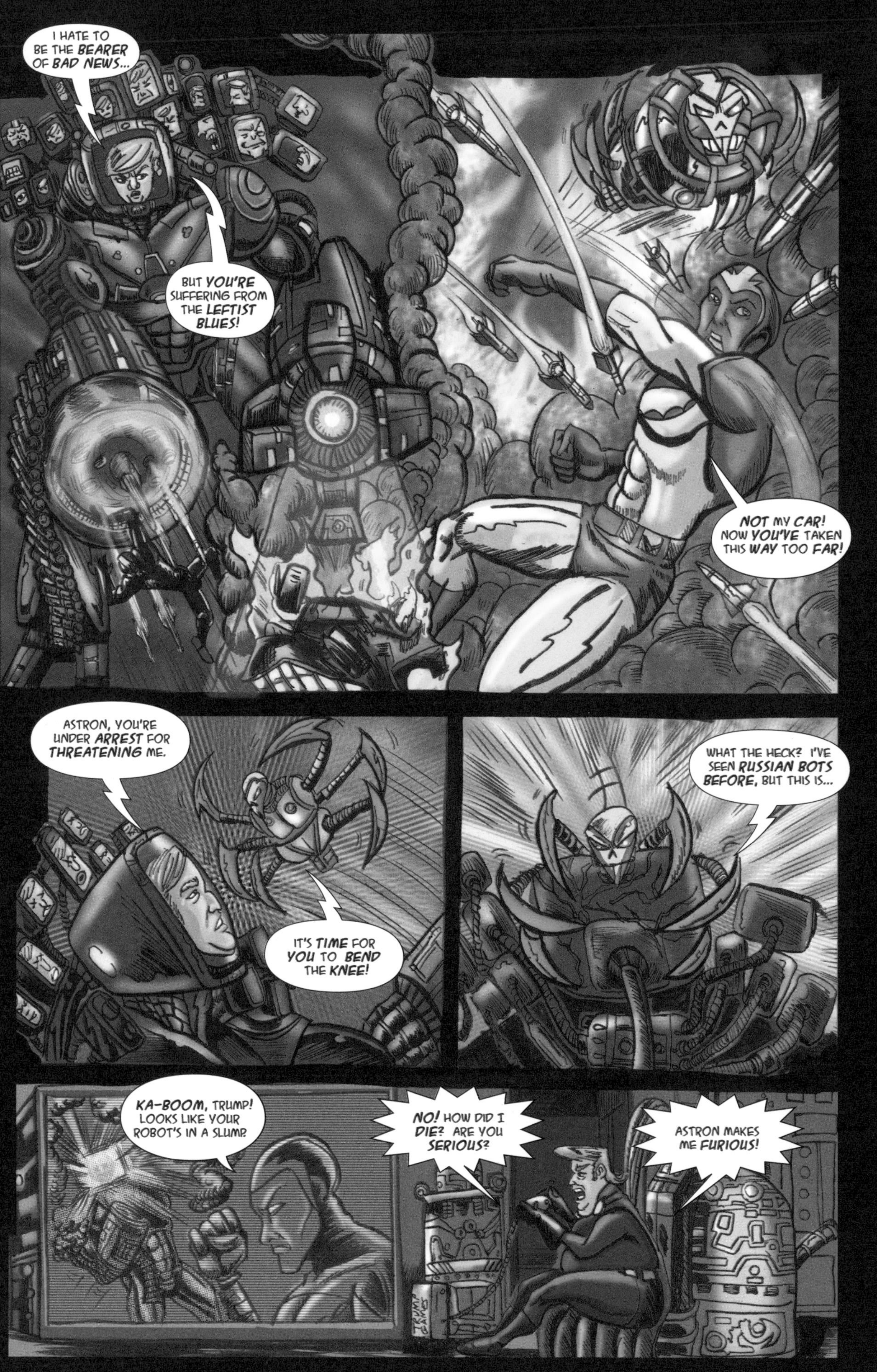
I HATE TO BE THE BEARER OF BAD NEWS...
BUT YOU'RE SUFFERING FROM THE LEFTIST BLUES!
NOT MY CAR! NOW YOU'VE TAKEN THIS WAY TOO FAR!
ASTRON, YOU'RE UNDER ARREST FOR THREATENING ME.
IT'S TIME FOR YOU TO BEND THE KNEE!
WHAT THE HECK? I'VE SEEN RUSSIAN BOTS BEFORE, BUT THIS IS...
KA-BOOM, TRUMP! LOOKS LIKE YOUR ROBOT'S IN A SLUMP.
NO! HOW DID I DIE? ARE YOU SERIOUS?
ASTRON MAKES ME FURIOUS!
TRUMP GAMES

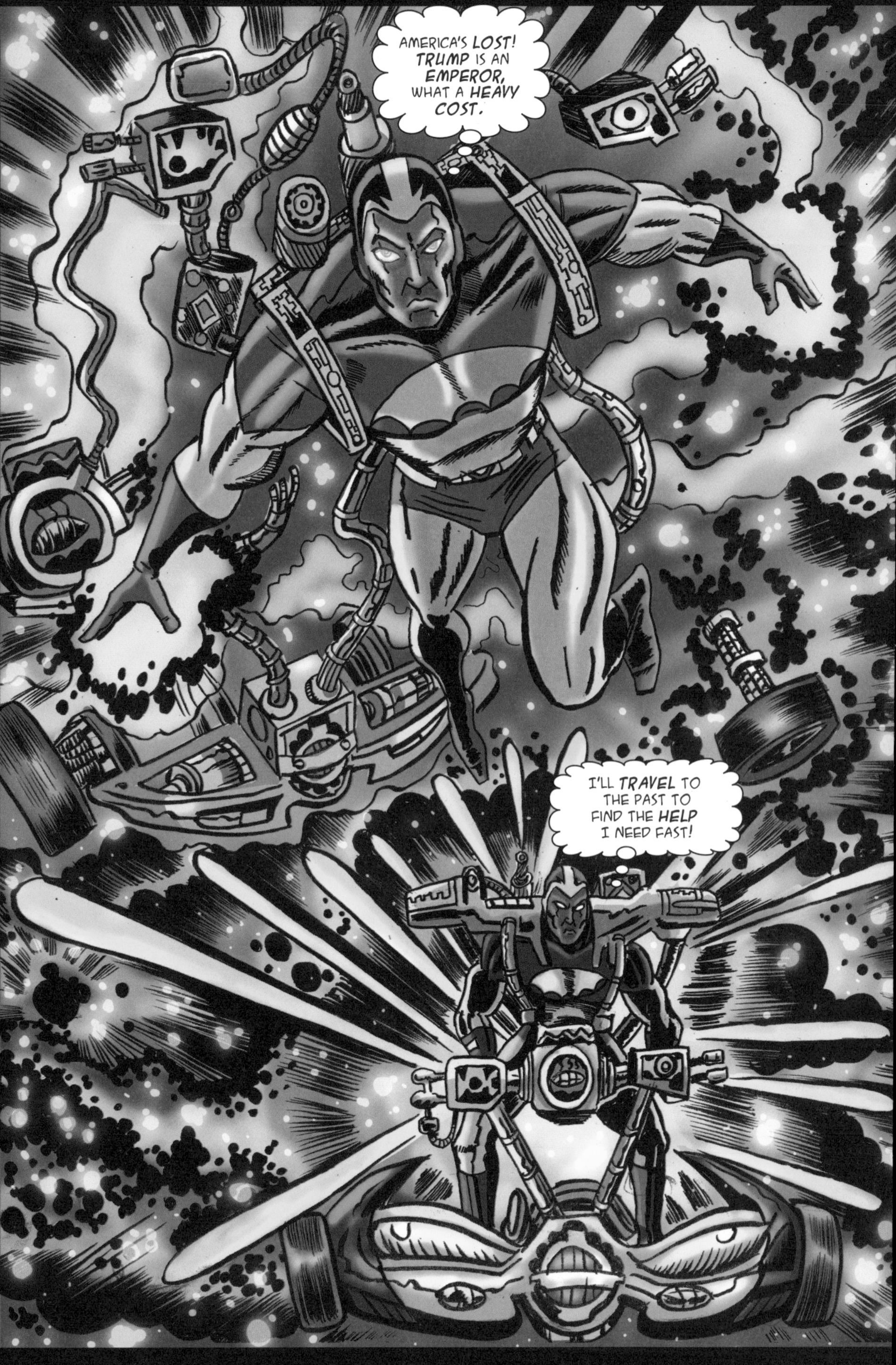
AMERICA'S LOST! TRUMP IS AN EMPEROR, WHAT A HEAVY COST.
I'LL TRAVEL TO THE PAST TO FIND THE HELP I NEED FAST!

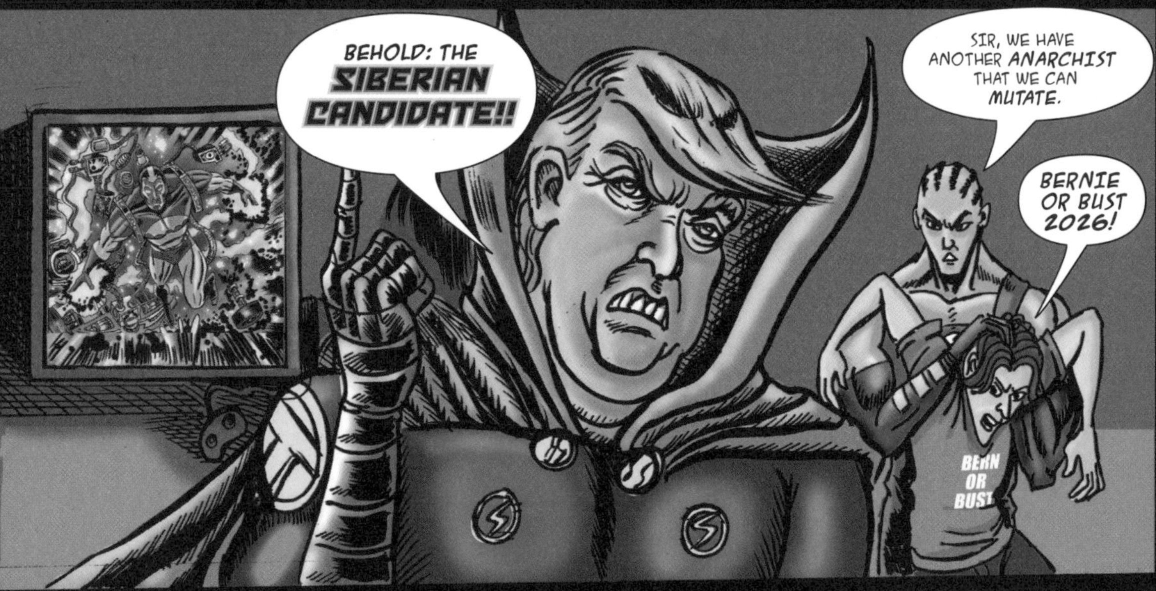
BEHOLD: THE SIBERIAN CANDIDATE!!
SIR, WE HAVE ANOTHER ANARCHIST THAT WE CAN MUTATE.
BERNIE OR BUST 2026!
BERN OR BUST

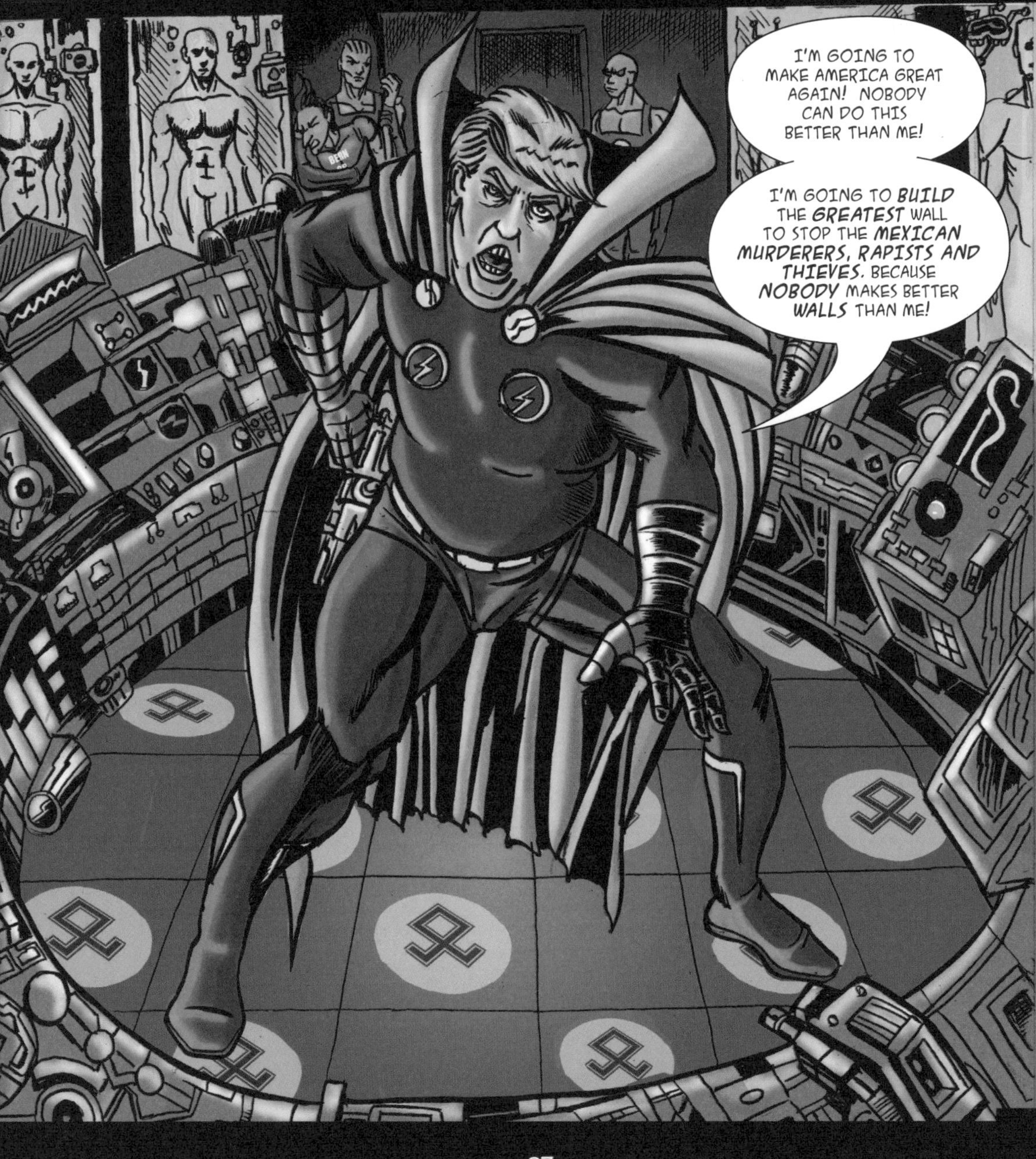
I'M GOING TO MAKE AMERICA GREAT AGAIN! NOBODY CAN DO THIS BETTER THAN ME!
I'M GOING TO BUILD THE GREATEST WALL TO STOP THE MEXICAN MURDERERS, RAPISTS AND THIEVES. BECAUSE NOBODY MAKES BETTER WALLS THAN ME!

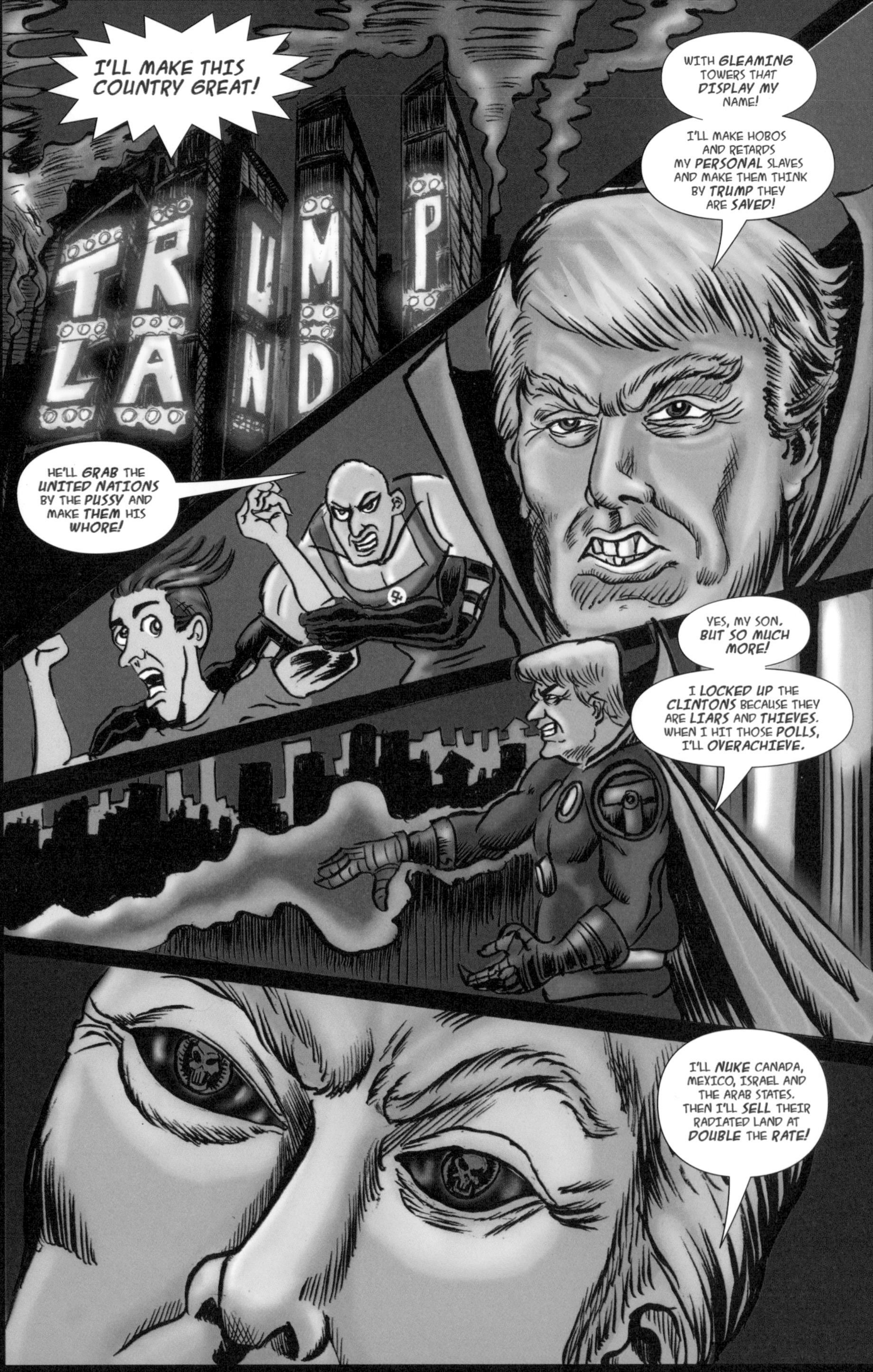
I'LL MAKE THIS COUNTRY GREAT!
WITH GLEAMING TOWERS THAT DISPLAY MY NAME!
I'LL MAKE HOBOS AND RETARDS MY PERSONAL SLAVES AND MAKE THEM THINK BY TRUMP THEY ARE SAVED!
TRUMP LAND
HE'LL GRAB THE UNITED NATIONS BY THE PUSSY AND MAKE THEM HIS WHORE!
YES, MY SON. BUT SO MUCH MORE!
I LOCKED UP THE CLINTONS BECAUSE THEY ARE LIARS AND THIEVES. WHEN I HIT THOSE POLLS, I'LL OVERACHIEVE.
I'LL NUKE CANADA, MEXICO, ISRAEL AND THE ARAB STATES. THEN I'LL SELL THEIR RADIATED LAND AT DOUBLE THE RATE!

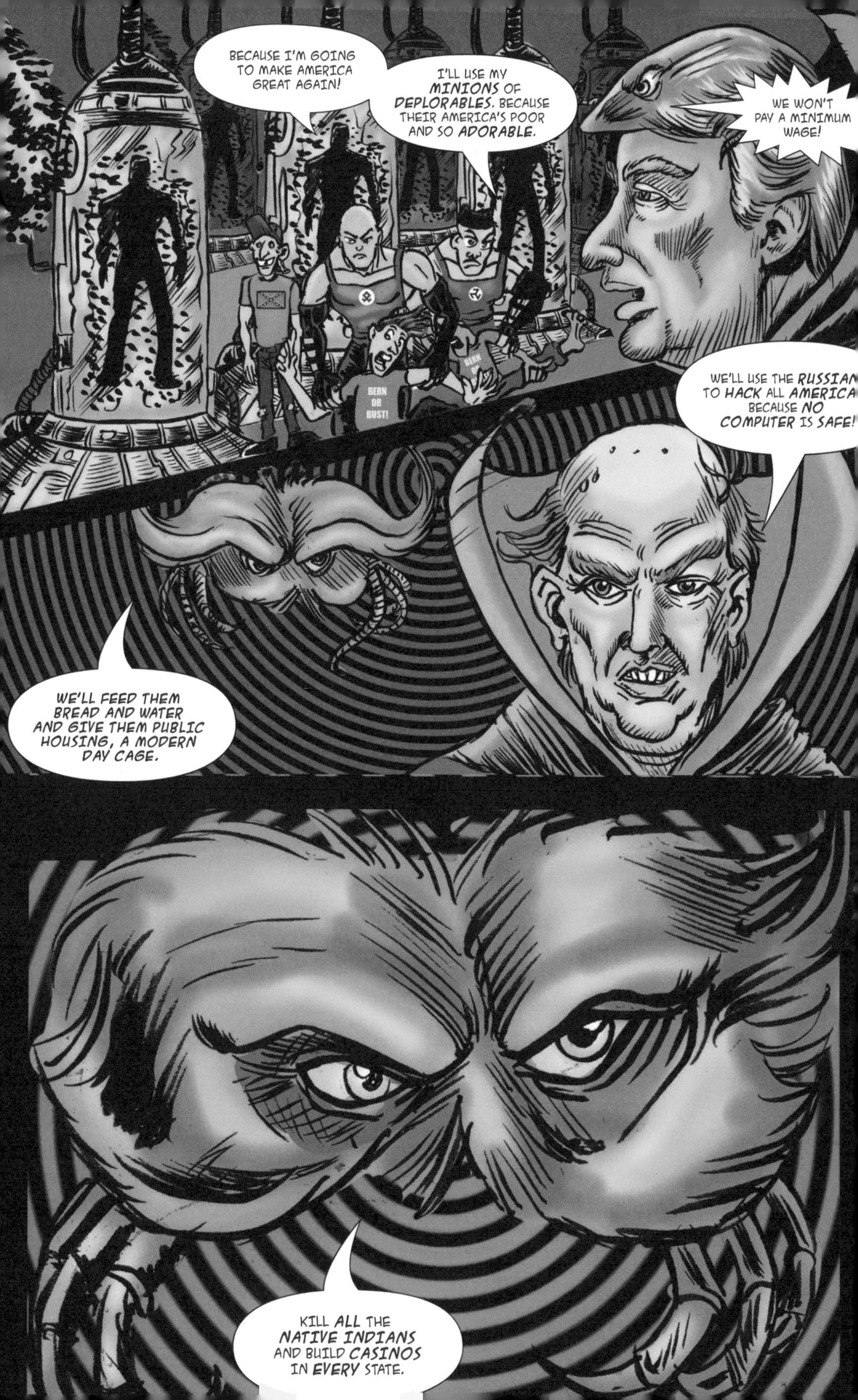
BECAUSE I'M GOING TO MAKE AMERICA GREAT AGAIN!
I'LL USE MY MINIONS OF DEPLORABLES. BECAUSE THEIR AMERICA'S POOR AND SO ADORABLE.
WE WON'T PAY A MINIMUM WAGE!
BERN OR BUST!
WE'LL USE THE RUSSIAN TO HACK ALL AMERICA BECAUSE NO COMPUTER IS SAFE!
WE'LL FEED THEM BREAD AND WATER AND GIVE THEM PUBLIC HOUSING, A MODERN DAY CAGE.
KILL ALL THE NATIVE INDIANS AND BUILD CASINOS IN EVERY STATE.

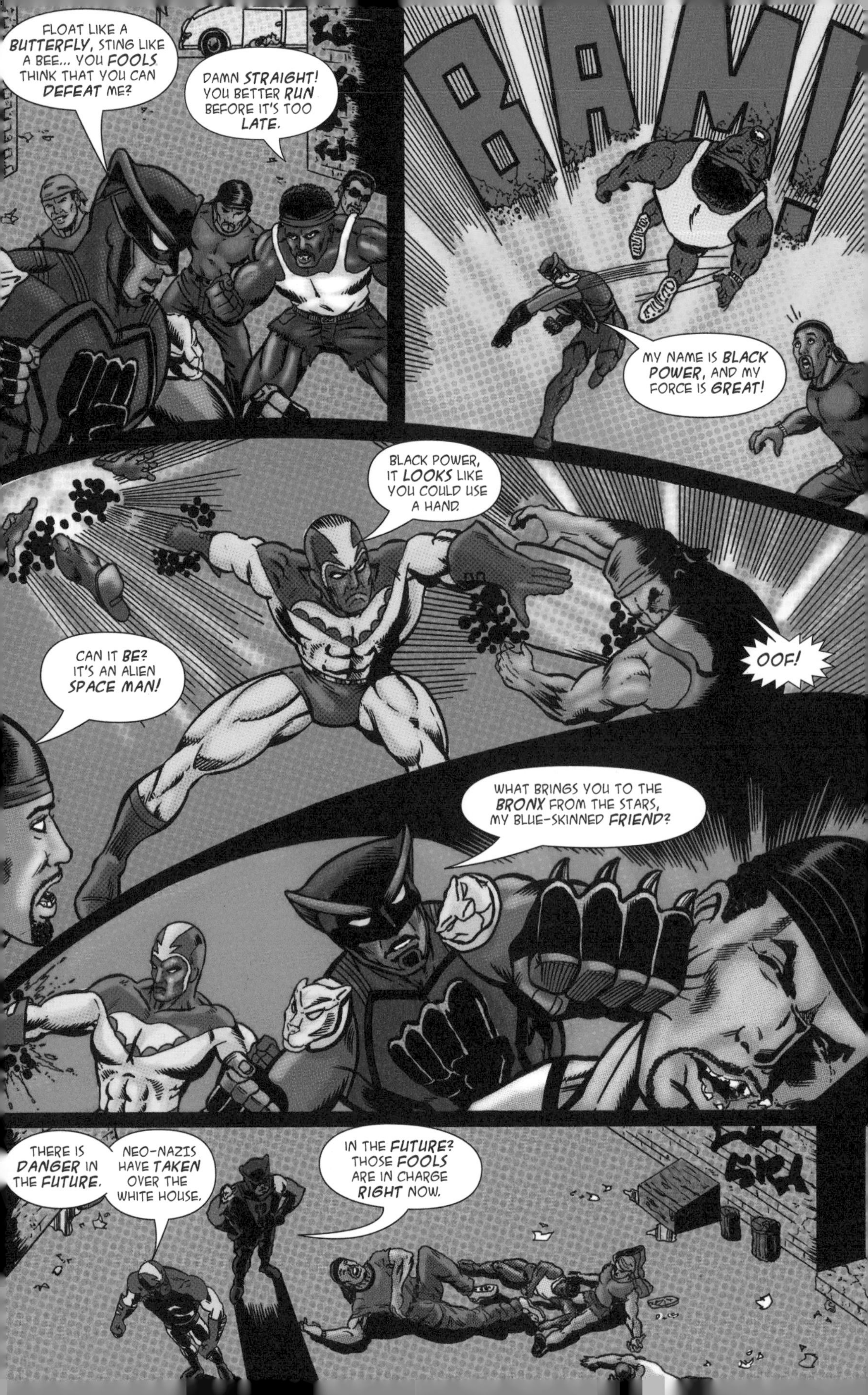

FLOAT LIKE A BUTTERFLY, STING LIKE A BEE... YOU FOOLS THINK THAT YOU CAN DEFEAT ME?
DAMN STRAIGHT! YOU BETTER RUN BEFORE IT'S TOO LATE.
BAM!
MY NAME IS BLACK POWER, AND MY FORCE IS GREAT!
BLACK POWER, IT LOOKS LIKE YOU COULD USE A HAND.
CAN IT BE? IT'S AN ALIEN SPACE MAN!
OOF!
WHAT BRINGS YOU TO THE BRONX FROM THE STARS, MY BLUE-SKINNED FRIEND?
THERE IS DANGER IN THE FUTURE.
NEO-NAZIS HAVE TAKEN OVER THE WHITE HOUSE.
IN THE FUTURE? THOSE FOOLS ARE IN CHARGE RIGHT NOW.

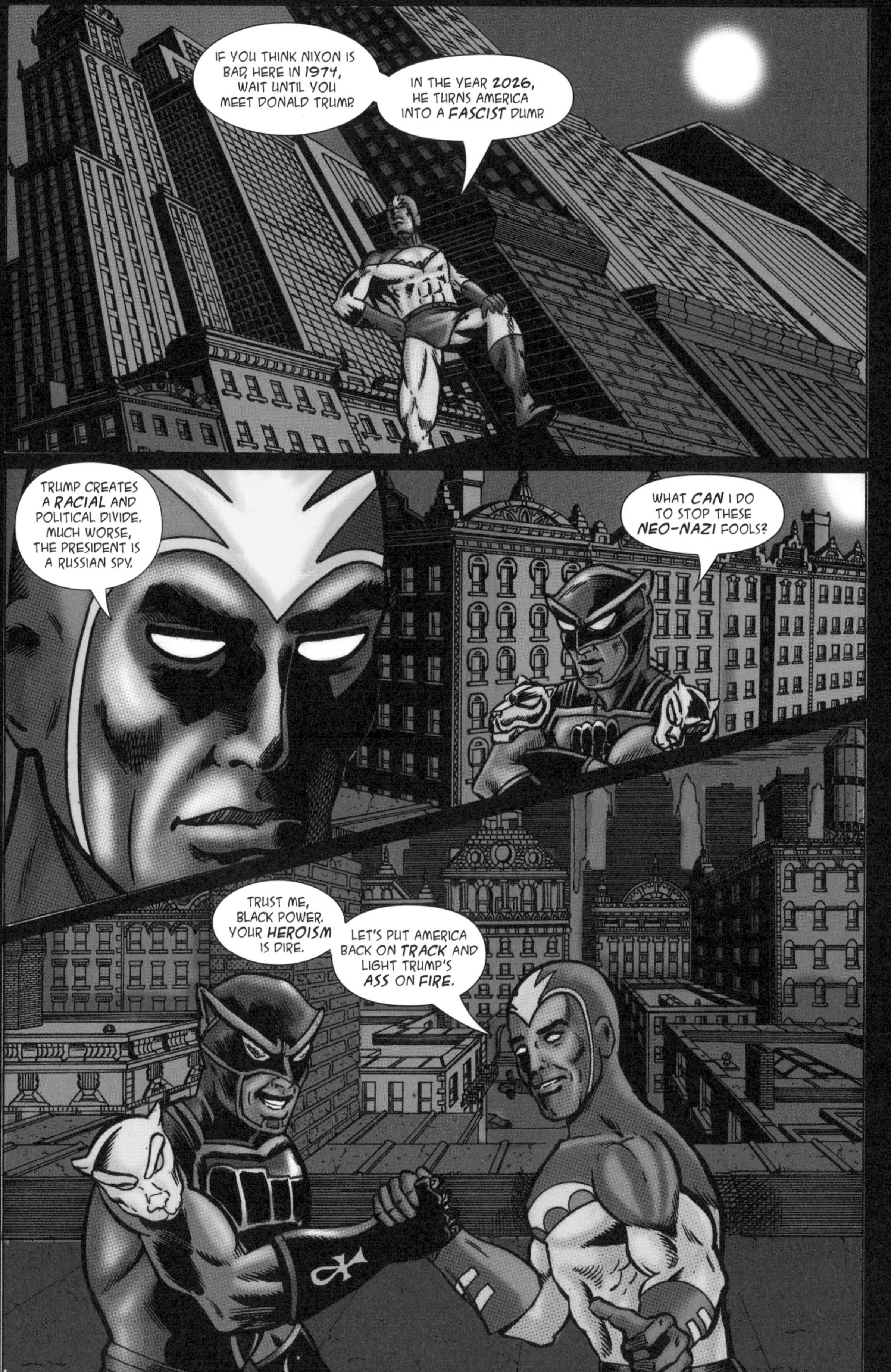
IF YOU THINK NIXON IS BAD, HERE IN 1974, WAIT UNTIL YOU MEET DONALD TRUMP.
IN THE YEAR 2026, HE TURNS AMERICA INTO A FASCIST DUMP.
TRUMP CREATES A RACIAL AND POLITICAL DIVIDE. MUCH WORSE, THE PRESIDENT IS A RUSSIAN SPY.
WHAT CAN I DO TO STOP THESE NEO-NAZI FOOLS?
TRUST ME, BLACK POWER. YOUR HEROISM IS DIRE.
LET'S PUT AMERICA BACK ON TRACK AND LIGHT TRUMP'S ASS ON FIRE.

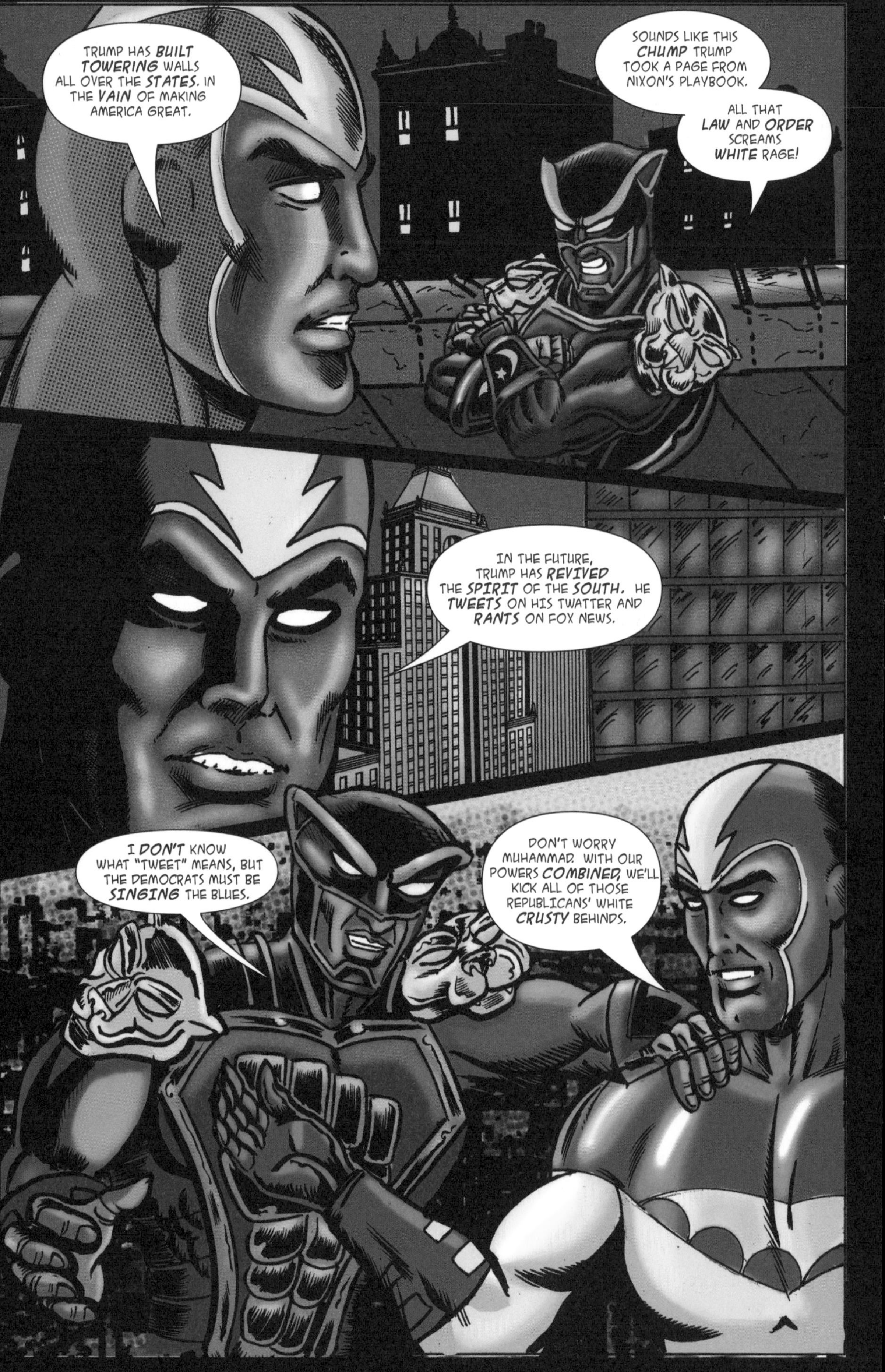
TRUMP HAS BUILT TOWERING WALLS ALL OVER THE STATES. IN THE VAIN OF MAKING AMERICA GREAT.
SOUNDS LIKE THIS CHUMP TRUMP TOOK A PAGE FROM NIXON'S PLAYBOOK.
ALL THAT LAW AND ORDER SCREAMS WHITE RAGE!
IN THE FUTURE, TRUMP HAS REVIVED THE SPIRIT OF THE SOUTH. HE TWEETS ON HIS TWATTER AND RANTS ON FOX NEWS.
I DON'T KNOW WHAT "TWEET" MEANS, BUT THE DEMOCRATS MUST BE SINGING THE BLUES.
DON'T WORRY MUHAMMAD. WITH OUR POWERS COMBINED, WE'LL KICK ALL OF THOSE REPUBLICANS' WHITE CRUSTY BEHINDS.

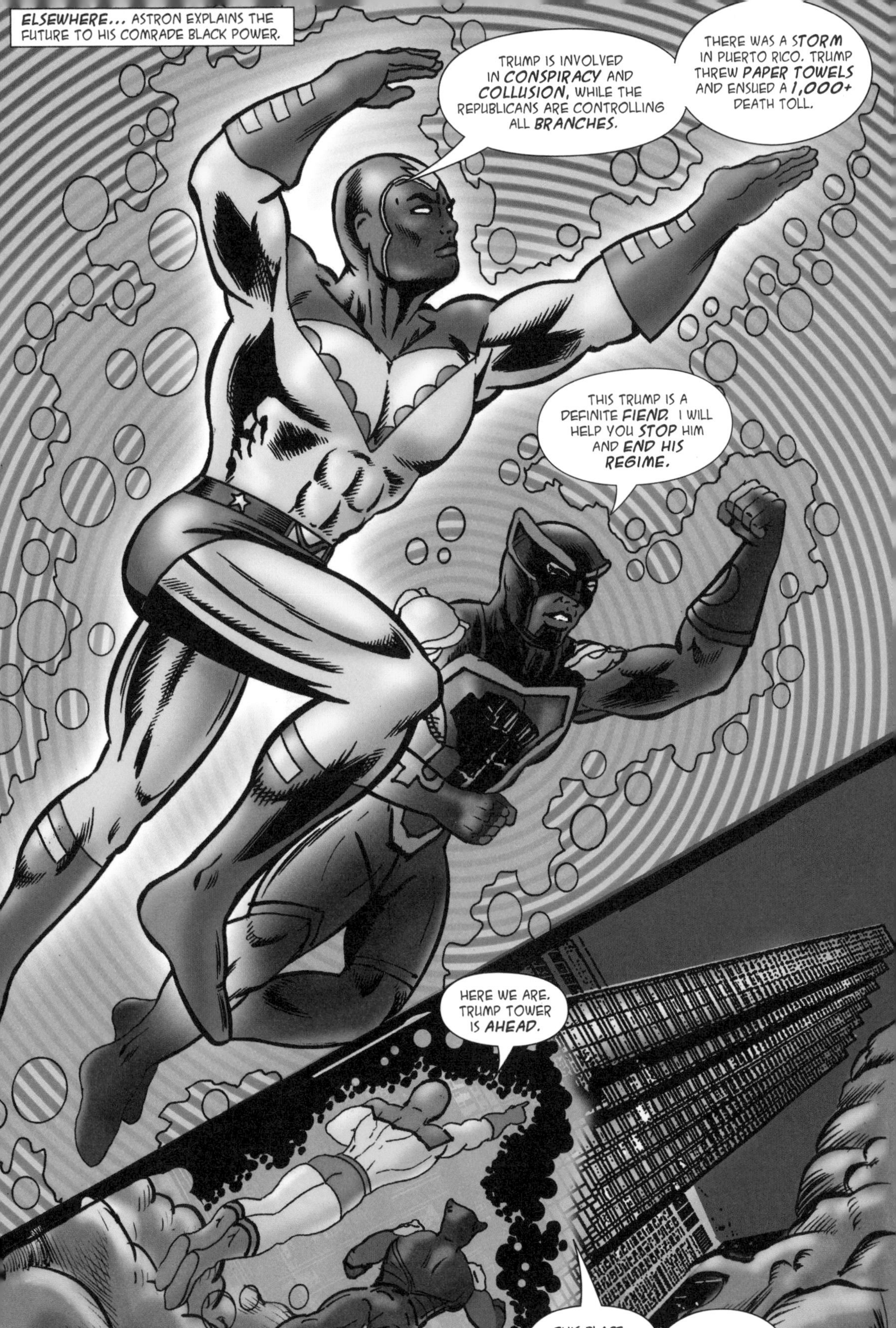
ELSEWHERE... ASTRON EXPLAINS THE FUTURE TO HIS COMRADE BLACK POWER.
TRUMP IS INVOLVED IN CONSPIRACY AND COLLUSION, WHILE THE REPUBLICANS ARE CONTROLLING ALL BRANCHES.
THERE WAS A STORM IN PUERTO RICO. TRUMP THREW PAPER TOWELS AND ENSUED A 1,000+ DEATH TOLL.
THIS TRUMP IS A DEFINITE FIEND. I WILL HELP YOU STOP HIM AND END HIS REGIME.
HERE WE ARE. TRUMP TOWER IS AHEAD.
THIS PLACE LOOKS CREEPY! I FEEL A SENSE OF DREAD.
LET'S GO KNOCK THAT MOP OFF HIS HEAD.

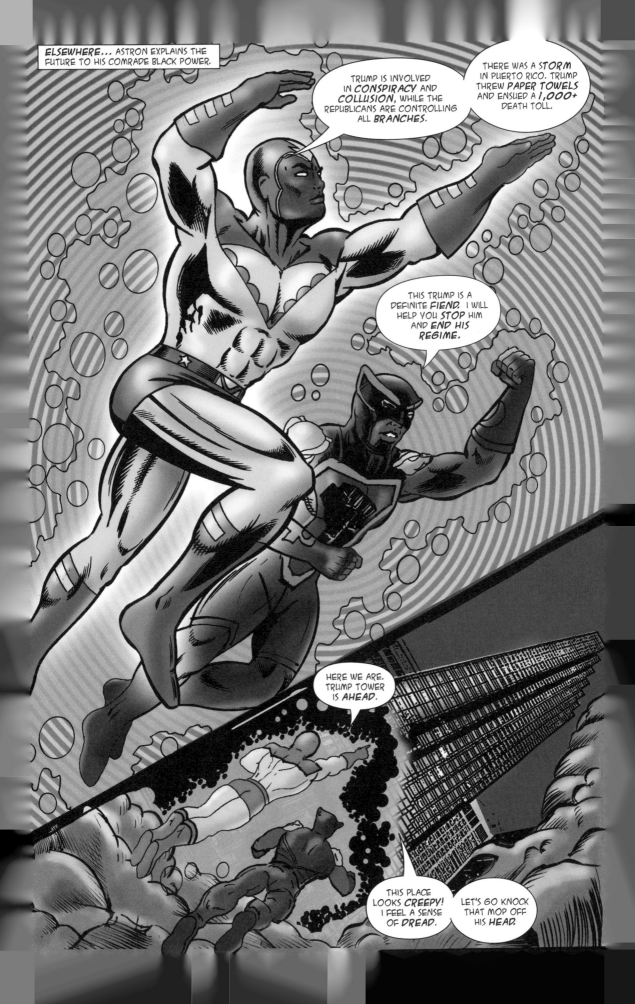

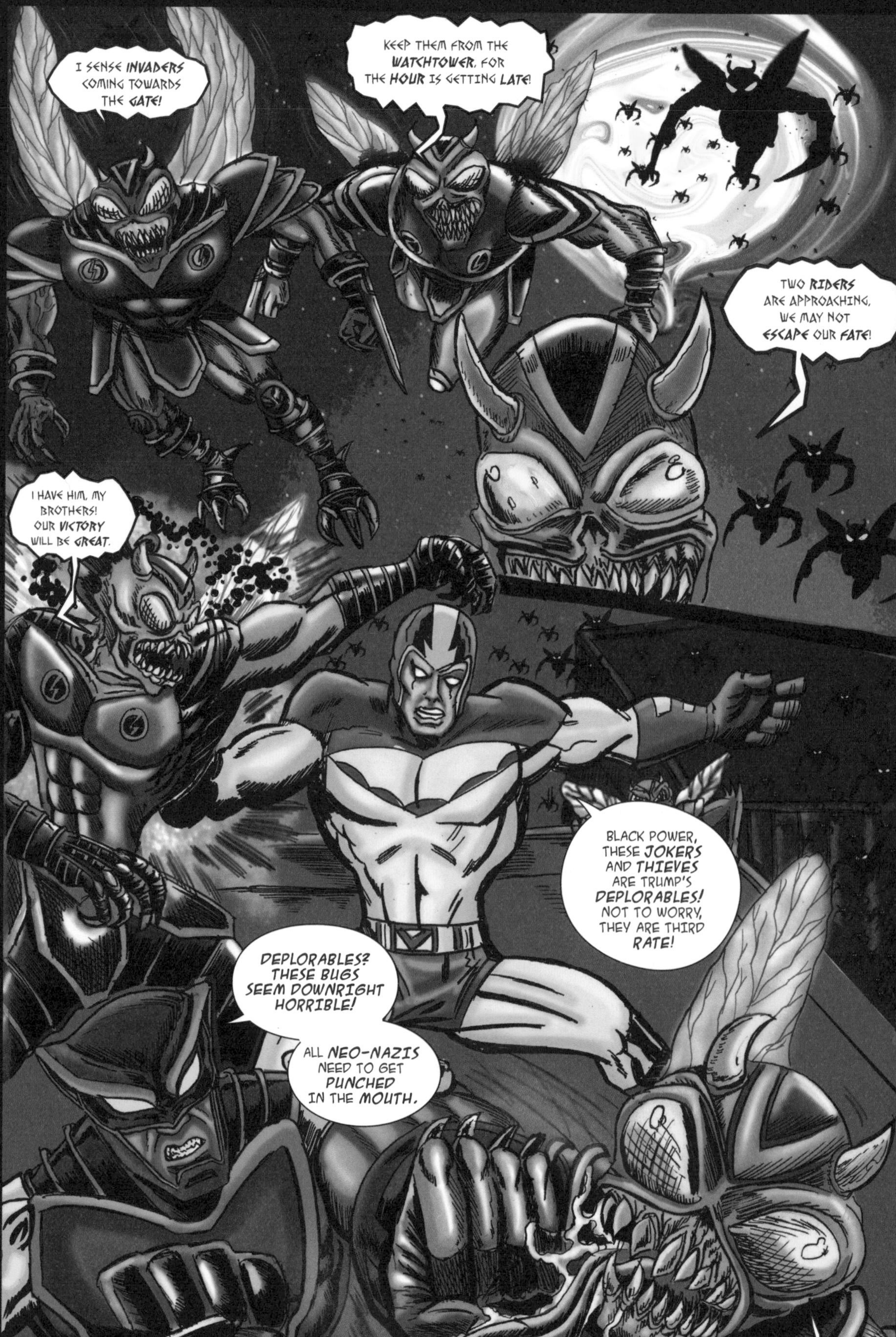
I SENSE INVADERS COMING TOWARDS THE GATE!
KEEP THEM FROM THE WATCHTOWER, FOR THE HOUR IS GETTING LATE!
TWO RIDERS ARE APPROACHING, WE MAY NOT ESCAPE OUR FATE!
I HAVE HIM, MY BROTHERS! OUR VICTORY WILL BE GREAT.
BLACK POWER, THESE JOKERS AND THIEVES ARE TRUMP'S DEPLORABLES! NOT TO WORRY, THEY ARE THIRD RATE!
DEPLORABLES? THESE BUGS SEEM DOWNRIGHT HORRIBLE!
ALL NEO-NAZIS NEED TO GET PUNCHED IN THE MOUTH.
LONG LIVE THE SOUTH!

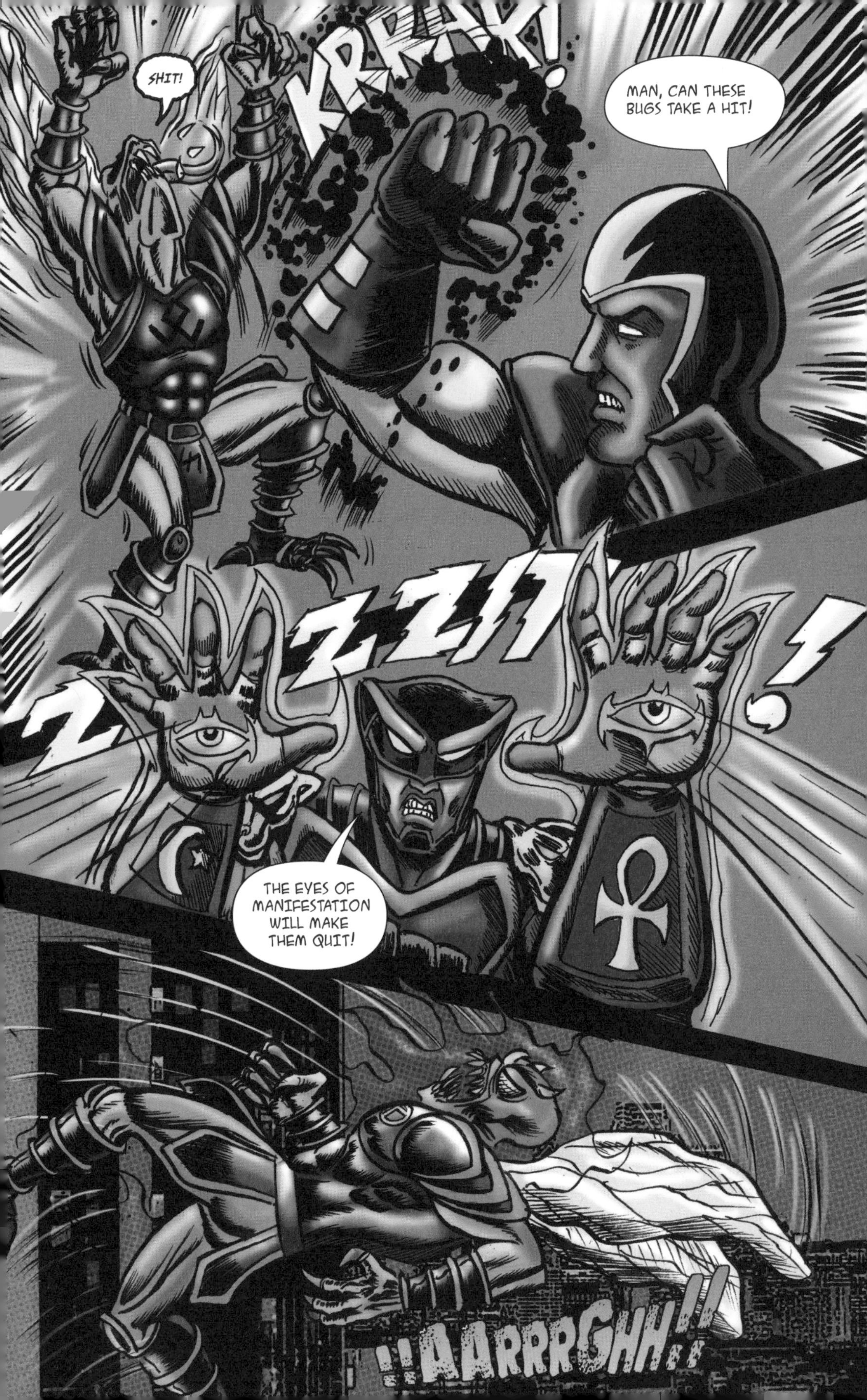
SHIT!
KRRAK!
MAN, CAN THESE BUGS TAKE A HIT!
ZZZZT!
THE EYES OF MANIFESTATION WILL MAKE THEM QUIT!
AARRRGHH!!

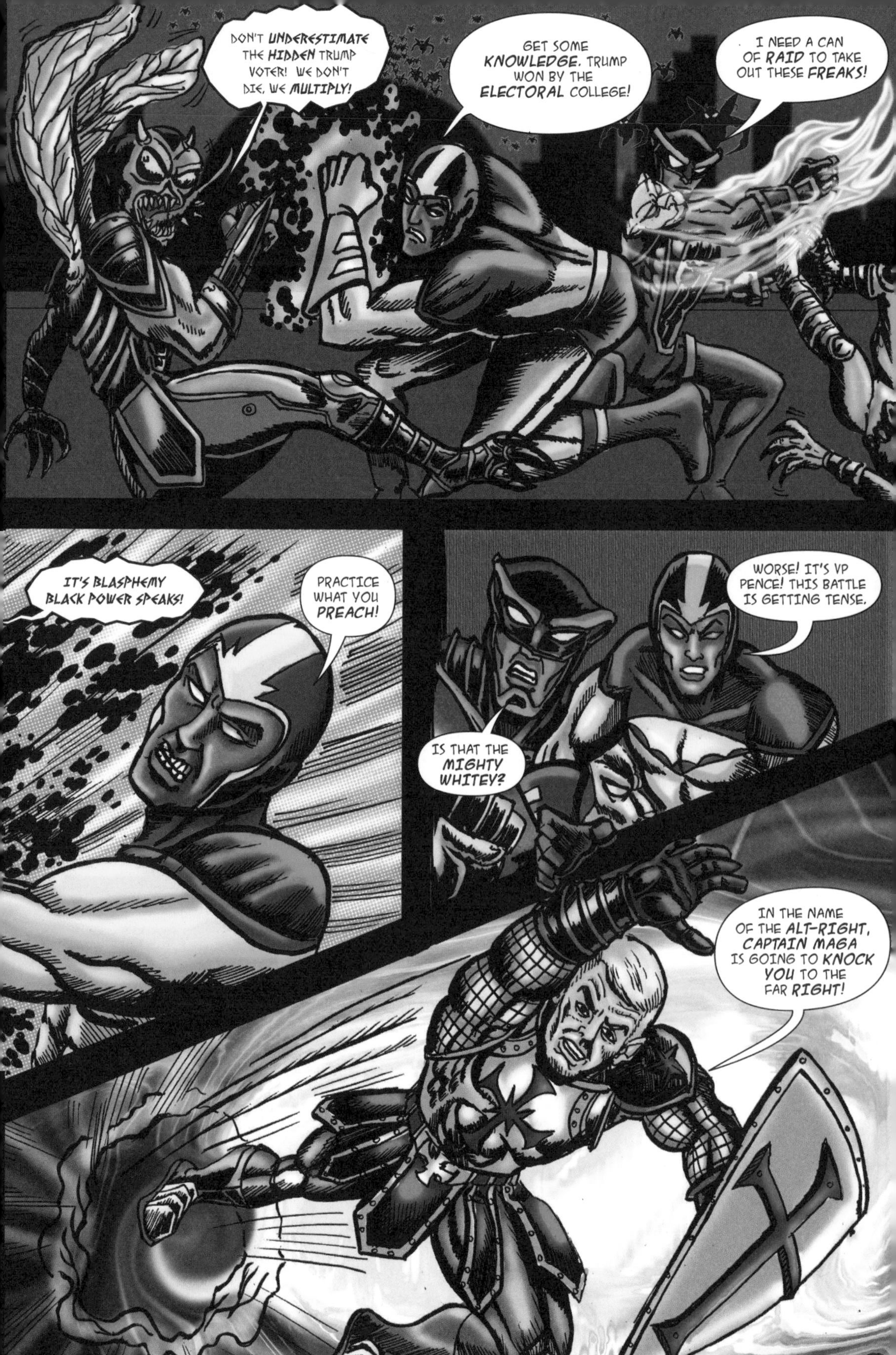
DON'T UNDERESTIMATE THE HIDDEN TRUMP VOTER! WE DON'T DIE, WE MULTIPLY!
GET SOME KNOWLEDGE. TRUMP WON BY THE ELECTORAL COLLEGE!
I NEED A CAN OF RAID TO TAKE OUT THESE FREAKS!
IT'S BLASPHEMY BLACK POWER SPEAKS!
PRACTICE WHAT YOU PREACH!
WORSE! IT'S VP PENCE! THIS BATTLE IS GETTING TENSE.
IS THAT THE MIGHTY WHITEY?
IN THE NAME OF THE ALT-RIGHT, CAPTAIN MAGA IS GOING TO KNOCK YOU TO THE FAR RIGHT!

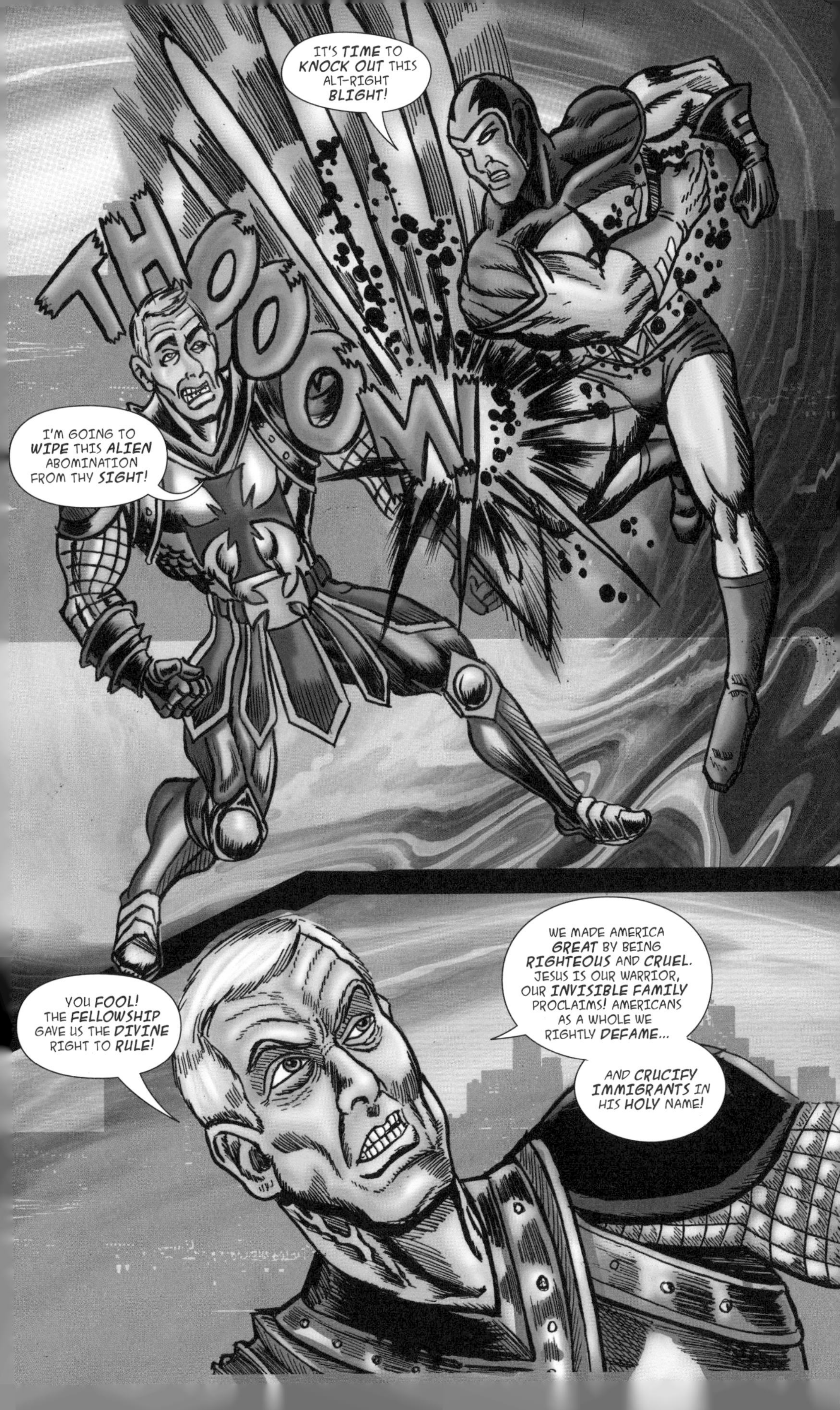
IT'S TIME TO KNOCK OUT THIS ALT-RIGHT BLIGHT!
THOOOM!
I'M GOING TO WIPE THIS ALIEN ABOMINATION FROM THY SIGHT!
YOU FOOL! THE FELLOWSHIP GAVE US THE DIVINE RIGHT TO RULE!
WE MADE AMERICA GREAT BY BEING RIGHTEOUS AND CRUEL. JESUS IS OUR WARRIOR, OUR INVISIBLE FAMILY PROCLAIMS! AMERICANS AS A WHOLE WE RIGHTLY DEFAME...
AND CRUCIFY IMMIGRANTS IN HIS HOLY NAME!

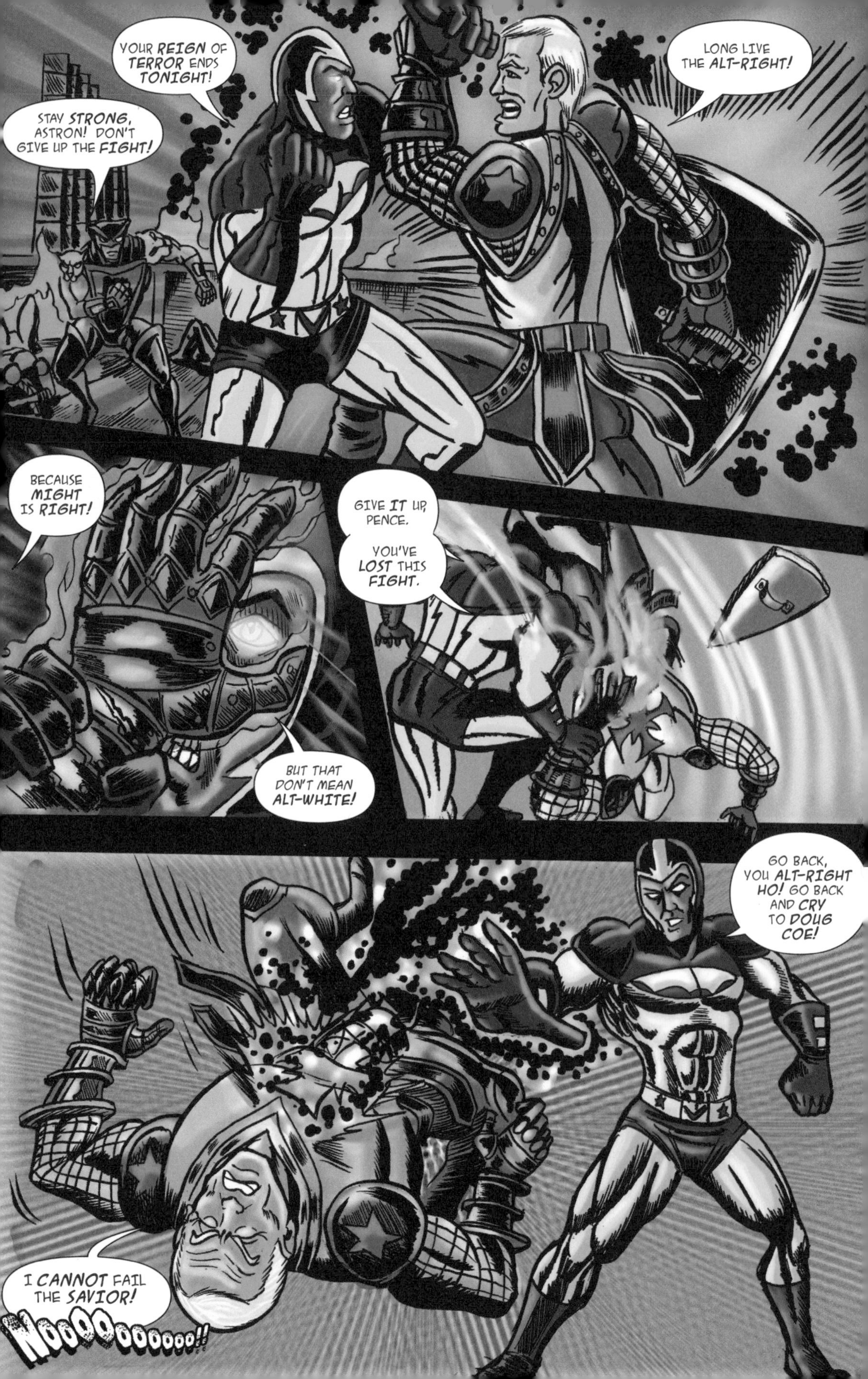
YOUR REIGN OF TERROR ENDS TONIGHT!
STAY STRONG, ASTRON! DON'T GIVE UP THE FIGHT!
LONG LIVE THE ALT-RIGHT!
BECAUSE MIGHT IS RIGHT!
BUT THAT DON'T MEAN ALT-WHITE!
GIVE IT UP, PENCE.
YOU'VE LOST THIS FIGHT.
GO BACK, YOU ALT-RIGHT HO! GO BACK AND CRY TO DOUG COE!
I CANNOT FAIL THE SAVIOR!
NOOOOoooooo!!

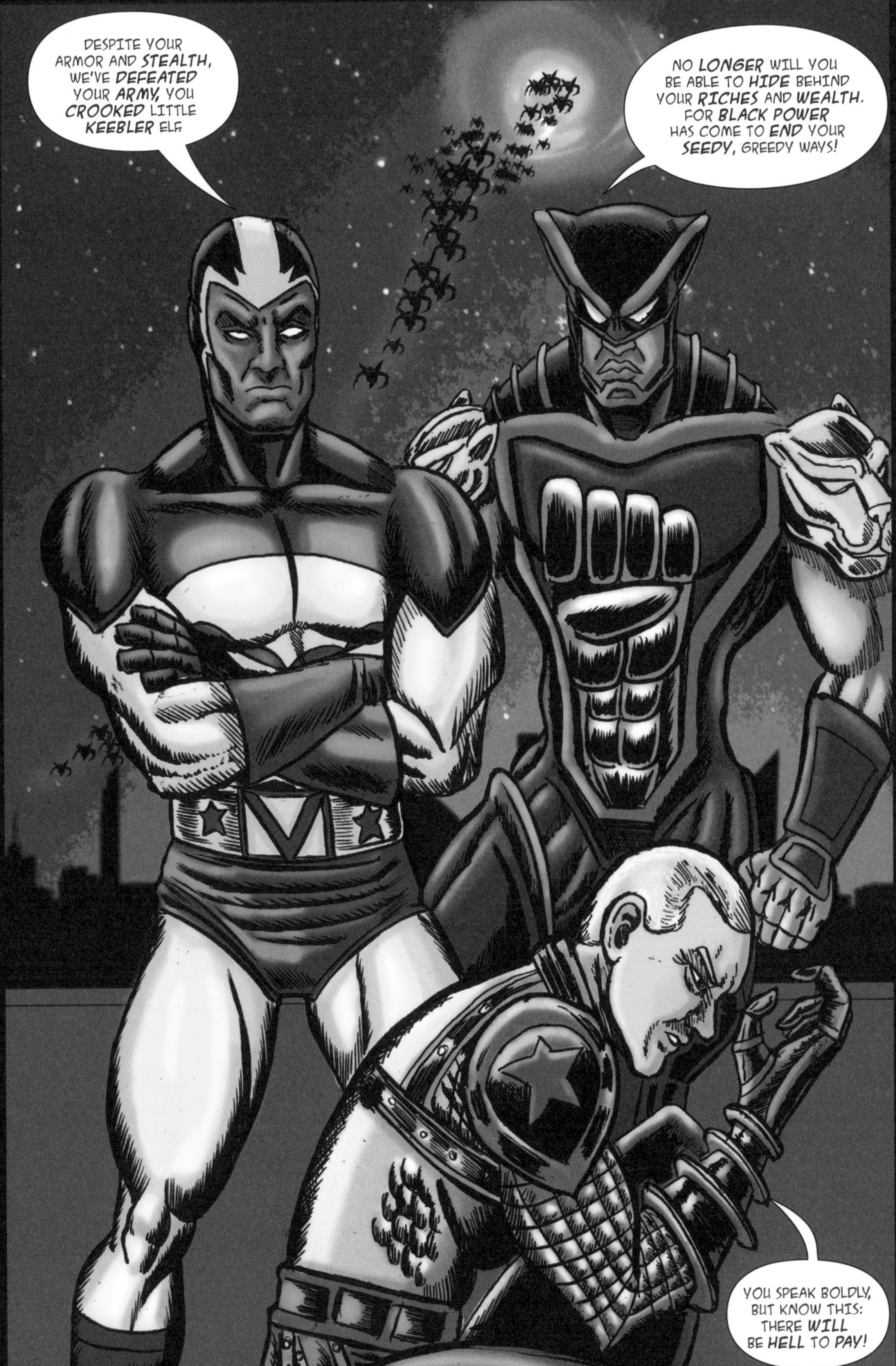
DESPITE YOUR ARMOR AND STEALTH, WE'VE DEFEATED YOUR ARMY, YOU CROOKED LITTLE KEEBLER ELF.
NO LONGER WILL YOU BE ABLE TO HIDE BEHIND YOUR RICHES AND WEALTH. FOR BLACK POWER HAS COME TO END YOUR SEEDY, GREEDY WAYS!
YOU SPEAK BOLDLY, BUT KNOW THIS: THERE WILL BE HELL TO PAY!

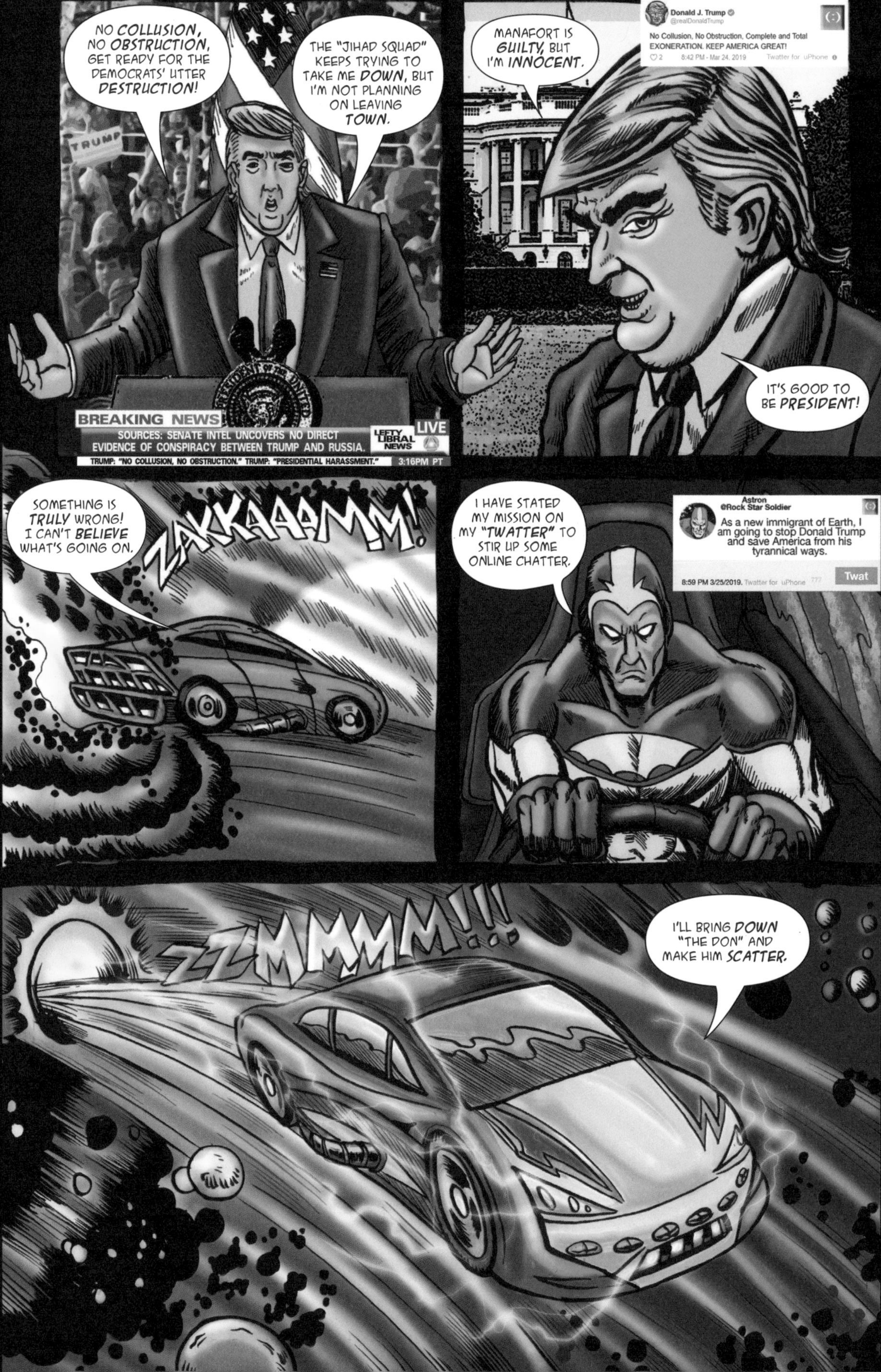

NO COLLUSION, NO OBSTRUCTION, GET READY FOR THE DEMOCRATS' UTTER DESTRUCTION!
THE "JIHAD SQUAD" KEEPS TRYING TO TAKE ME DOWN, BUT I'M NOT PLANNING ON LEAVING TOWN.
TRUMP
BREAKING NEWS
SOURCES: SENATE INTEL UNCOVERS NO DIRECT EVIDENCE OF CONSPIRACY BETWEEN TRUMP AND RUSSIA.
LEFTY LIBRAL NEWS
LIVE
TRUMP: "NO COLLUSION, NO OBSTRUCTION." TRUMP: "PRESIDENTIAL HARASSMENT."
3:16PM PT
MANAFORT IS GUILTY, BUT I'M INNOCENT.
Donald J. Trump
@realDonaldTrump
No Collusion, No Obstruction, Complete and Total EXONERATION. KEEP AMERICA GREAT!
2
8:42 PM - Mar 24, 2019
Twatter for uPhone
IT'S GOOD TO BE PRESIDENT!
SOMETHING IS TRULY WRONG! I CAN'T BELIEVE WHAT'S GOING ON.
ZAKKAAAMMM!
I HAVE STATED MY MISSION ON MY "TWATTER" TO STIR UP SOME ONLINE CHATTER.
Astron
@Rock Star Soldier
As a new immigrant of Earth, I am going to stop Donald Trump and save America from his tyrannical ways.
8:59 PM 3/25/2019. Twatter for uPhone
Twat
ZZMMMMM!!!
I'LL BRING DOWN "THE DON" AND MAKE HIM SCATTER.

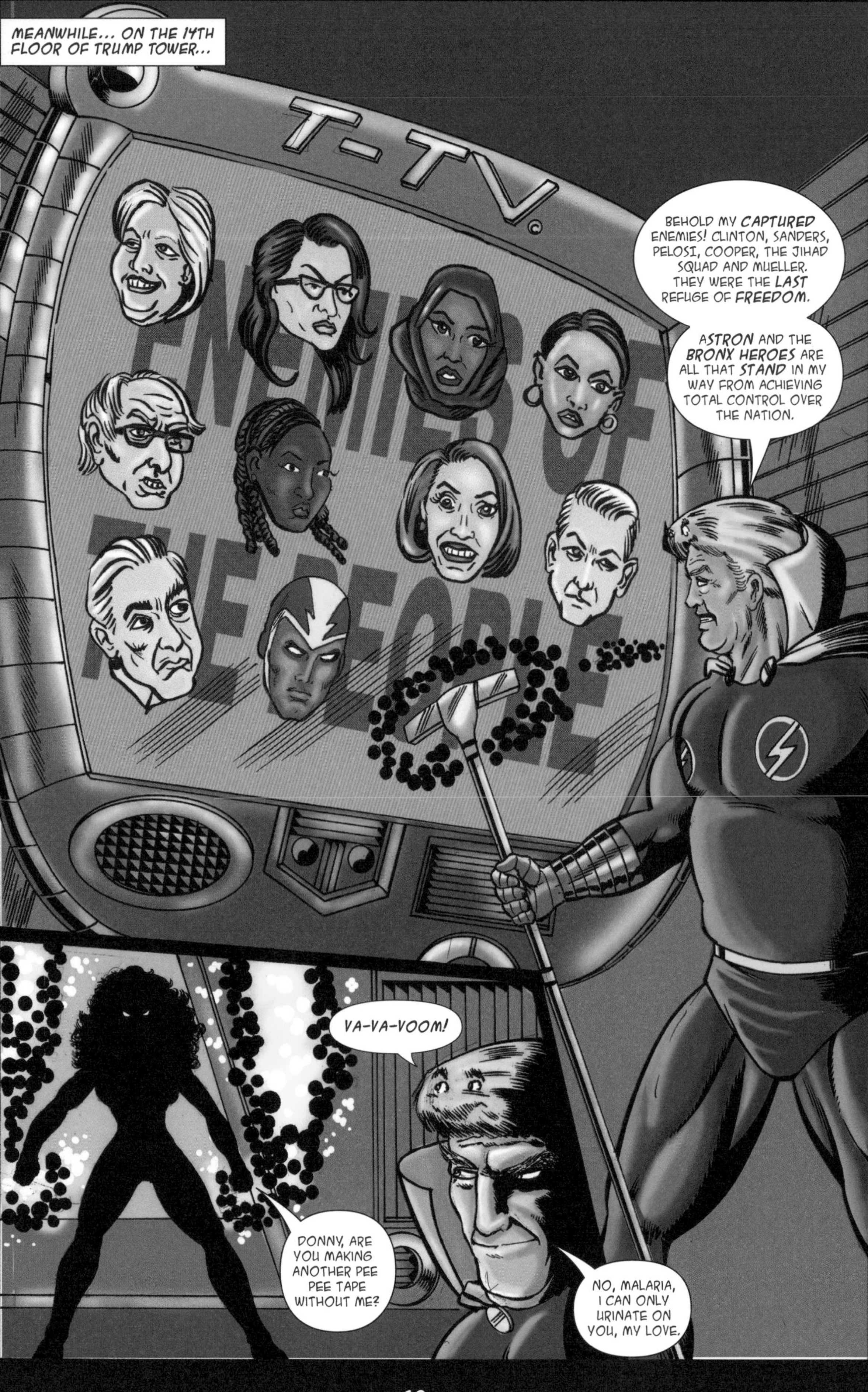
MEANWHILE... ON THE 14TH FLOOR OF TRUMP TOWER...
T-TV.
ENEMIES OF THE PEOPLE
BEHOLD MY CAPTURED ENEMIES! CLINTON, SANDERS, PELOSI, COOPER, THE JIHAD SQUAD AND MUELLER. THEY WERE THE LAST REFUGE OF FREEDOM.
ASTRON AND THE BRONX HEROES ARE ALL THAT STAND IN MY WAY FROM ACHIEVING TOTAL CONTROL OVER THE NATION.
VA-VA-VOOM!
DONNY, ARE YOU MAKING ANOTHER PEE PEE TAPE WITHOUT ME?
NO, MALARIA, I CAN ONLY URINATE ON YOU, MY LOVE.

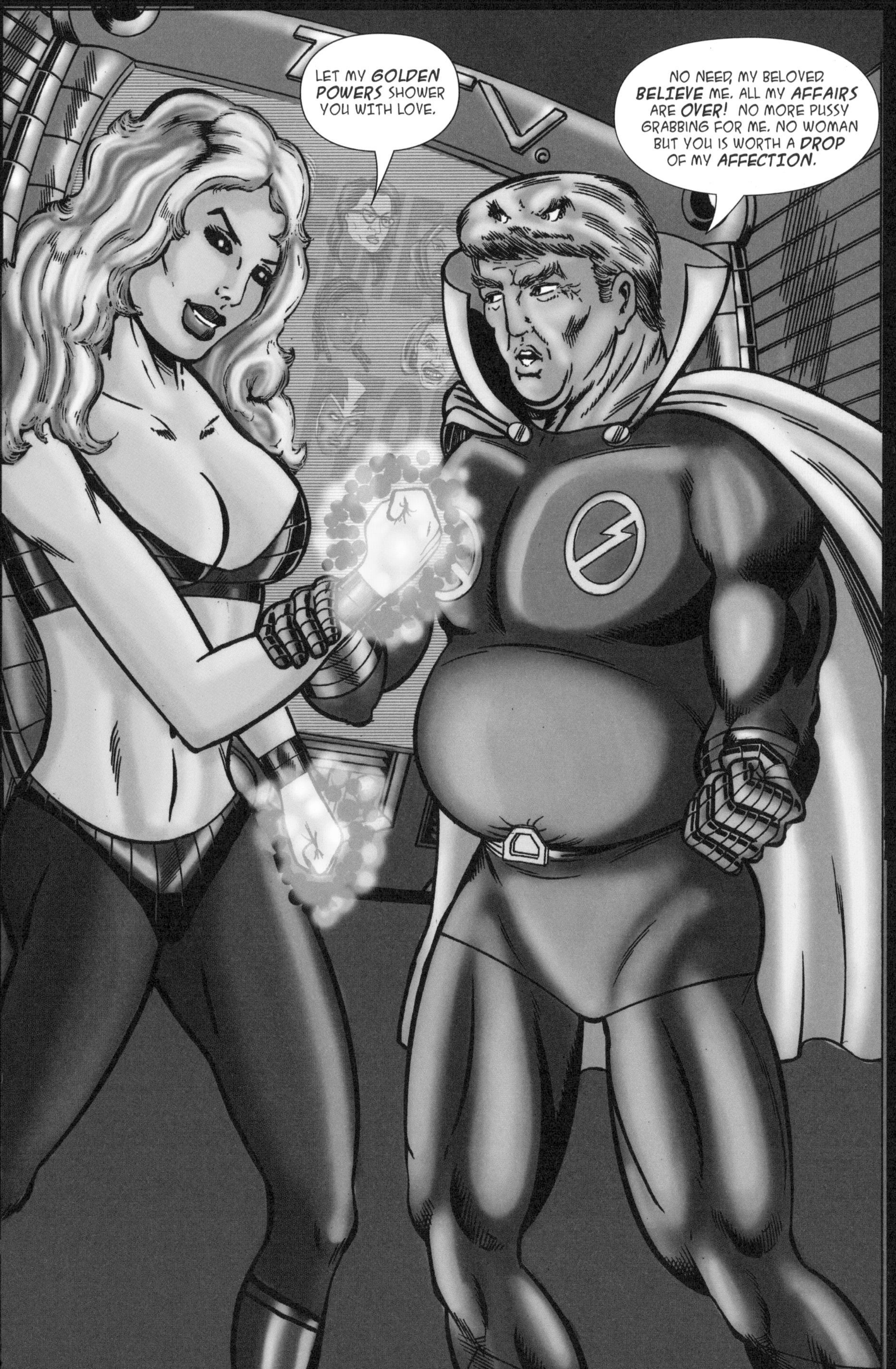
LET MY GOLDEN POWERS SHOWER YOU WITH LOVE.
NO NEED, MY BELOVED. BELIEVE ME. ALL MY AFFAIRS ARE OVER! NO MORE PUSSY GRABBING FOR ME. NO WOMAN BUT YOU IS WORTH A DROP OF MY AFFECTION.

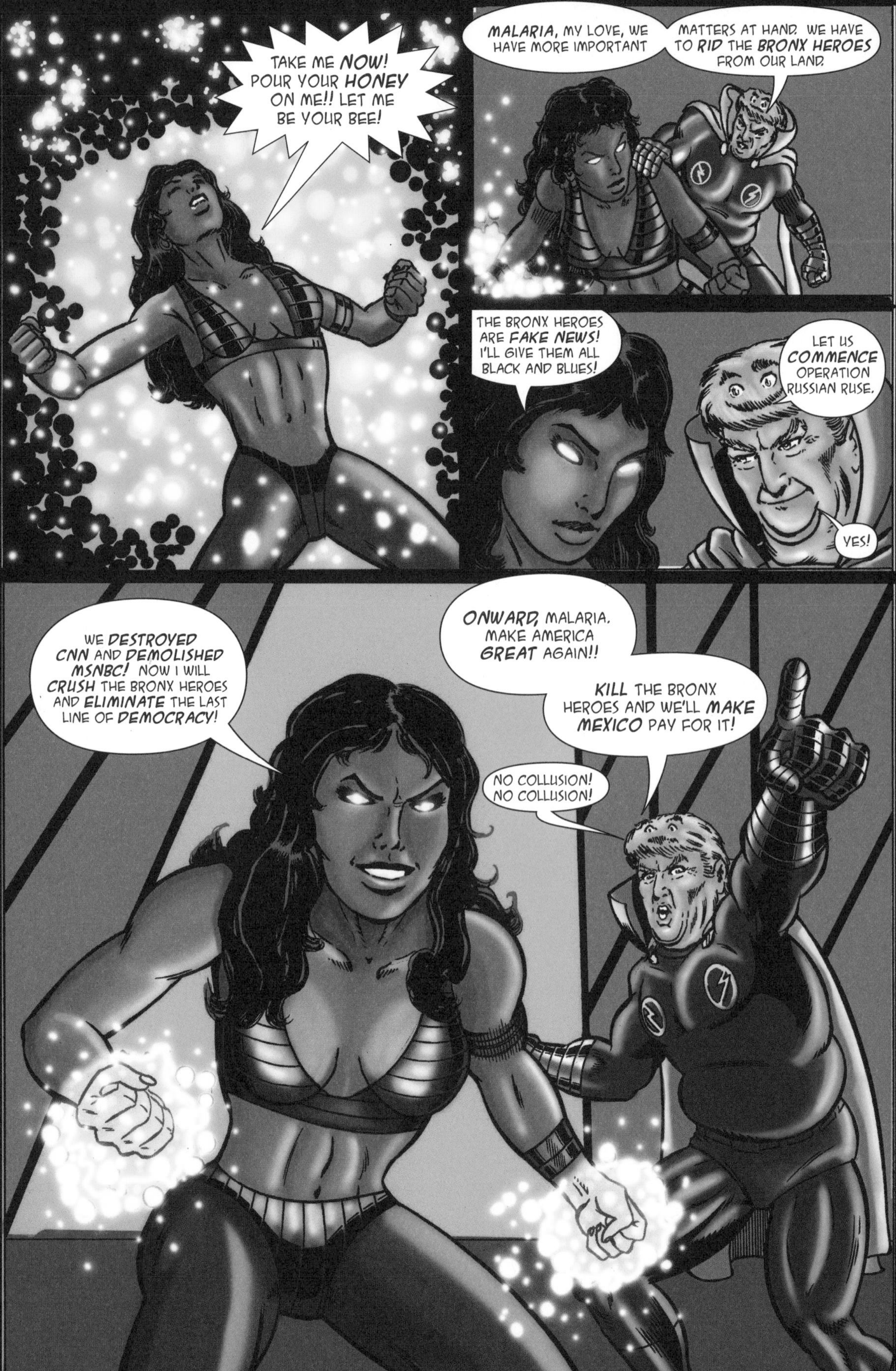
TAKE ME NOW! POUR YOUR HONEY ON ME!! LET ME BE YOUR BEE!
MALARIA, MY LOVE, WE HAVE MORE IMPORTANT
MATTERS AT HAND. WE HAVE TO RID THE BRONX HEROES FROM OUR LAND.
THE BRONX HEROES ARE FAKE NEWS! I'LL GIVE THEM ALL BLACK AND BLUES!
LET US COMMENCE OPERATION RUSSIAN RUSE.
YES!
WE DESTROYED CNN AND DEMOLISHED MSNBC! NOW I WILL CRUSH THE BRONX HEROES AND ELIMINATE THE LAST LINE OF DEMOCRACY!
ONWARD, MALARIA. MAKE AMERICA GREAT AGAIN!!
KILL THE BRONX HEROES AND WE'LL MAKE MEXICO PAY FOR IT!
NO COLLUSION! NO COLLUSION!

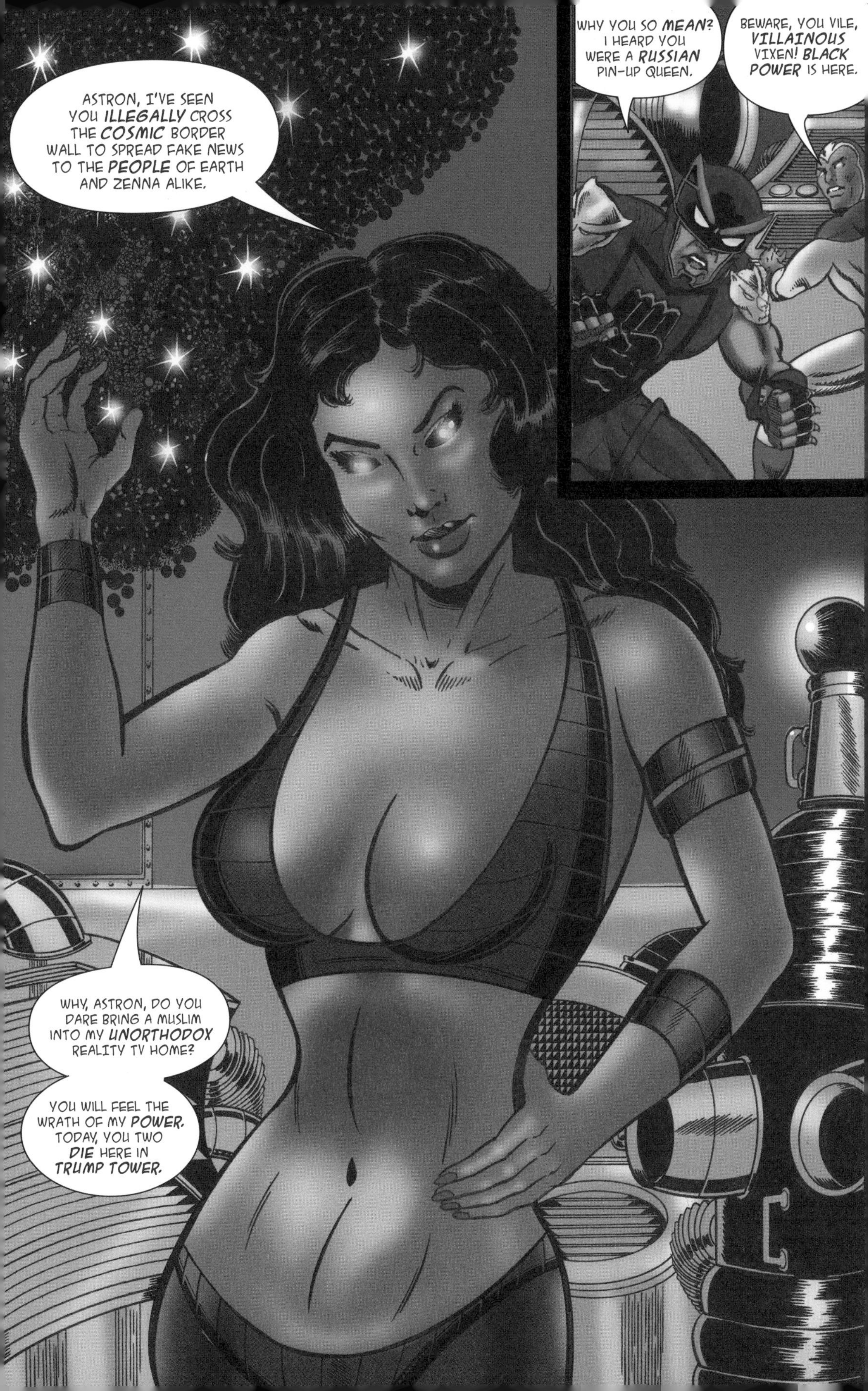
ASTRON, I'VE SEEN YOU ILLEGALLY CROSS THE COSMIC BORDER WALL TO SPREAD FAKE NEWS TO THE PEOPLE OF EARTH AND ZENNA ALIKE.
WHY YOU SO MEAN? I HEARD YOU WERE A RUSSIAN PIN-UP QUEEN.
BEWARE, YOU VILE, VILLAINOUS VIXEN! BLACK POWER IS HERE.
WHY, ASTRON, DO YOU DARE BRING A MUSLIM INTO MY UNORTHODOX REALITY TV HOME?
YOU WILL FEEL THE WRATH OF MY POWER. TODAY, YOU TWO DIE HERE IN TRUMP TOWER.

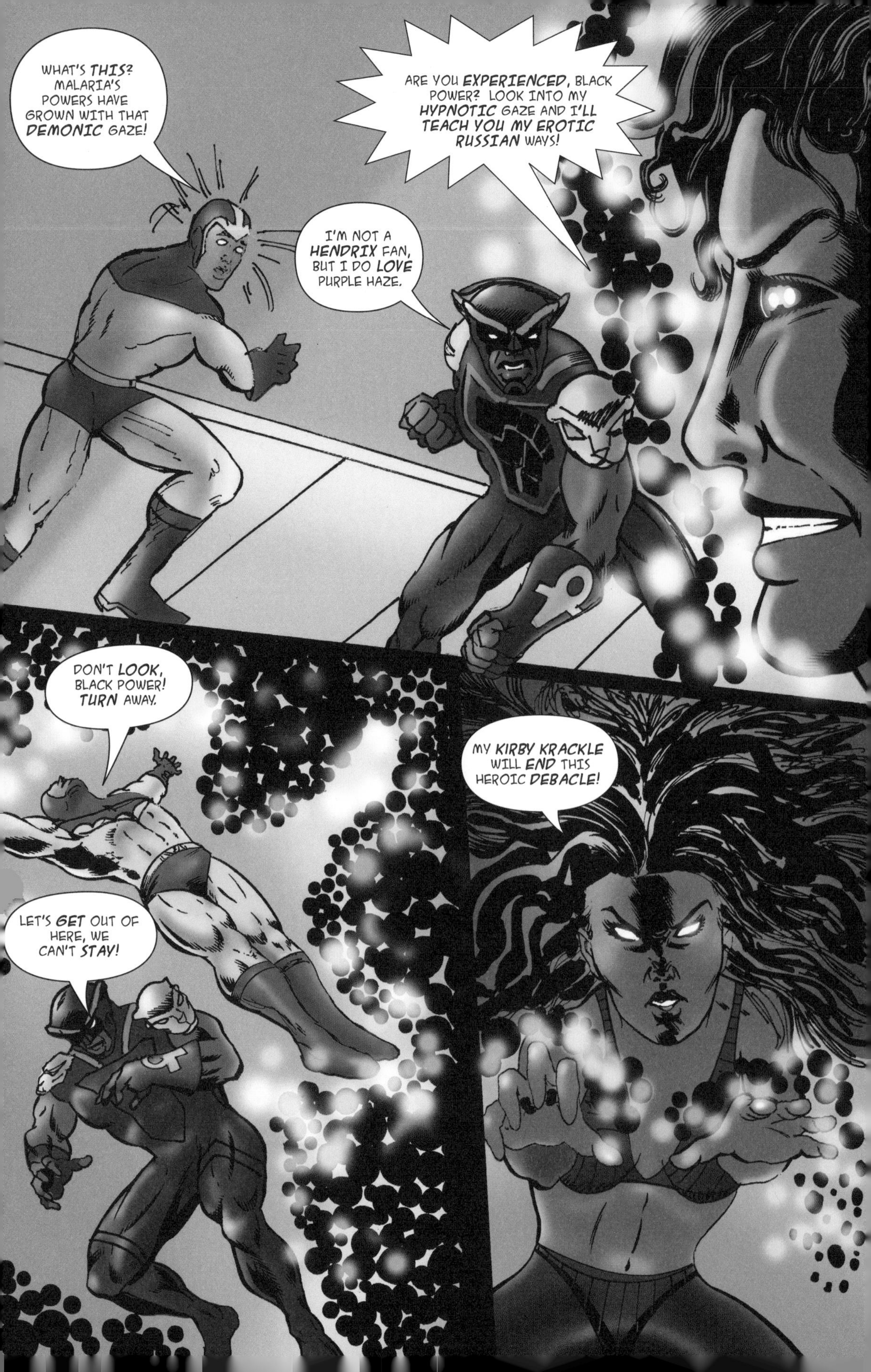
WHAT'S THIS? MALARIA'S POWERS HAVE GROWN WITH THAT DEMONIC GAZE!
ARE YOU EXPERIENCED, BLACK POWER? LOOK INTO MY HYPNOTIC GAZE AND I'LL TEACH YOU MY EROTIC RUSSIAN WAYS!
I'M NOT A HENDRIX FAN, BUT I DO LOVE PURPLE HAZE.
DON'T LOOK, BLACK POWER! TURN AWAY.
LET'S GET OUT OF HERE, WE CAN'T STAY!
MY KIRBY KRACKLE WILL END THIS HEROIC DEBACLE!

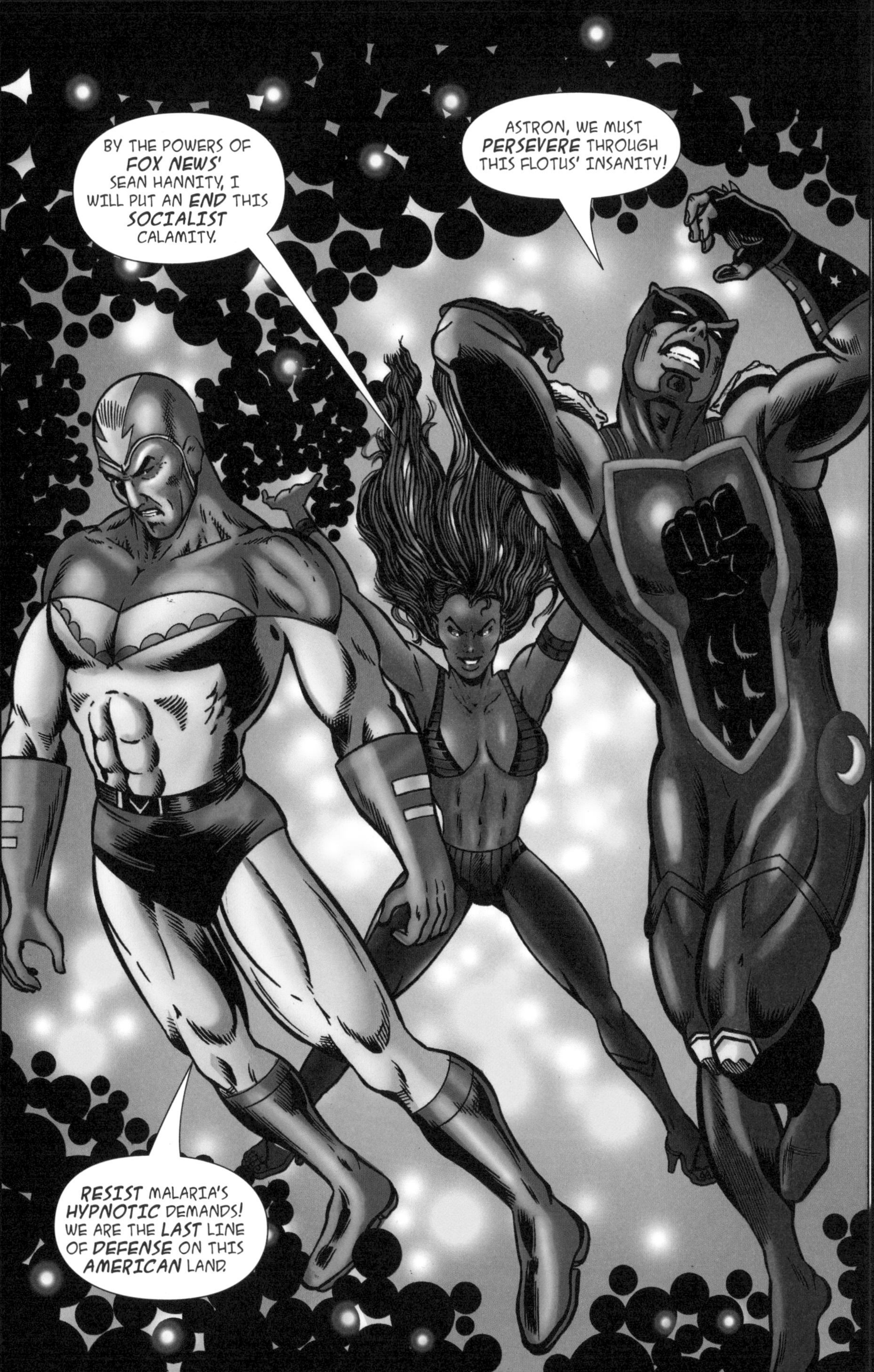
BY THE POWERS OF FOX NEWS' SEAN HANNITY, I WILL PUT AN END THIS SOCIALIST CALAMITY.
ASTRON, WE MUST PERSEVERE THROUGH THIS FLOTUS' INSANITY!
RESIST MALARIA'S HYPNOTIC DEMANDS! WE ARE THE LAST LINE OF DEFENSE ON THIS AMERICAN LAND.

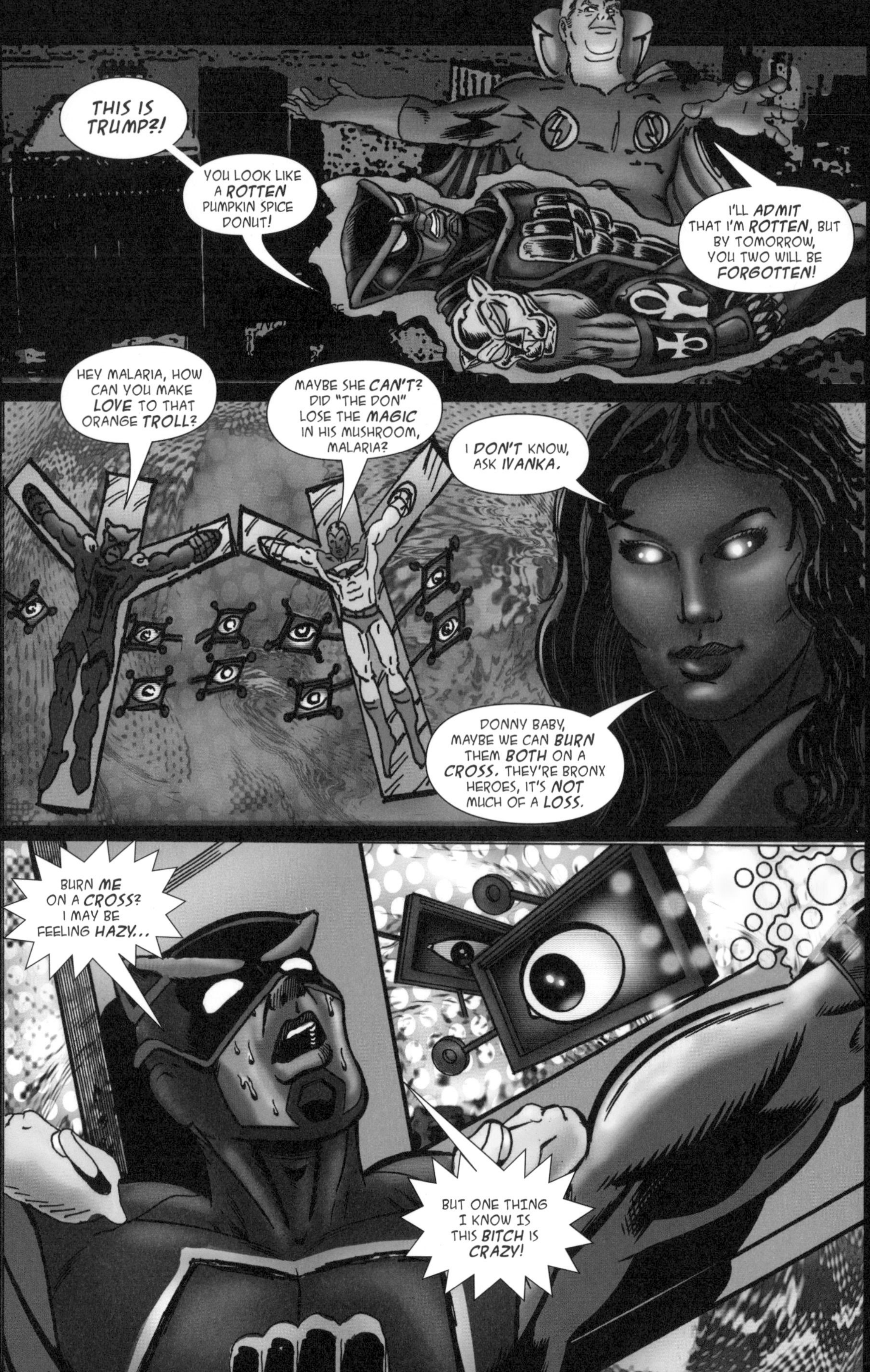
THIS IS TRUMP?!
YOU LOOK LIKE A ROTTEN PUMPKIN SPICE DONUT!
I'LL ADMIT THAT I'M ROTTEN, BUT BY TOMORROW, YOU TWO WILL BE FORGOTTEN!
HEY MALARIA, HOW CAN YOU MAKE LOVE TO THAT ORANGE TROLL?
MAYBE SHE CAN'T? DID "THE DON" LOSE THE MAGIC IN HIS MUSHROOM, MALARIA?
I DON'T KNOW, ASK IVANKA.
DONNY BABY, MAYBE WE CAN BURN THEM BOTH ON A CROSS. THEY'RE BRONX HEROES, IT'S NOT MUCH OF A LOSS.
BURN ME ON A CROSS? I MAY BE FEELING HAZY...
BUT ONE THING I KNOW IS THIS BITCH IS CRAZY!

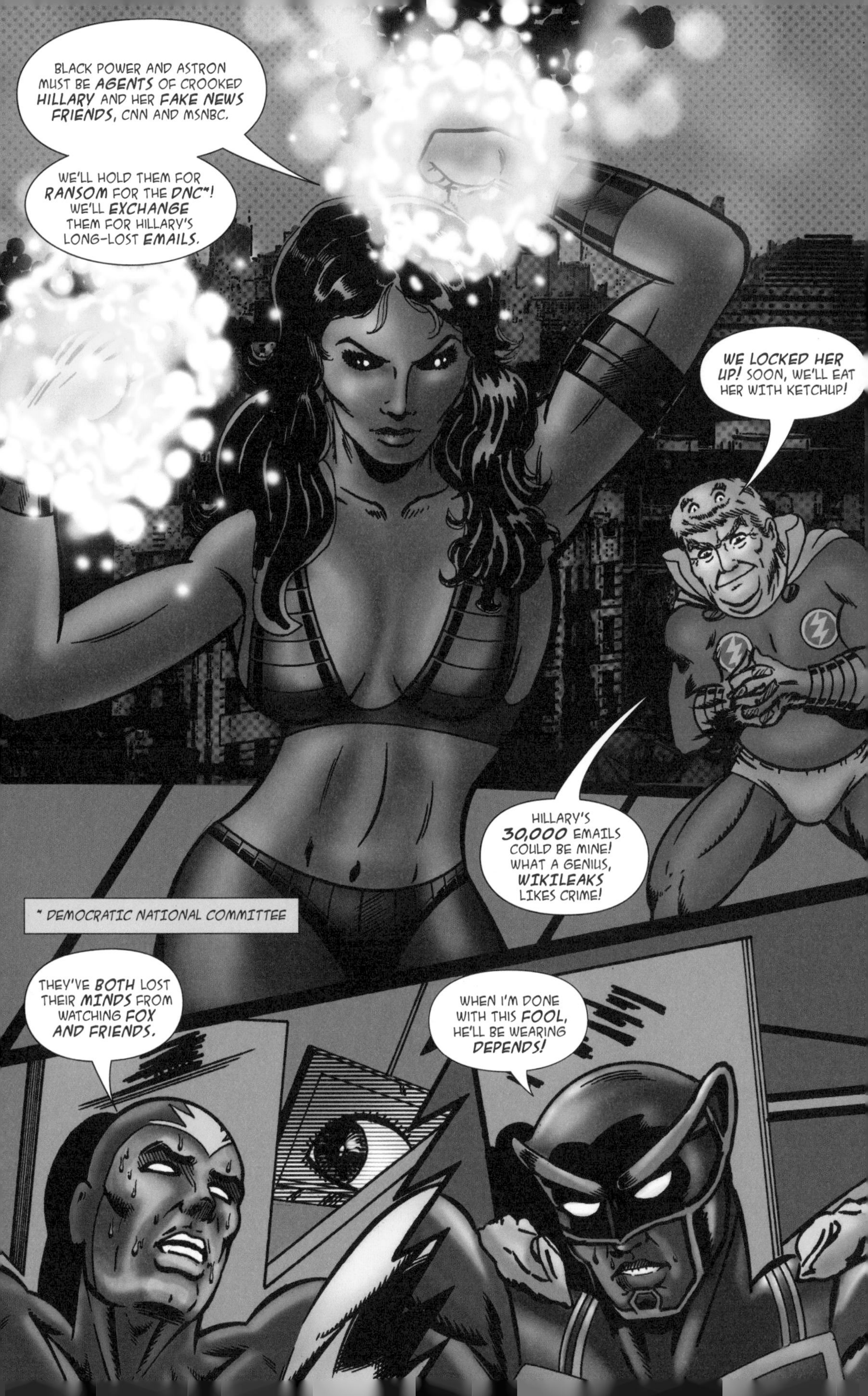

BLACK POWER AND ASTRON MUST BE AGENTS OF CROOKED HILLARY AND HER FAKE NEWS FRIENDS, CNN AND MSNBC.
WE'LL HOLD THEM FOR RANSOM FOR THE DNC*! WE'LL EXCHANGE THEM FOR HILLARY'S LONG-LOST EMAILS.
WE LOCKED HER UP! SOON, WE'LL EAT HER WITH KETCHUP!
HILLARY'S 30,000 EMAILS COULD BE MINE! WHAT A GENIUS, WIKILEAKS LIKES CRIME!
* DEMOCRATIC NATIONAL COMMITTEE
THEY'VE BOTH LOST THEIR MINDS FROM WATCHING FOX AND FRIENDS.
WHEN I'M DONE WITH THIS FOOL, HE'LL BE WEARING DEPENDS!

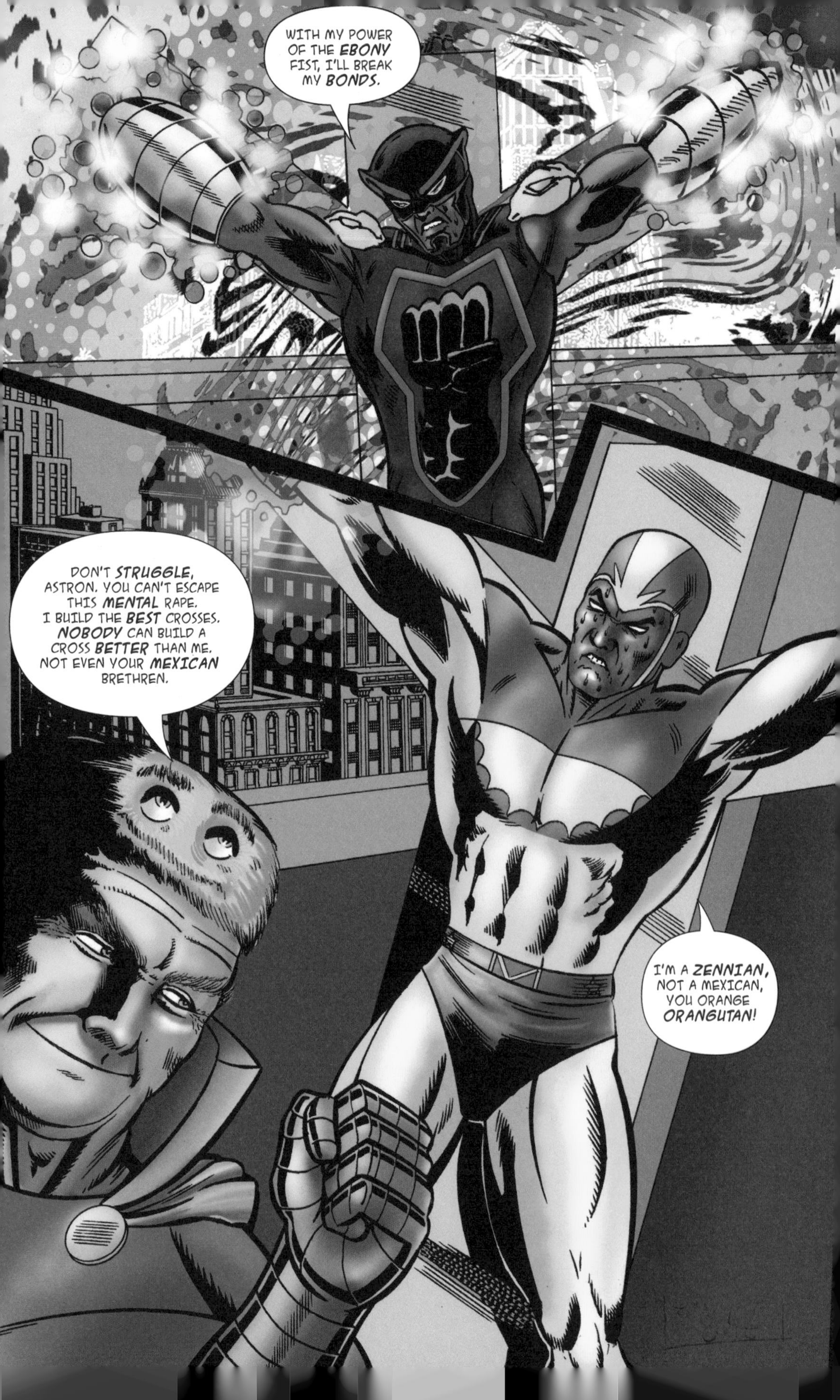
WITH MY POWER OF THE EBONY FIST, I'LL BREAK MY BONDS.
DON'T STRUGGLE, ASTRON. YOU CAN'T ESCAPE THIS MENTAL RAPE. I BUILD THE BEST CROSSES. NOBODY CAN BUILD A CROSS BETTER THAN ME. NOT EVEN YOUR MEXICAN BRETHREN.
I'M A ZENNIAN, NOT A MEXICAN, YOU ORANGE ORANGUTAN!

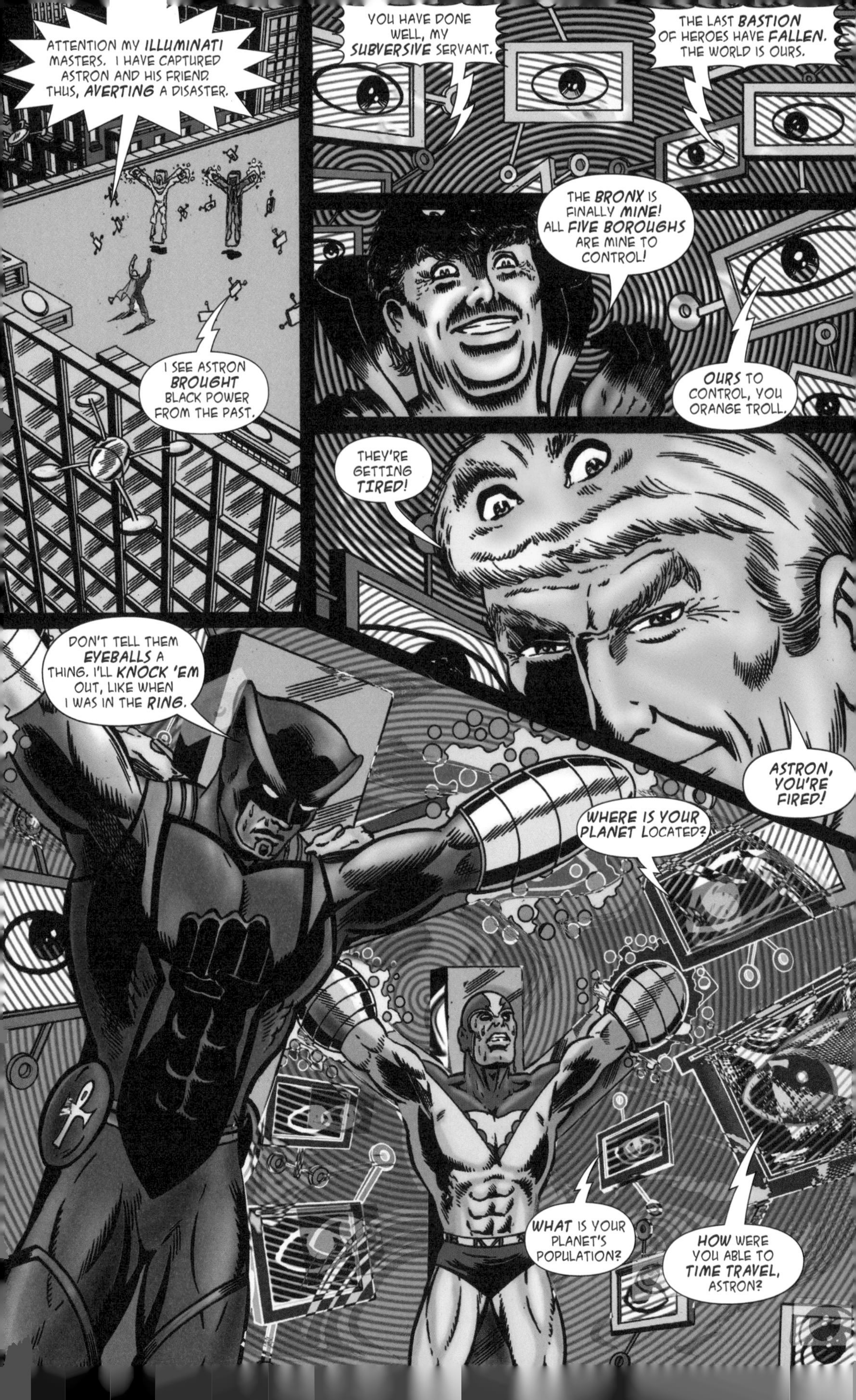
ATTENTION MY ILLUMINATI MASTERS. I HAVE CAPTURED ASTRON AND HIS FRIEND. THUS, AVERTING A DISASTER.
I SEE ASTRON BROUGHT BLACK POWER FROM THE PAST.
YOU HAVE DONE WELL, MY SUBVERSIVE SERVANT.
THE LAST BASTION OF HEROES HAVE FALLEN. THE WORLD IS OURS.
THE BRONX IS FINALLY MINE! ALL FIVE BOROUGHS ARE MINE TO CONTROL!
OURS TO CONTROL, YOU ORANGE TROLL.
THEY'RE GETTING TIRED!
ASTRON, YOU'RE FIRED!
DON'T TELL THEM EYEBALLS A THING. I'LL KNOCK 'EM OUT, LIKE WHEN I WAS IN THE RING.
WHERE IS YOUR PLANET LOCATED?
WHAT IS YOUR PLANET'S POPULATION?
HOW WERE YOU ABLE TO TIME TRAVEL, ASTRON?

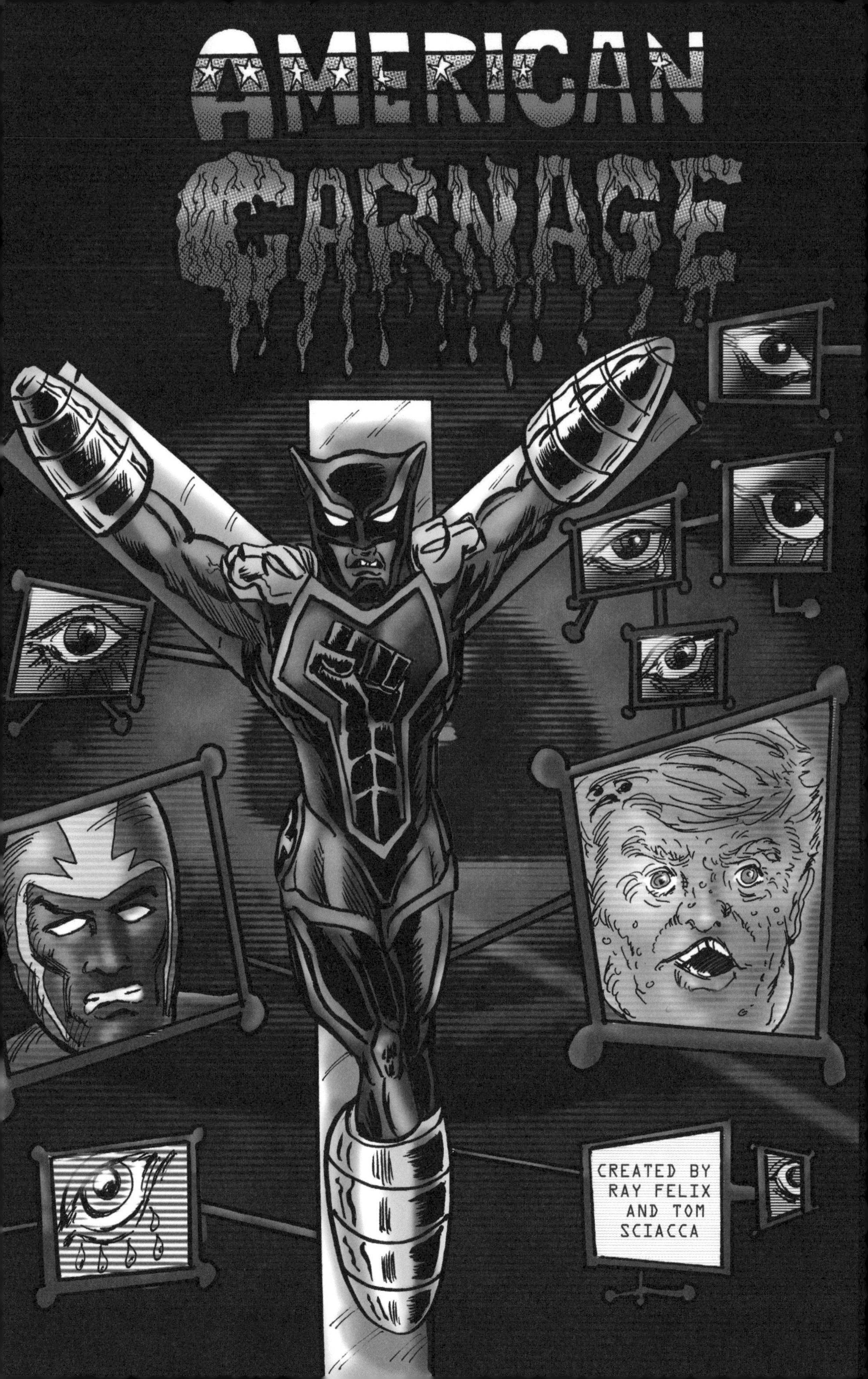
AMERICAN
CARNAGE
CREATED BY
RAY FELIX
AND TOM
SCIACCA

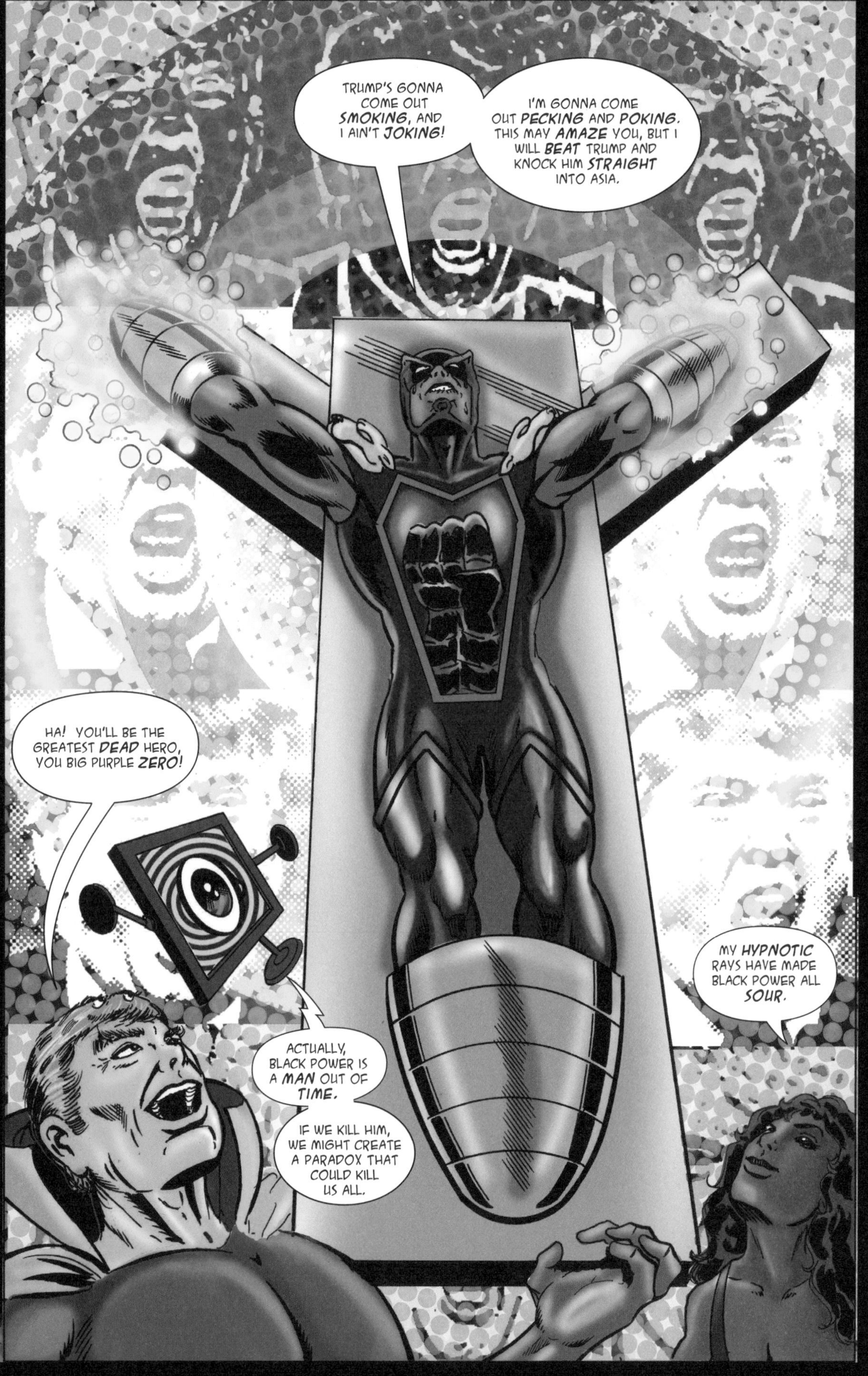
TRUMP'S GONNA COME OUT SMOKING, AND I AIN'T JOKING!
I'M GONNA COME OUT PECKING AND POKING. THIS MAY AMAZE YOU, BUT I WILL BEAT TRUMP AND KNOCK HIM STRAIGHT INTO ASIA.
HA! YOU'LL BE THE GREATEST DEAD HERO, YOU BIG PURPLE ZERO!
MY HYPNOTIC RAYS HAVE MADE BLACK POWER ALL SOUR.
ACTUALLY, BLACK POWER IS A MAN OUT OF TIME.
IF WE KILL HIM, WE MIGHT CREATE A PARADOX THAT COULD KILL US ALL.

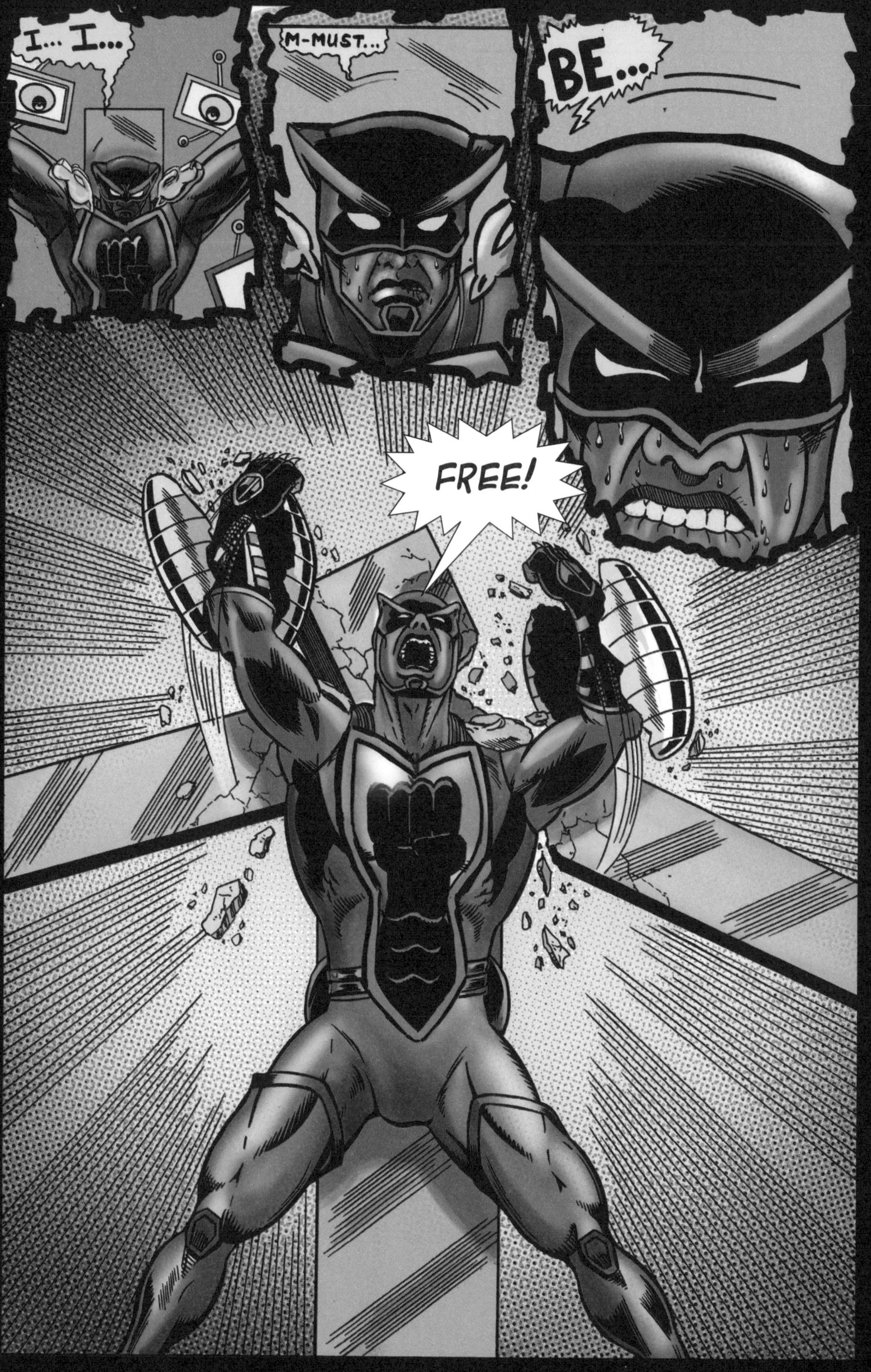

I... I...
M-MUST...
BE...
FREE!

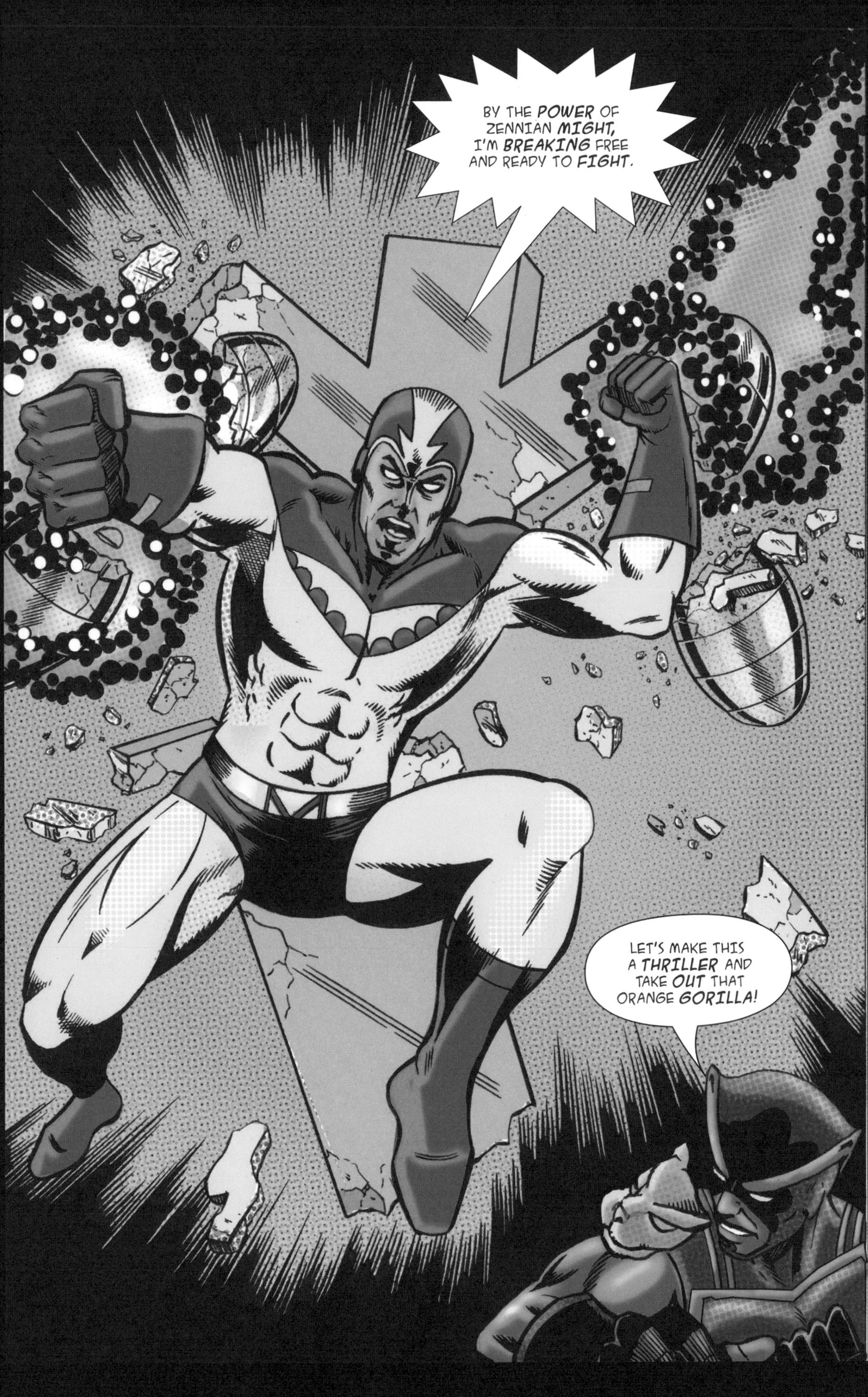
BY THE POWER OF ZENNIAN MIGHT, I'M BREAKING FREE AND READY TO FIGHT.
LET'S MAKE THIS A THRILLER AND TAKE OUT THAT ORANGE GORILLA!

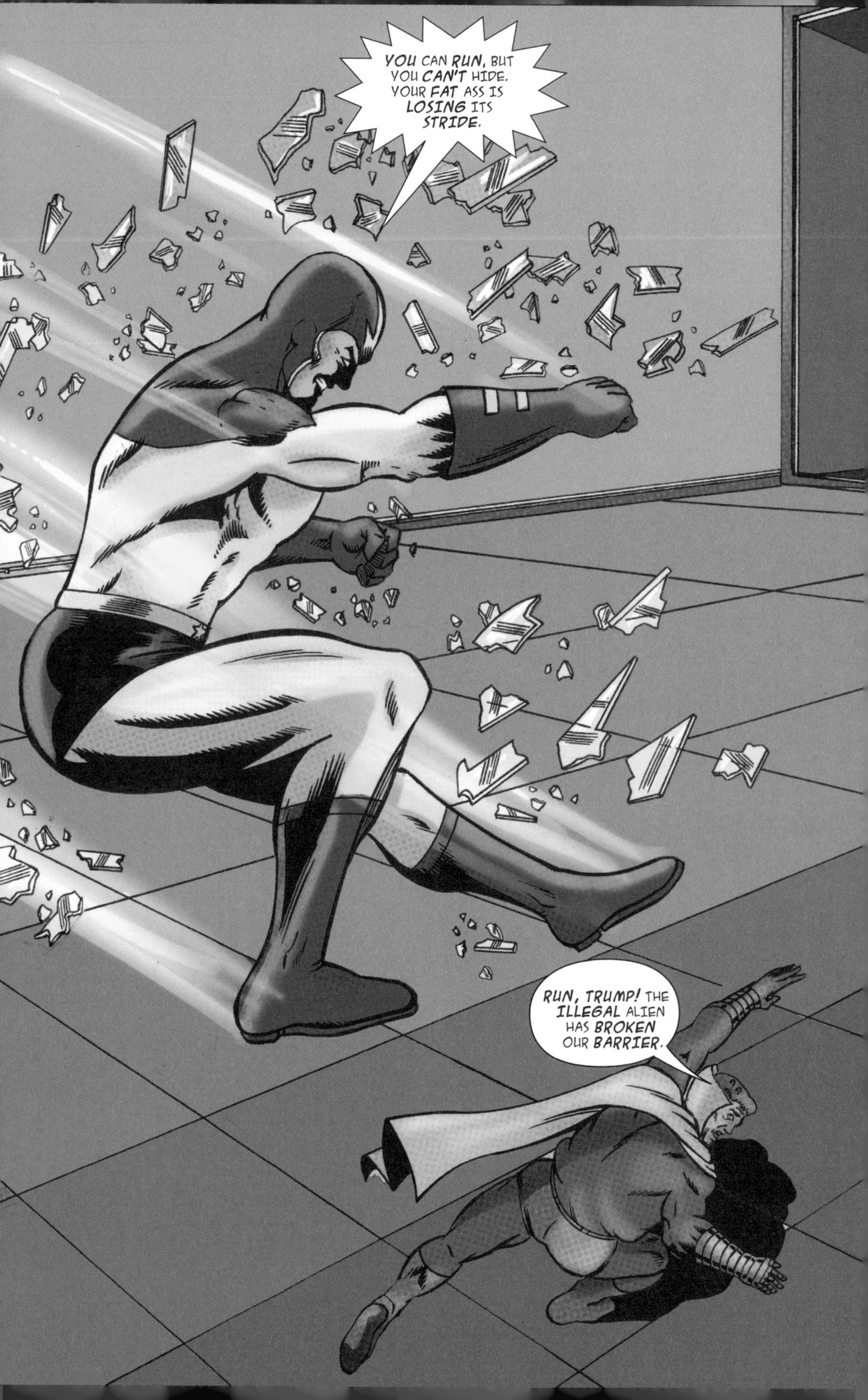
YOU CAN RUN, BUT YOU CAN'T HIDE. YOUR FAT ASS IS LOSING ITS STRIDE.
RUN, TRUMP! THE ILLEGAL ALIEN HAS BROKEN OUR BARRIER.

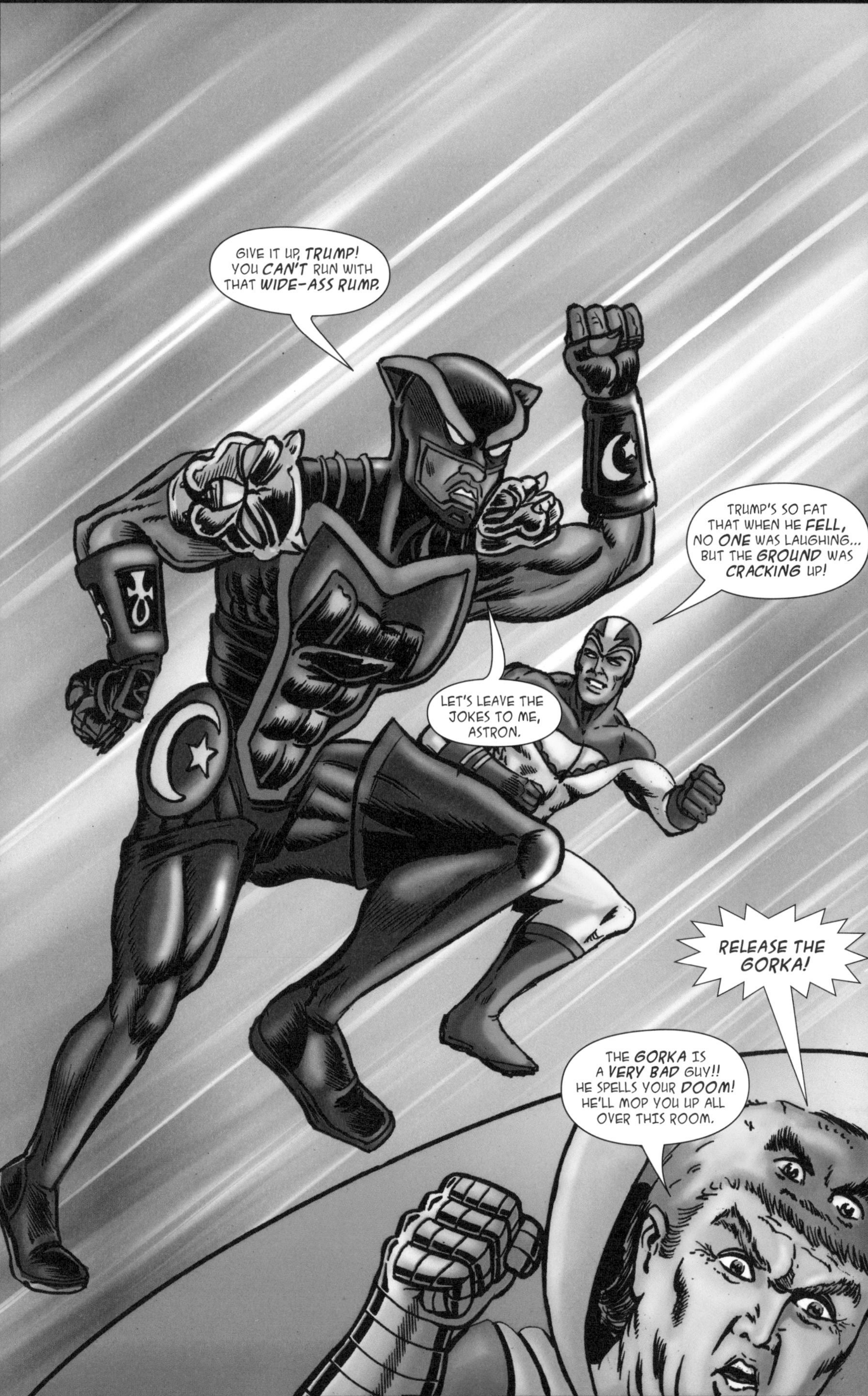
GIVE IT UP, TRUMP! YOU CAN'T RUN WITH THAT WIDE-ASS RUMP.
TRUMP'S SO FAT THAT WHEN HE FELL, NO ONE WAS LAUGHING... BUT THE GROUND WAS CRACKING UP!
LET'S LEAVE THE JOKES TO ME, ASTRON.
RELEASE THE GORKA!
THE GORKA IS A VERY BAD GUY!! HE SPELLS YOUR DOOM! HE'LL MOP YOU UP ALL OVER THIS ROOM.

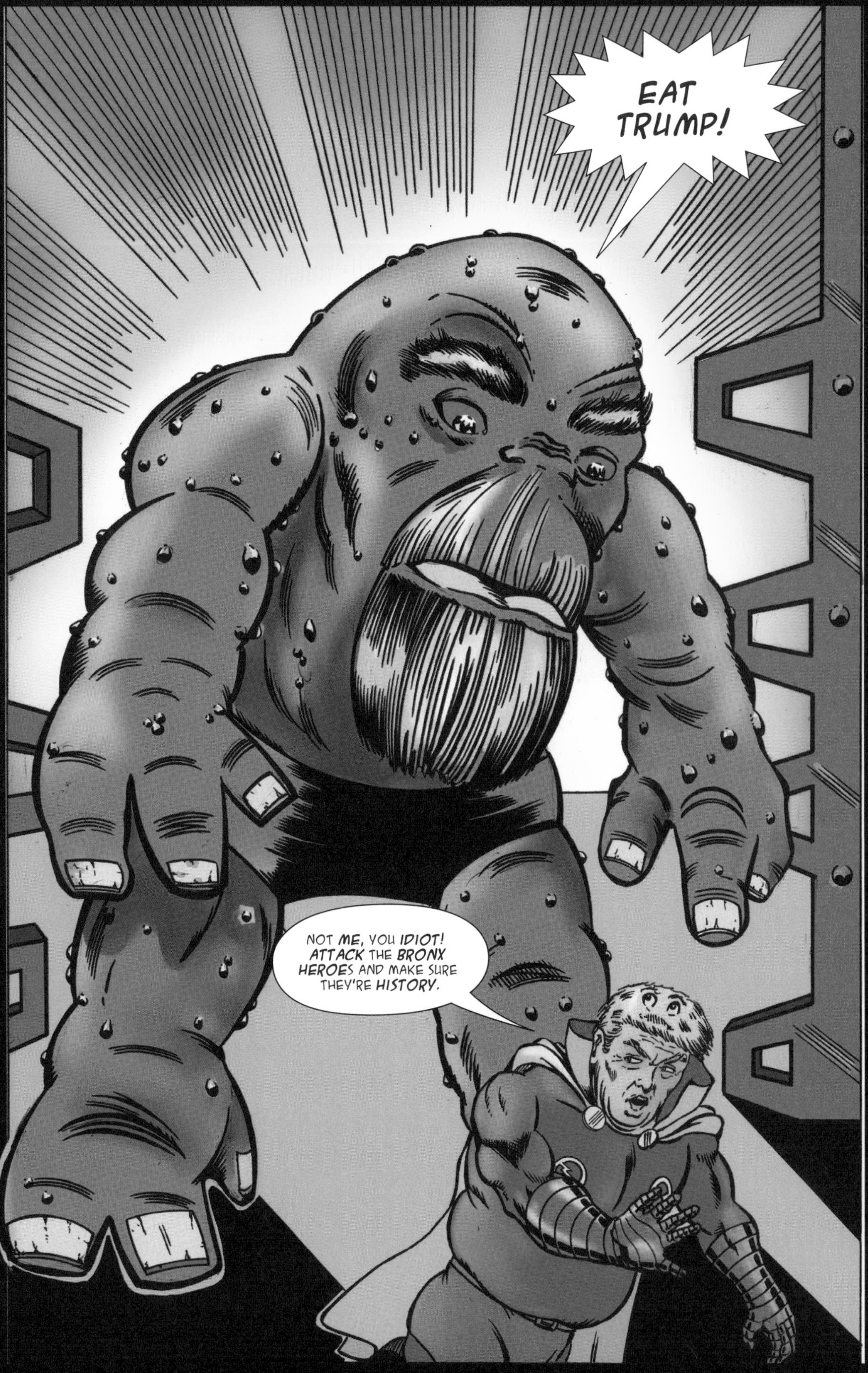
EAT TRUMP!
NOT ME, YOU IDIOT! ATTACK THE BRONX HEROES AND MAKE SURE THEY'RE HISTORY.

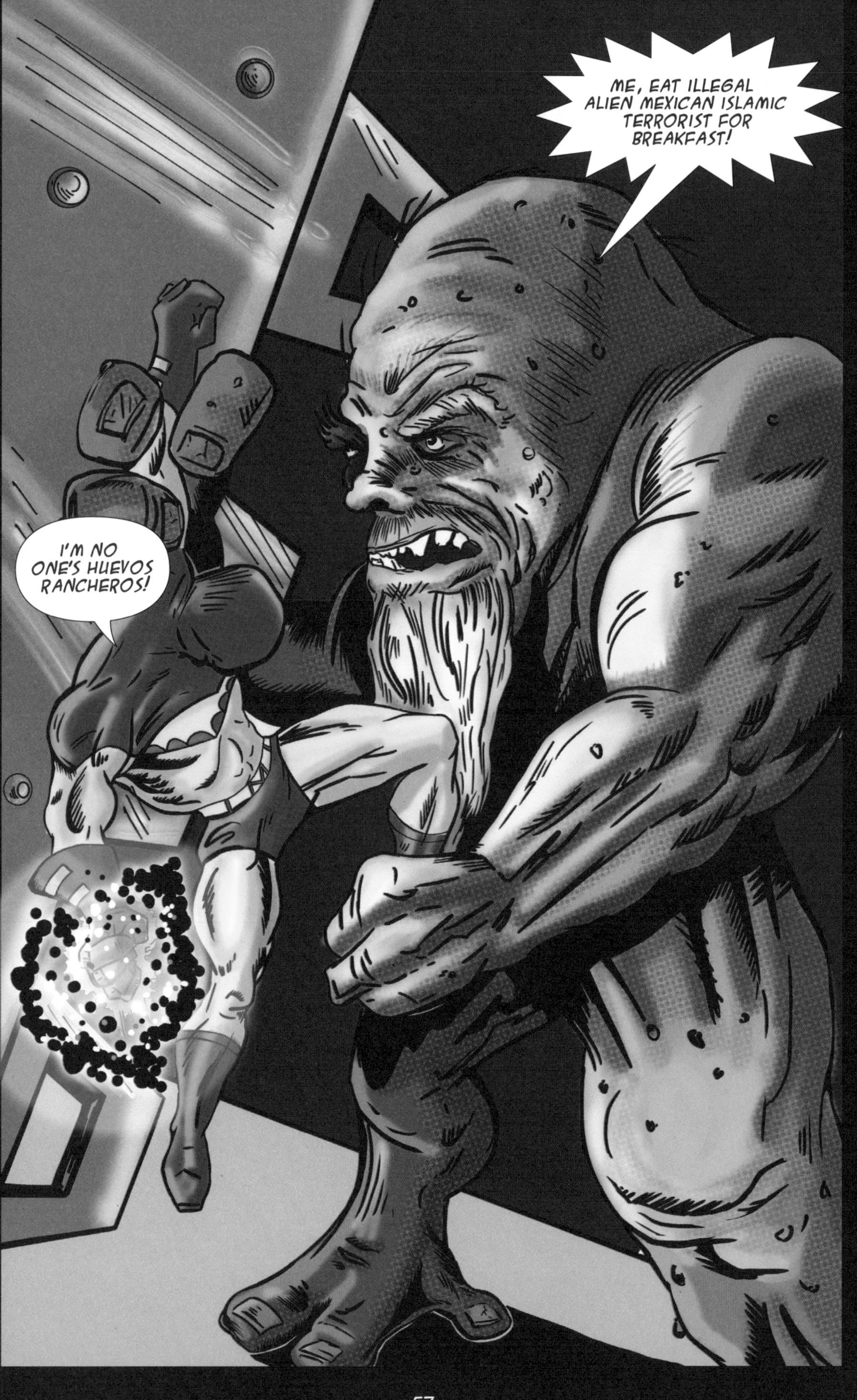
ME, EAT ILLEGAL ALIEN MEXICAN ISLAMIC TERRORIST FOR BREAKFAST!
I'M NO ONE'S HUEVOS RANCHEROS!

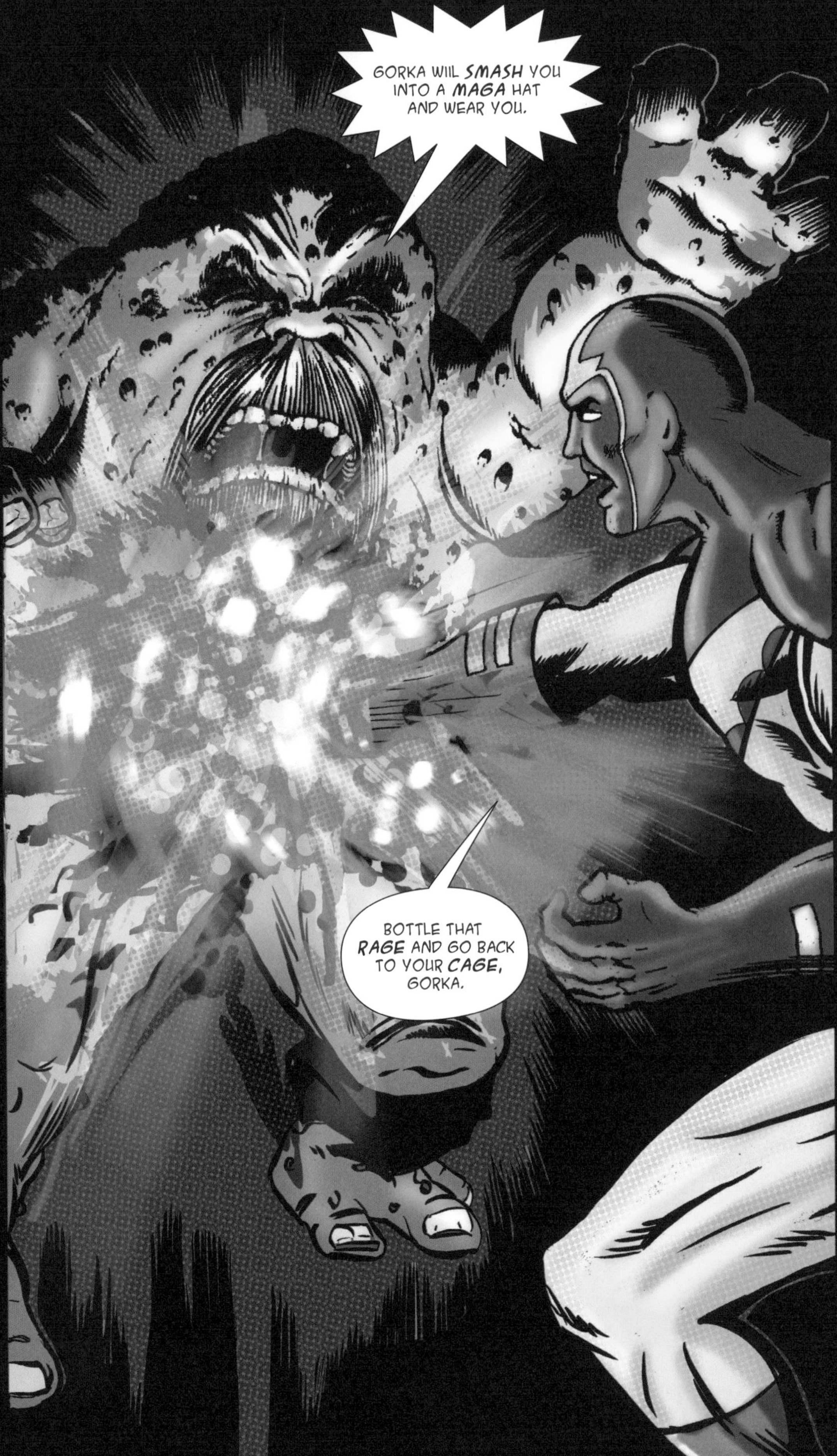
GORKA WIIL SMASH YOU INTO A MAGA HAT AND WEAR YOU.
BOTTLE THAT RAGE AND GO BACK TO YOUR CAGE, GORKA.

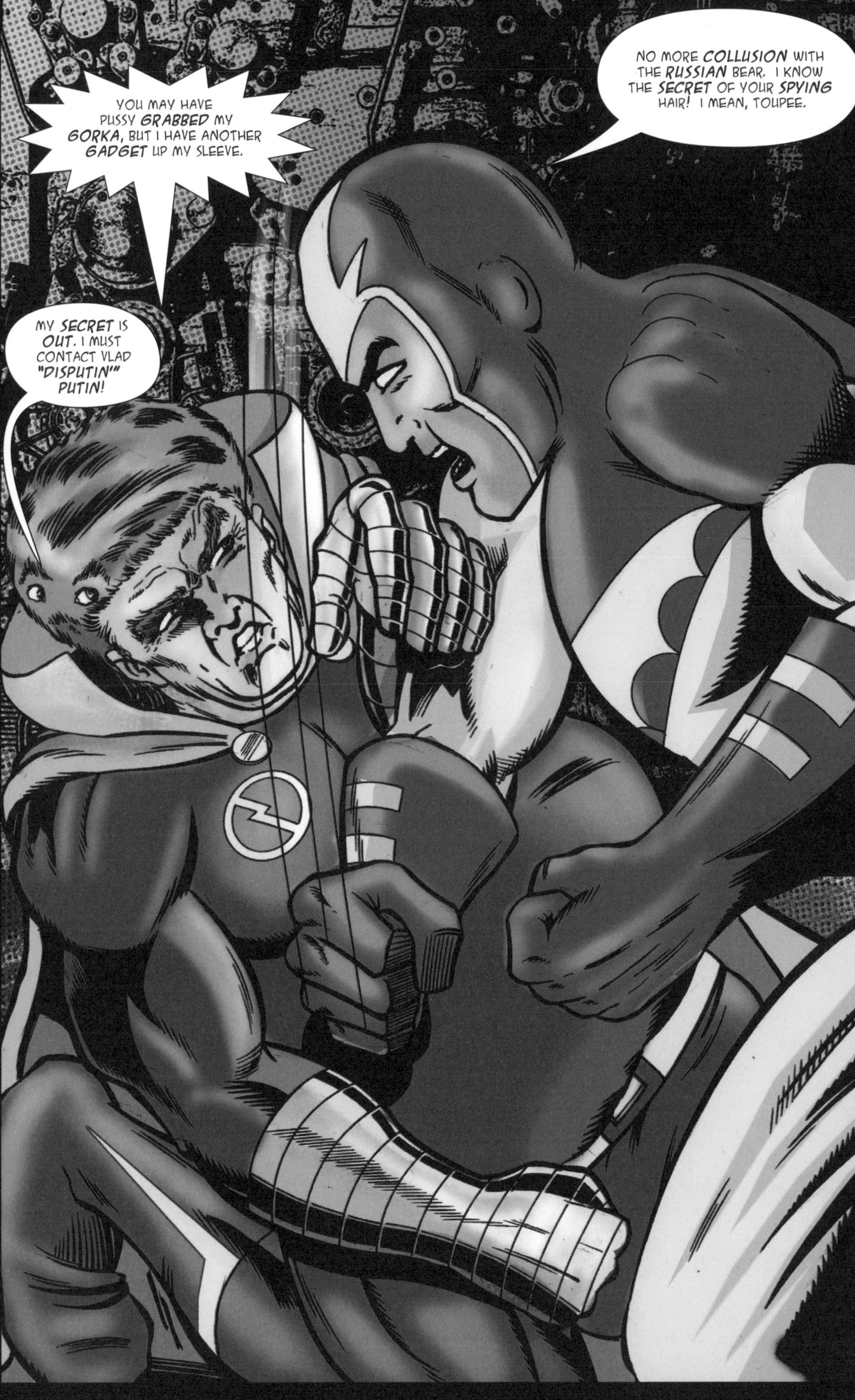
YOU MAY HAVE PUSSY GRABBED MY GORKA, BUT I HAVE ANOTHER GADGET UP MY SLEEVE.
NO MORE COLLUSION WITH THE RUSSIAN BEAR. I KNOW THE SECRET OF YOUR SPYING HAIR! I MEAN, TOUPEE.
MY SECRET IS OUT. I MUST CONTACT VLAD "DISPUTIN'" PUTIN!

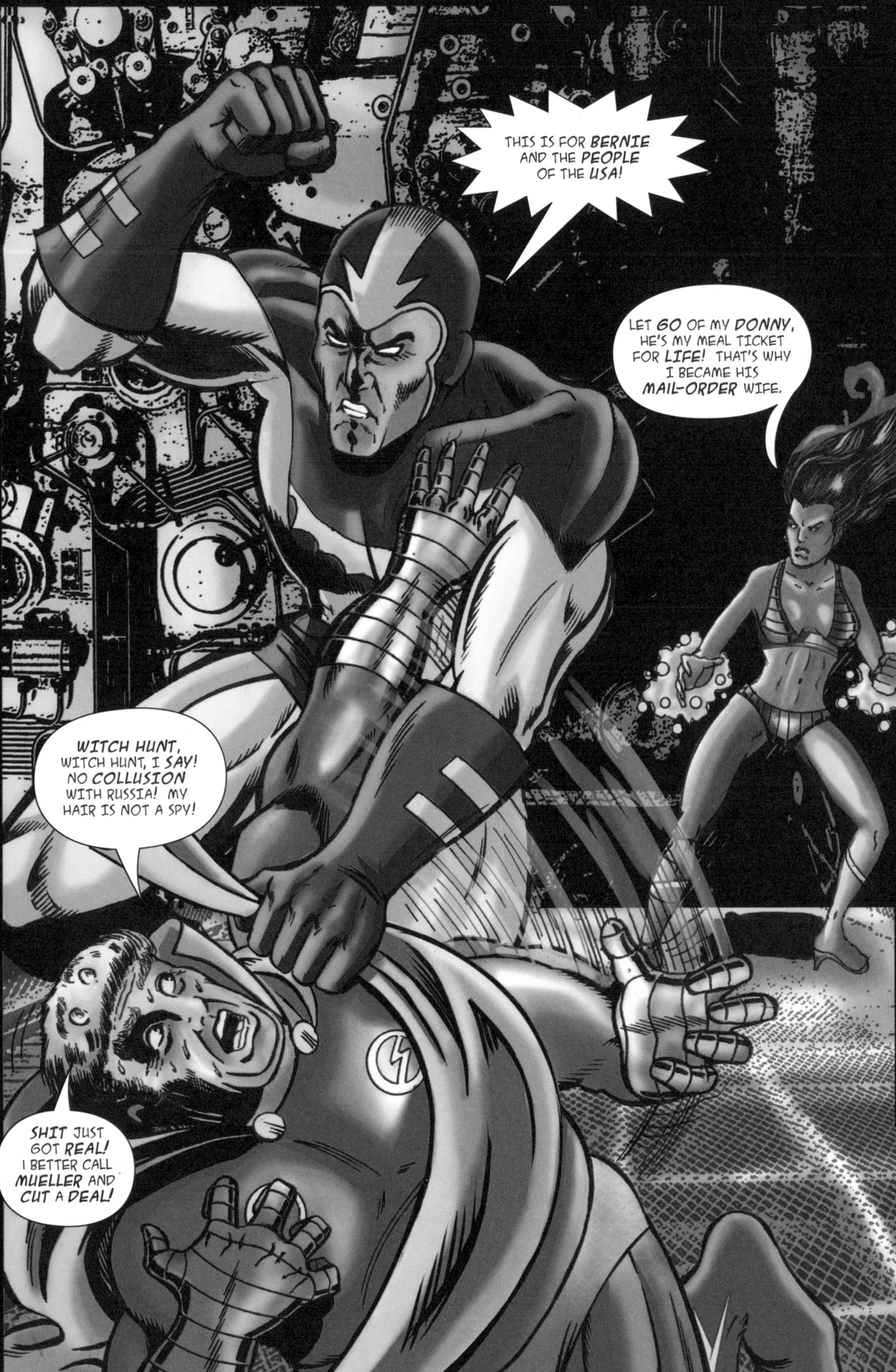
THIS IS FOR BERNIE AND THE PEOPLE OF THE USA!
LET GO OF MY DONNY, HE'S MY MEAL TICKET FOR LIFE! THAT'S WHY I BECAME HIS MAIL-ORDER WIFE.
WITCH HUNT, WITCH HUNT, I SAY! NO COLLUSION WITH RUSSIA! MY HAIR IS NOT A SPY!
SHIT JUST GOT REAL! I BETTER CALL MUELLER AND CUT A DEAL!

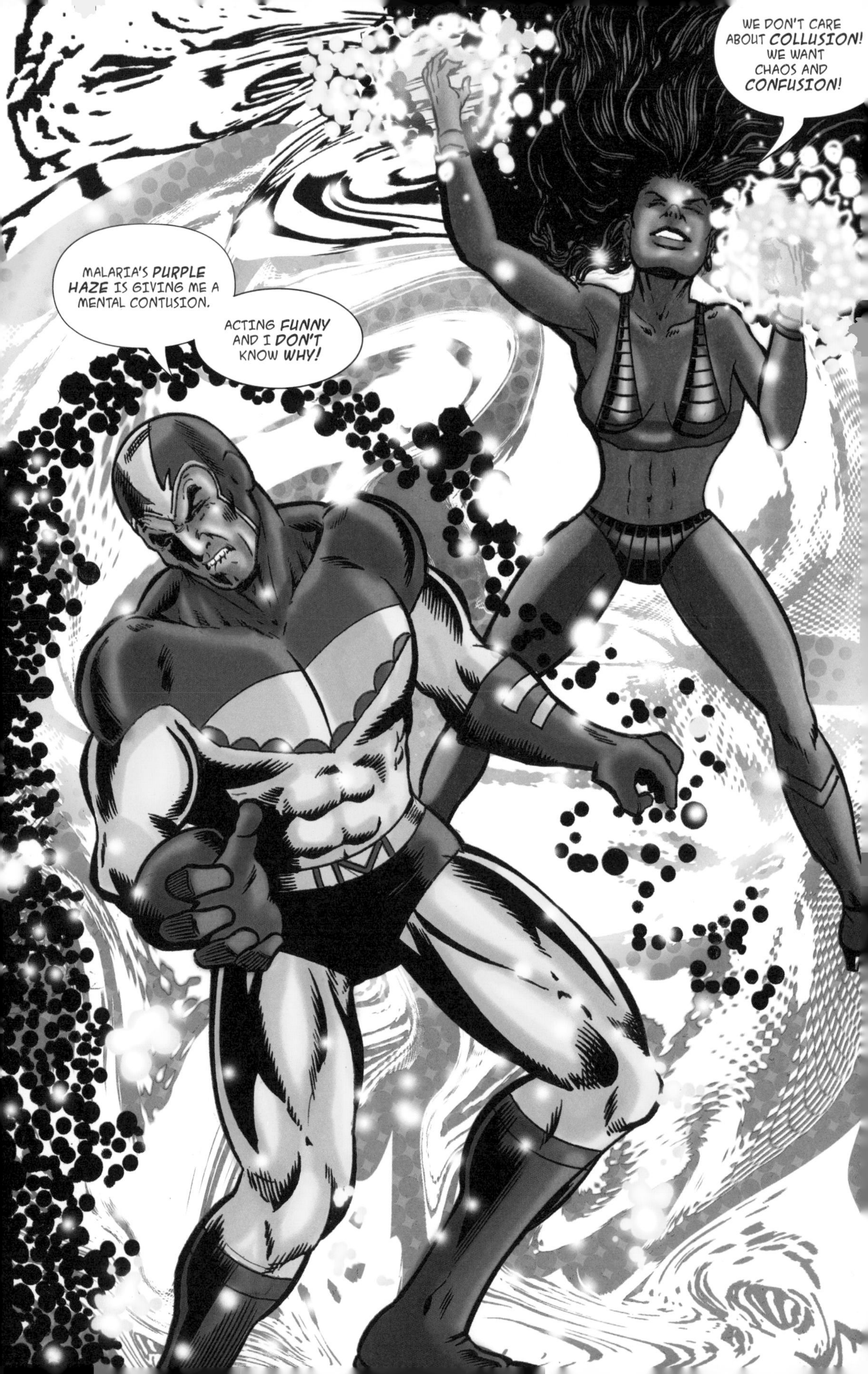
MALARIA'S PURPLE HAZE IS GIVING ME A MENTAL CONTUSION.
ACTING FUNNY AND I DON'T KNOW WHY!
WE DON'T CARE ABOUT COLLUSION! WE WANT CHAOS AND CONFUSION!

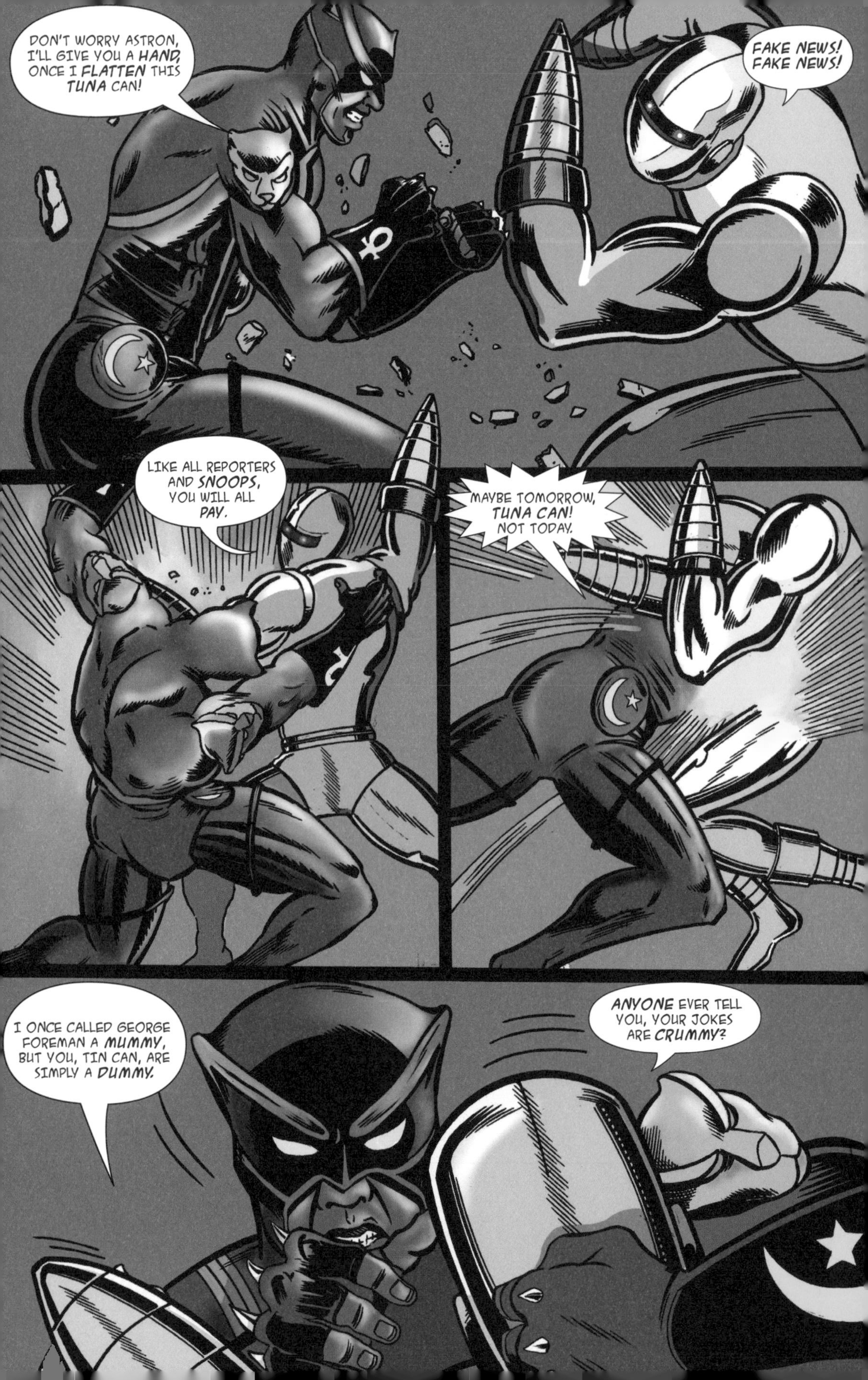
DON'T WORRY ASTRON, I'LL GIVE YOU A HAND, ONCE I FLATTEN THIS TUNA CAN!
FAKE NEWS! FAKE NEWS!
LIKE ALL REPORTERS AND SNOOPS, YOU WILL ALL PAY.
MAYBE TOMORROW, TUNA CAN! NOT TODAY.
I ONCE CALLED GEORGE FOREMAN A MUMMY, BUT YOU, TIN CAN, ARE SIMPLY A DUMMY.
ANYONE EVER TELL YOU, YOUR JOKES ARE CRUMMY?

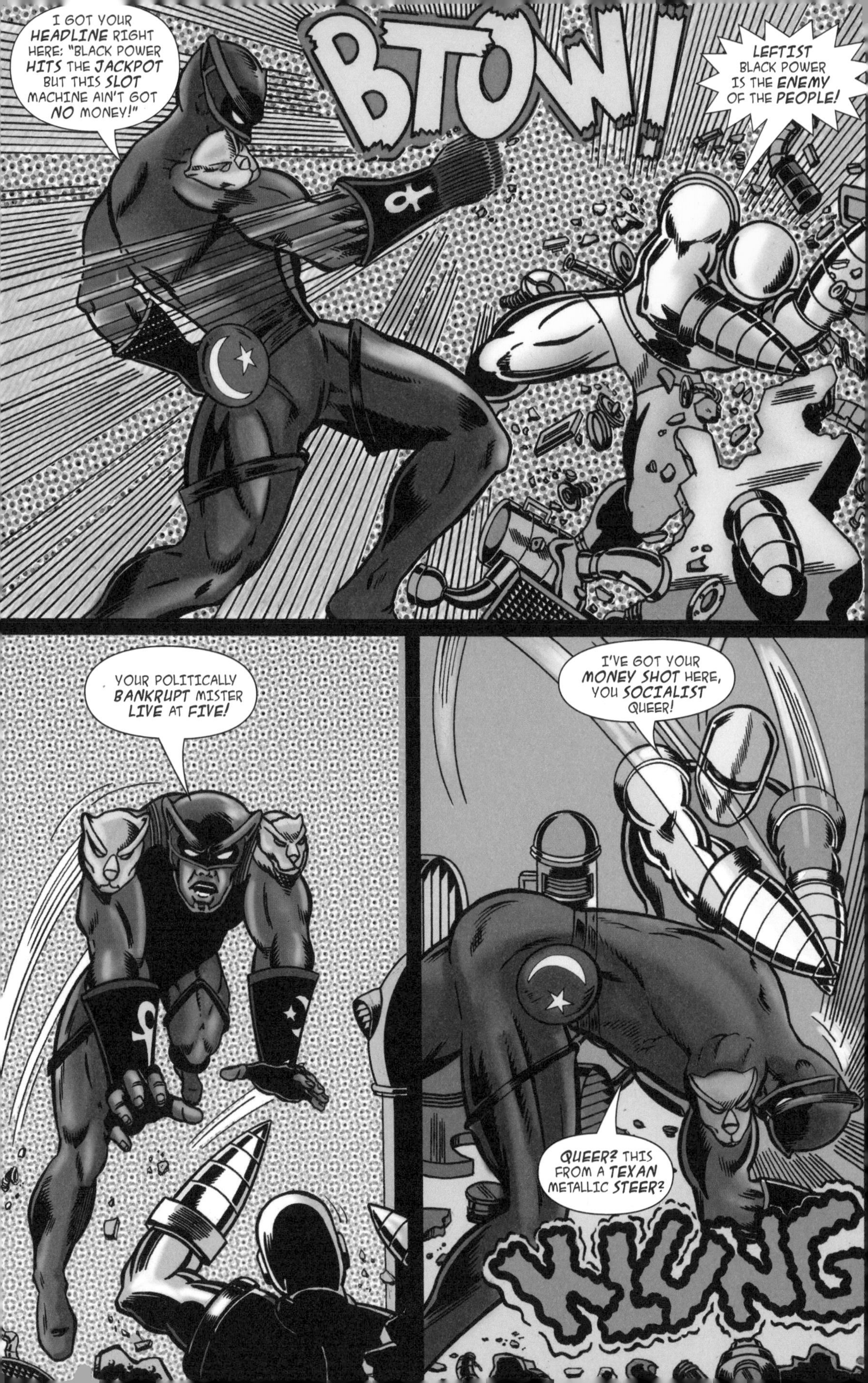
I GOT YOUR HEADLINE RIGHT HERE: "BLACK POWER HITS THE JACKPOT BUT THIS SLOT MACHINE AIN'T GOT NO MONEY!"
BTOW!
LEFTIST BLACK POWER IS THE ENEMY OF THE PEOPLE!
YOUR POLITICALLY BANKRUPT MISTER LIVE AT FIVE!
I'VE GOT YOUR MONEY SHOT HERE, YOU SOCIALIST QUEER!
QUEER? THIS FROM A TEXAN METALLIC STEER?
KLUNG

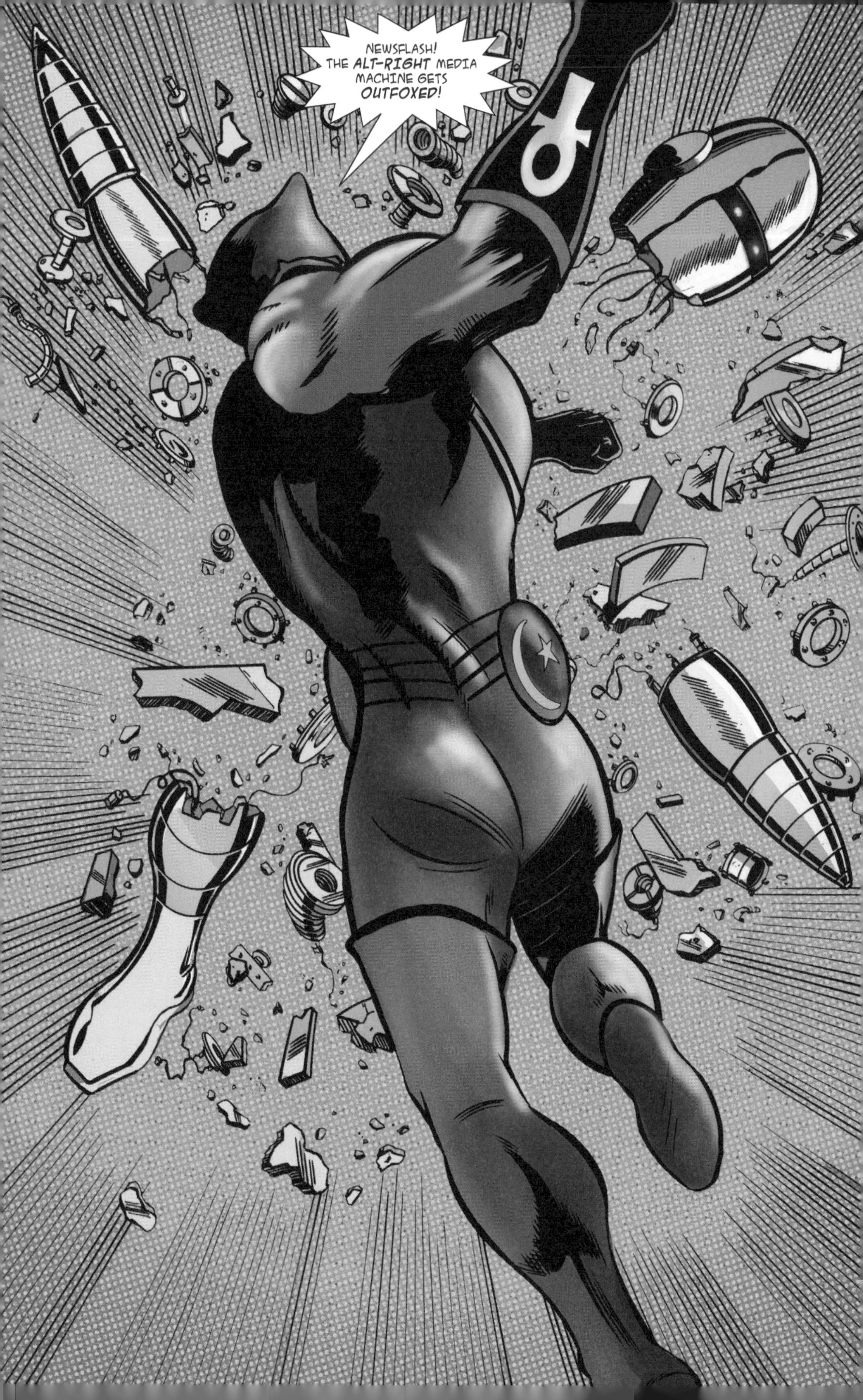
NEWSFLASH! THE ALT-RIGHT MEDIA MACHINE GETS OUTFOXED!

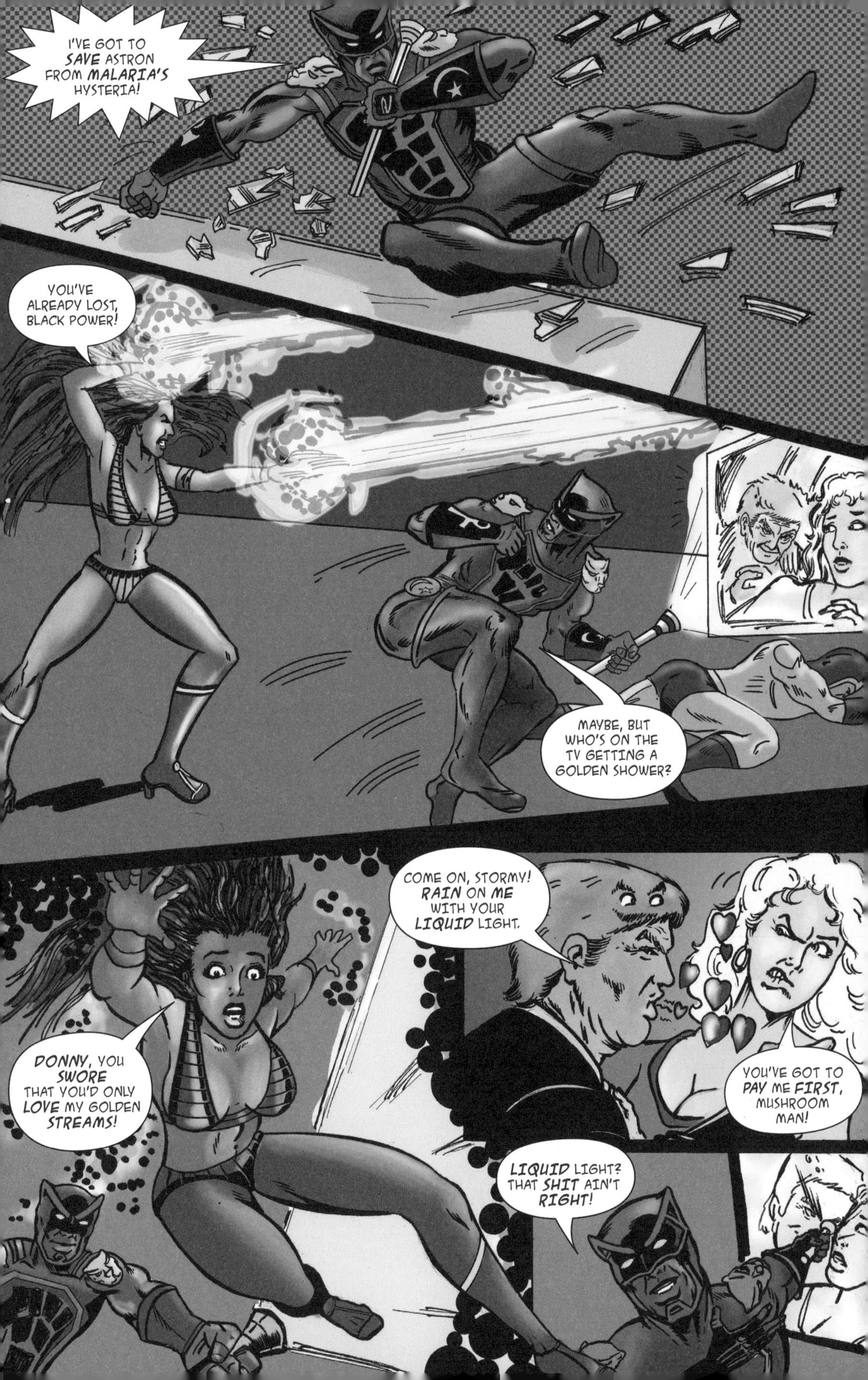

I'VE GOT TO SAVE ASTRON FROM MALARIA'S HYSTERIA!
YOU'VE ALREADY LOST, BLACK POWER!
MAYBE, BUT WHO'S ON THE TV GETTING A GOLDEN SHOWER?
COME ON, STORMY! RAIN ON ME WITH YOUR LIQUID LIGHT.
YOU'VE GOT TO PAY ME FIRST, MUSHROOM MAN!
DONNY, YOU SWORE THAT YOU'D ONLY LOVE MY GOLDEN STREAMS!
LIQUID LIGHT? THAT SHIT AIN'T RIGHT!

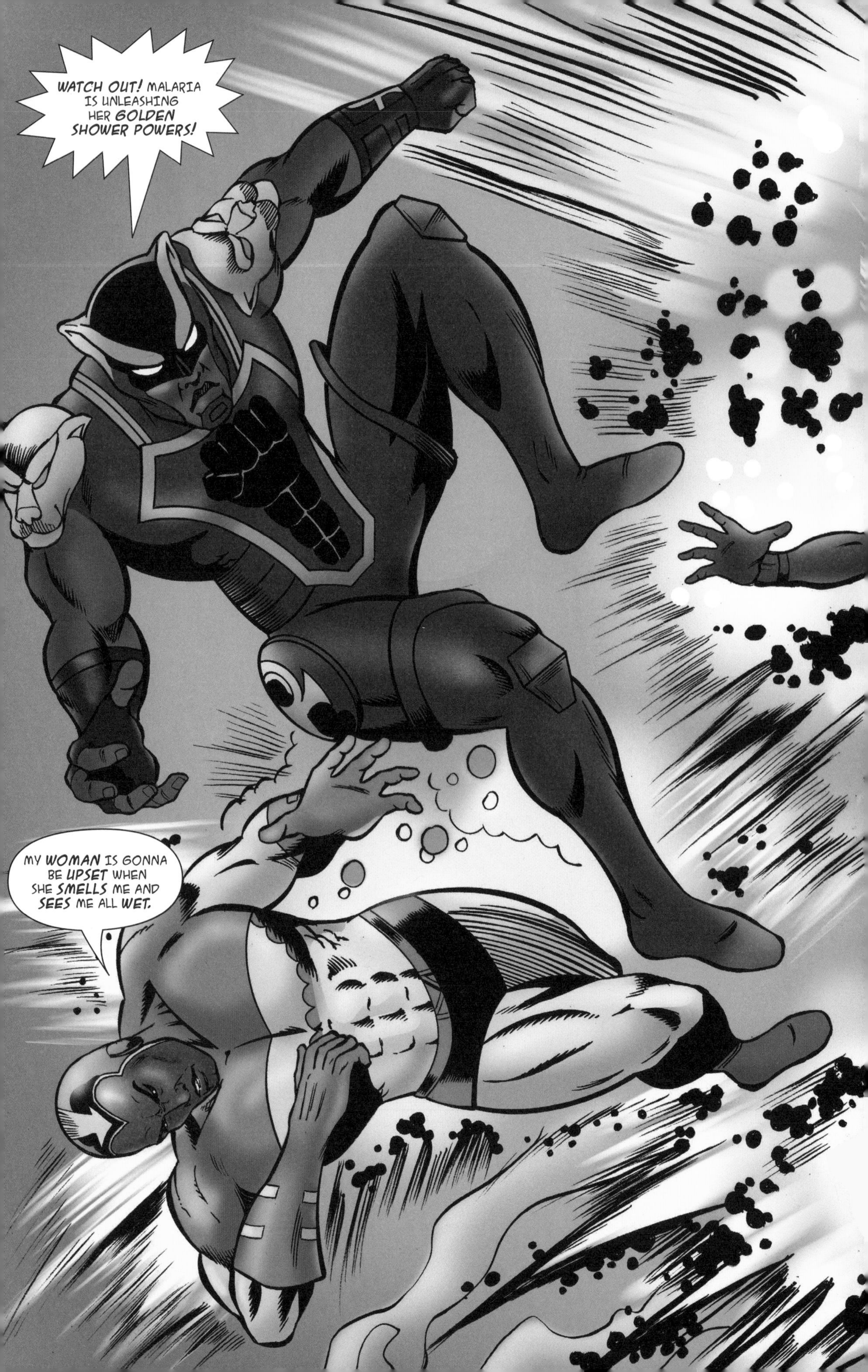
WATCH OUT! MALARIA IS UNLEASHING HER GOLDEN SHOWER POWERS!
MY WOMAN IS GONNA BE UPSET WHEN SHE SMELLS ME AND SEES ME ALL WET.

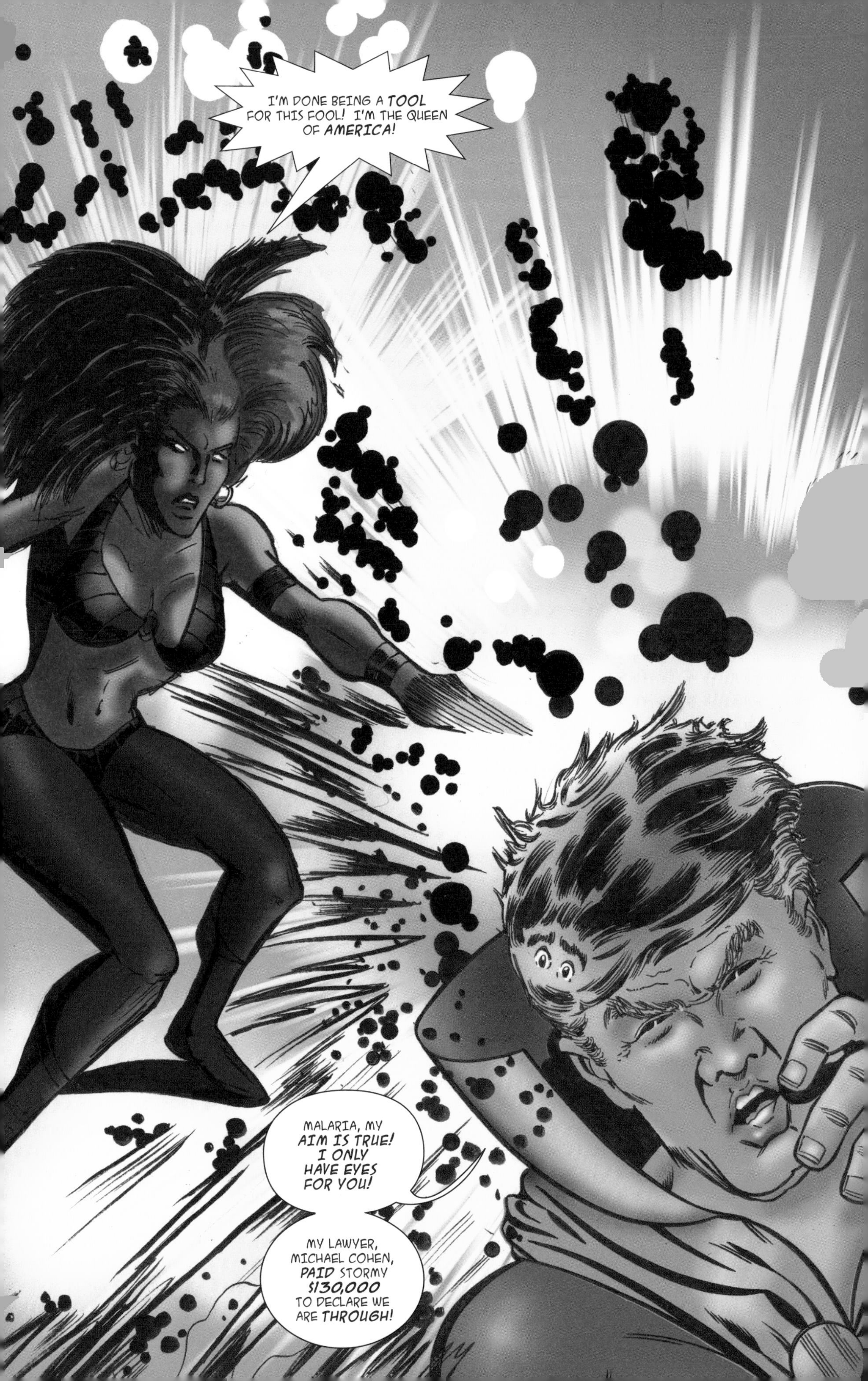

I'M DONE BEING A TOOL FOR THIS FOOL! I'M THE QUEEN OF AMERICA!
MALARIA, MY AIM IS TRUE! I ONLY HAVE EYES FOR YOU!
MY LAWYER, MICHAEL COHEN, PAID STORMY $130,000 TO DECLARE WE ARE THROUGH!

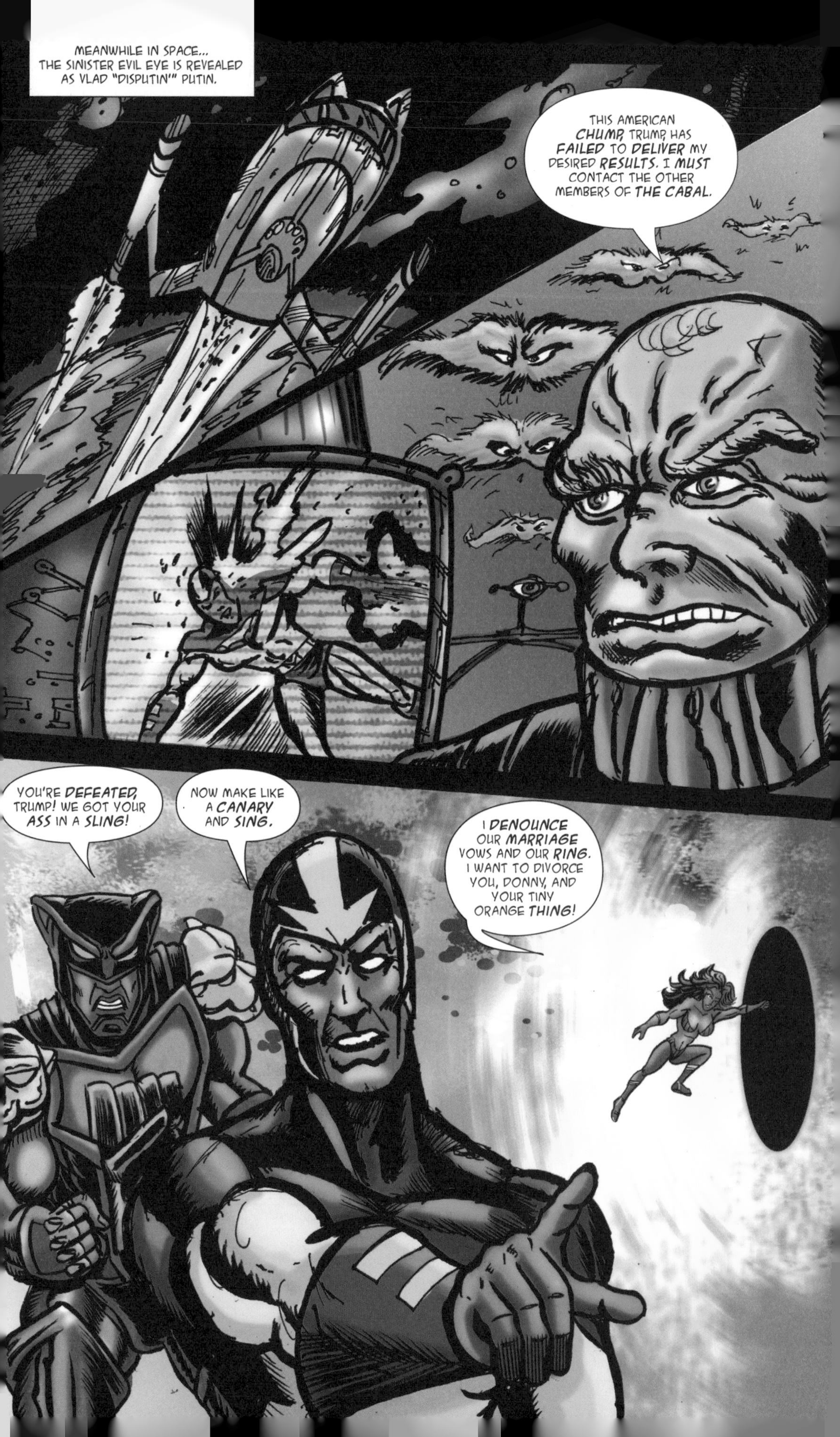
MEANWHILE IN SPACE... THE SINISTER EVIL EYE IS REVEALED AS VLAD "DISPUTIN'" PUTIN.
THIS AMERICAN CHUMP, TRUMP, HAS FAILED TO DELIVER MY DESIRED RESULTS. I MUST CONTACT THE OTHER MEMBERS OF THE CABAL.
YOU'RE DEFEATED, TRUMP! WE GOT YOUR ASS IN A SLING!
NOW MAKE LIKE A CANARY AND SING.
I DENOUNCE OUR MARRIAGE VOWS AND OUR RING. I WANT TO DIVORCE YOU, DONNY, AND YOUR TINY ORANGE THING!

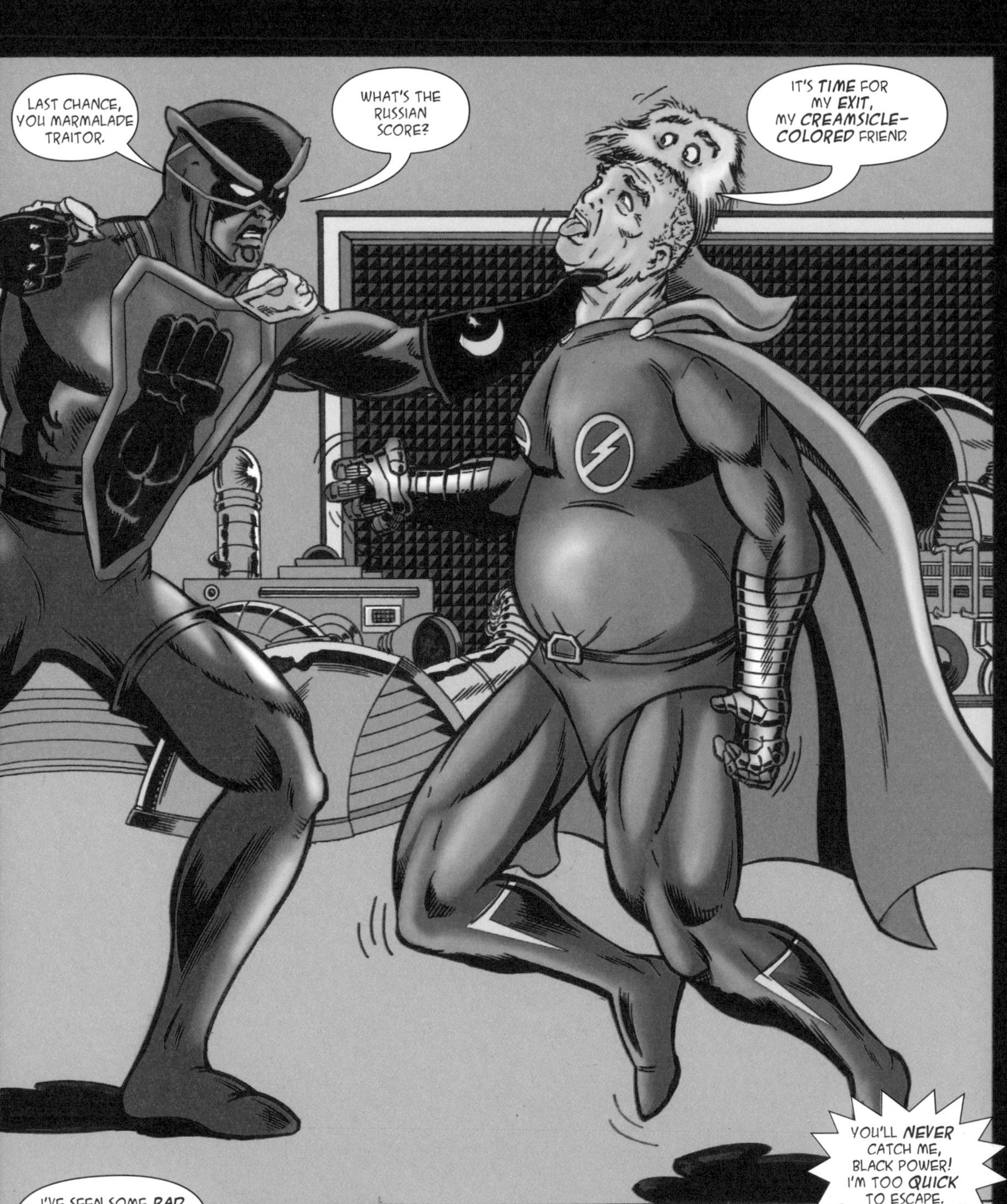
LAST CHANCE, YOU MARMALADE TRAITOR.
WHAT'S THE RUSSIAN SCORE?
IT'S TIME FOR MY EXIT, MY CREAMSICLE-COLORED FRIEND.

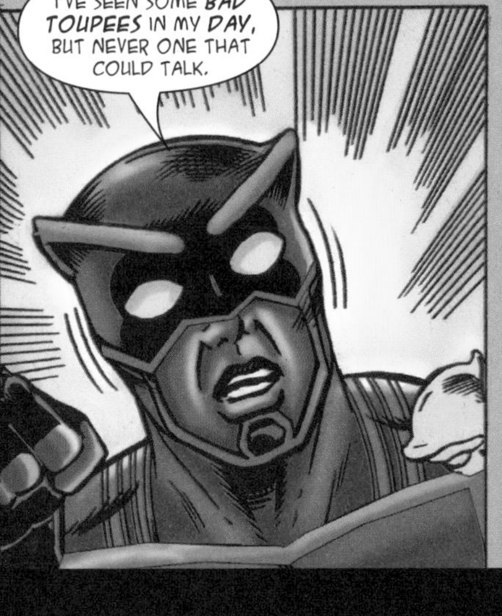
I'VE SEEN SOME BAD TOUPEES IN MY DAY, BUT NEVER ONE THAT COULD TALK.

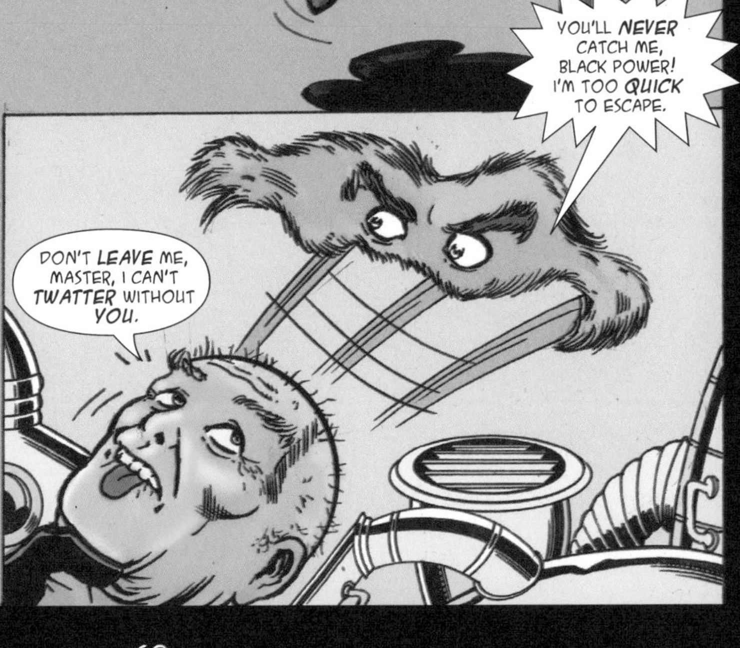
YOU'LL NEVER CATCH ME, BLACK POWER! I'M TOO QUICK TO ESCAPE.
DON'T LEAVE ME, MASTER, I CAN'T TWATTER WITHOUT YOU.

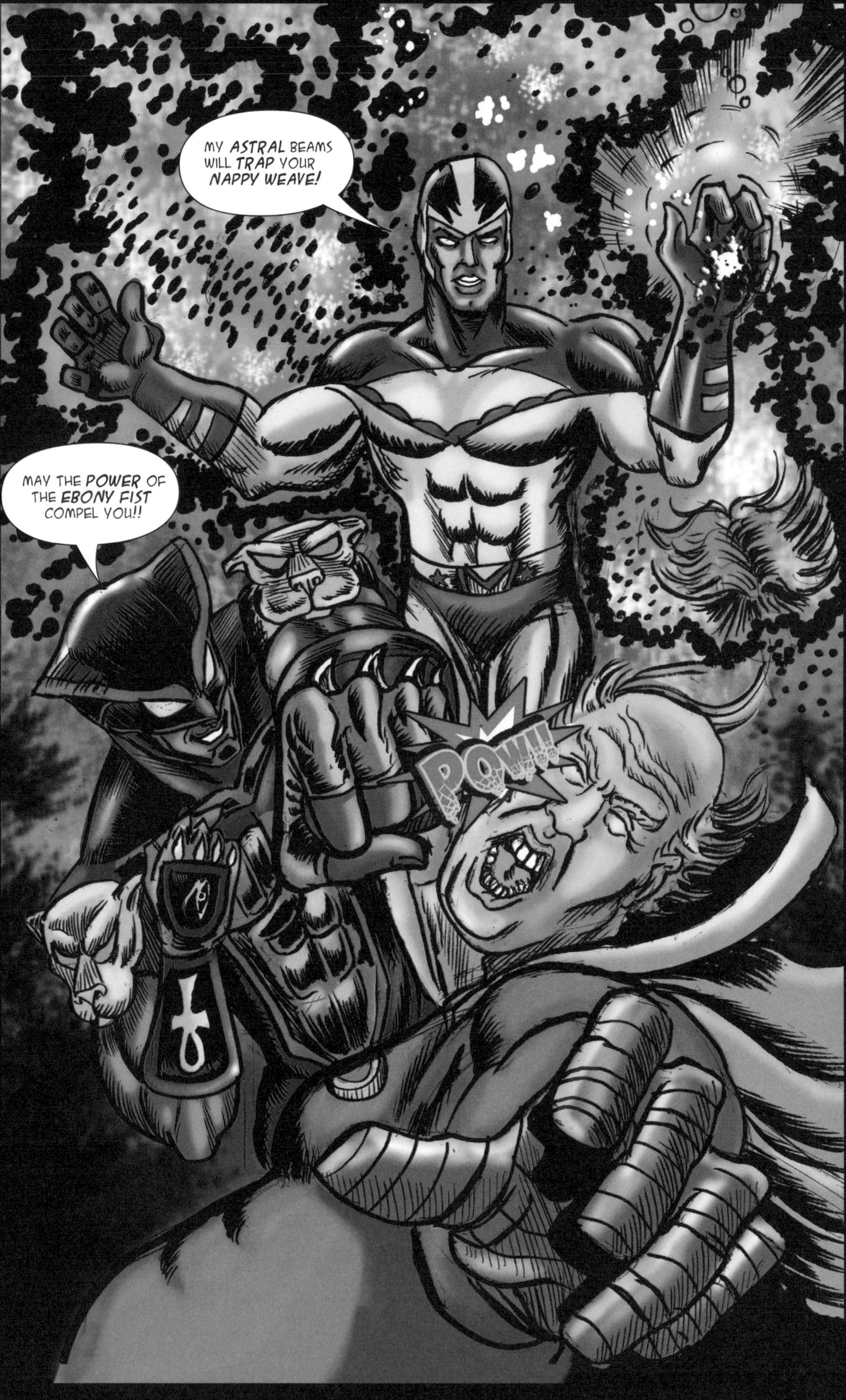
MY ASTRAL BEAMS WILL TRAP YOUR NAPPY WEAVE!
MAY THE POWER OF THE EBONY FIST COMPEL YOU!!
POW!!

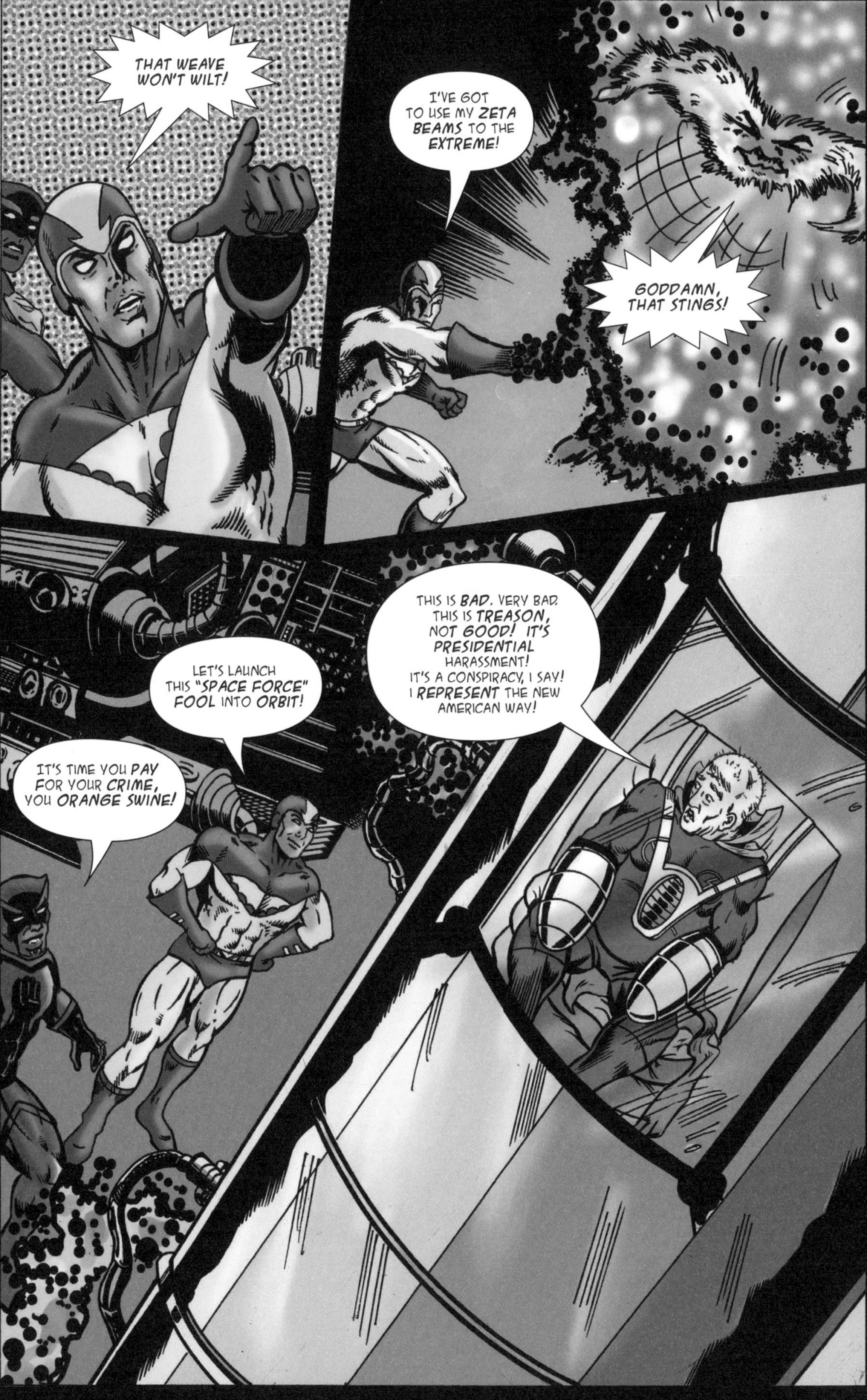

THAT WEAVE WON'T WILT!
I'VE GOT TO USE MY ZETA BEAMS TO THE EXTREME!
GODDAMN, THAT STINGS!
THIS IS BAD. VERY BAD. THIS IS TREASON, NOT GOOD! IT'S PRESIDENTIAL HARASSMENT! IT'S A CONSPIRACY, I SAY! I REPRESENT THE NEW AMERICAN WAY!
LET'S LAUNCH THIS "SPACE FORCE" FOOL INTO ORBIT!
IT'S TIME YOU PAY FOR YOUR CRIME, YOU ORANGE SWINE!

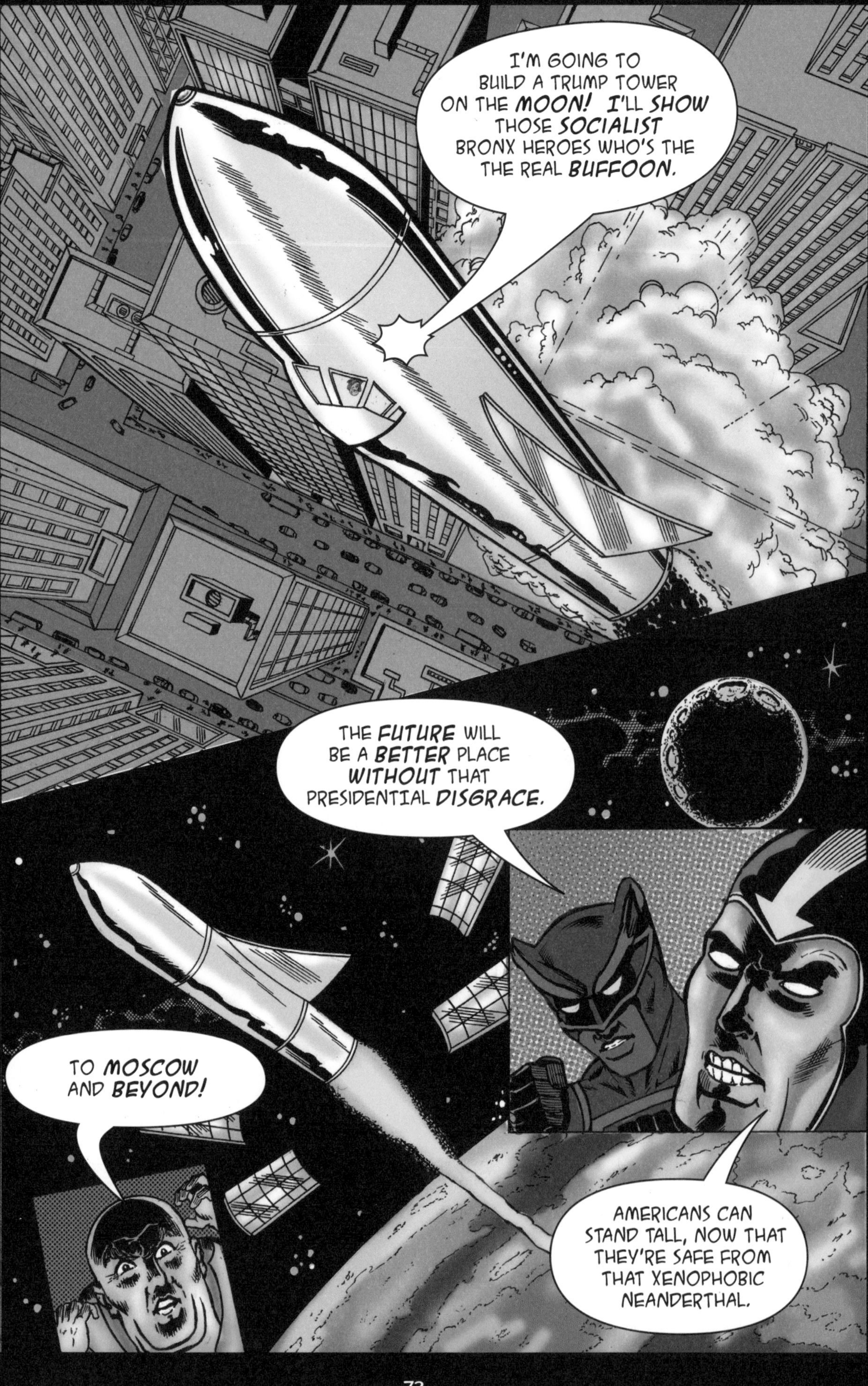

I'M GOING TO BUILD A TRUMP TOWER ON THE MOON! I'LL SHOW THOSE SOCIALIST BRONX HEROES WHO'S THE THE REAL BUFFOON.
THE FUTURE WILL BE A BETTER PLACE WITHOUT THAT PRESIDENTIAL DISGRACE.
TO MOSCOW AND BEYOND!
AMERICANS CAN STAND TALL, NOW THAT THEY'RE SAFE FROM THAT XENOPHOBIC NEANDERTHAL.

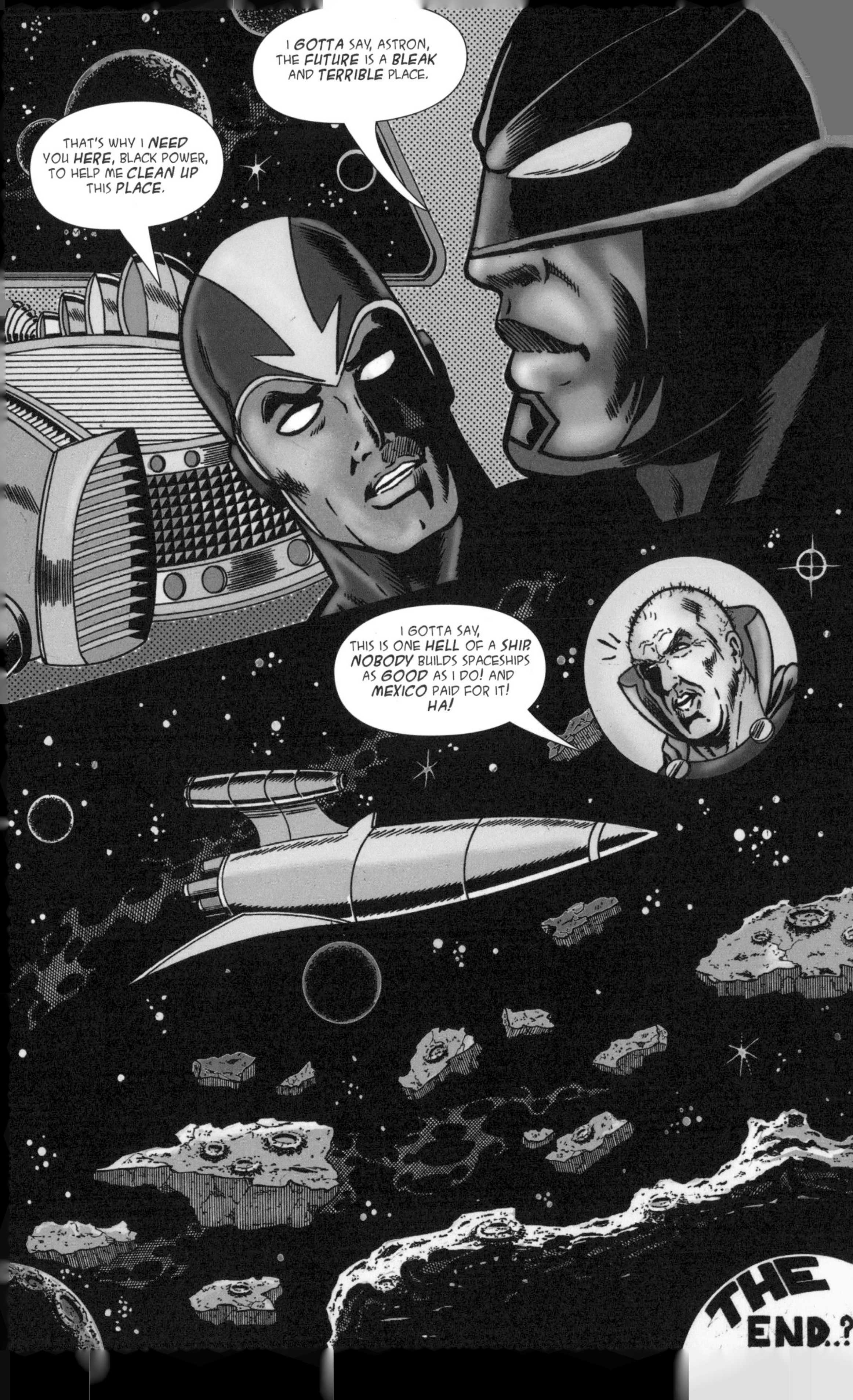
I GOTTA SAY, ASTRON, THE FUTURE IS A BLEAK AND TERRIBLE PLACE.
THAT'S WHY I NEED YOU HERE, BLACK POWER, TO HELP ME CLEAN UP THIS PLACE.
I GOTTA SAY, THIS IS ONE HELL OF A SHIP. NOBODY BUILDS SPACESHIPS AS GOOD AS I DO! AND MEXICO PAID FOR IT! HA!
THE END..?

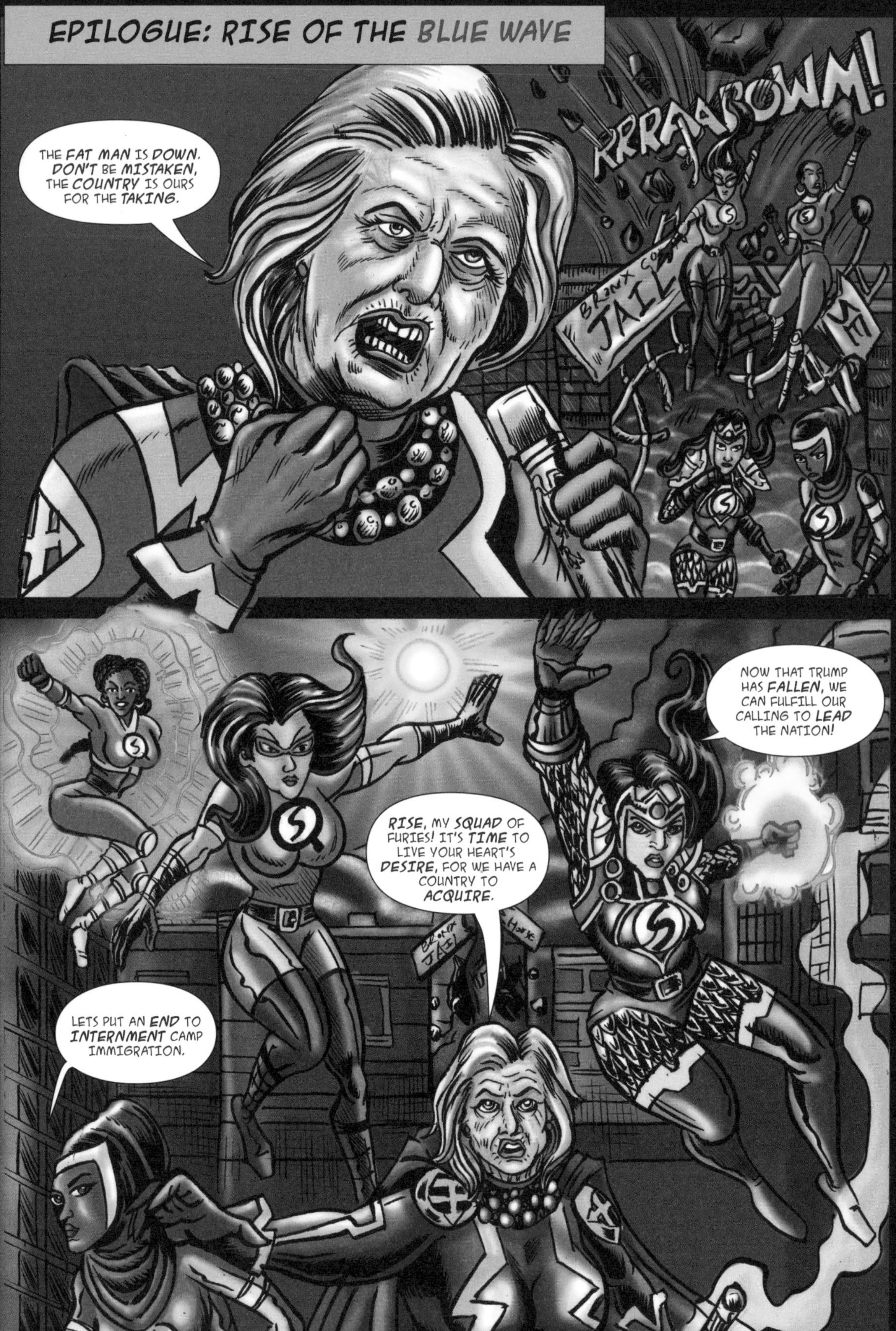
EPILOGUE: RISE OF THE BLUE WAVE
THE FAT MAN IS DOWN. DON'T BE MISTAKEN, THE COUNTRY IS OURS FOR THE TAKING.
KRRAABOWM!
JAIL
NOW THAT TRUMP HAS FALLEN, WE CAN FULFILL OUR CALLING TO LEAD THE NATION!
RISE, MY SQUAD OF FURIES! IT'S TIME TO LIVE YOUR HEART'S DESIRE, FOR WE HAVE A COUNTRY TO ACQUIRE.
LETS PUT AN END TO INTERNMENT CAMP IMMIGRATION.

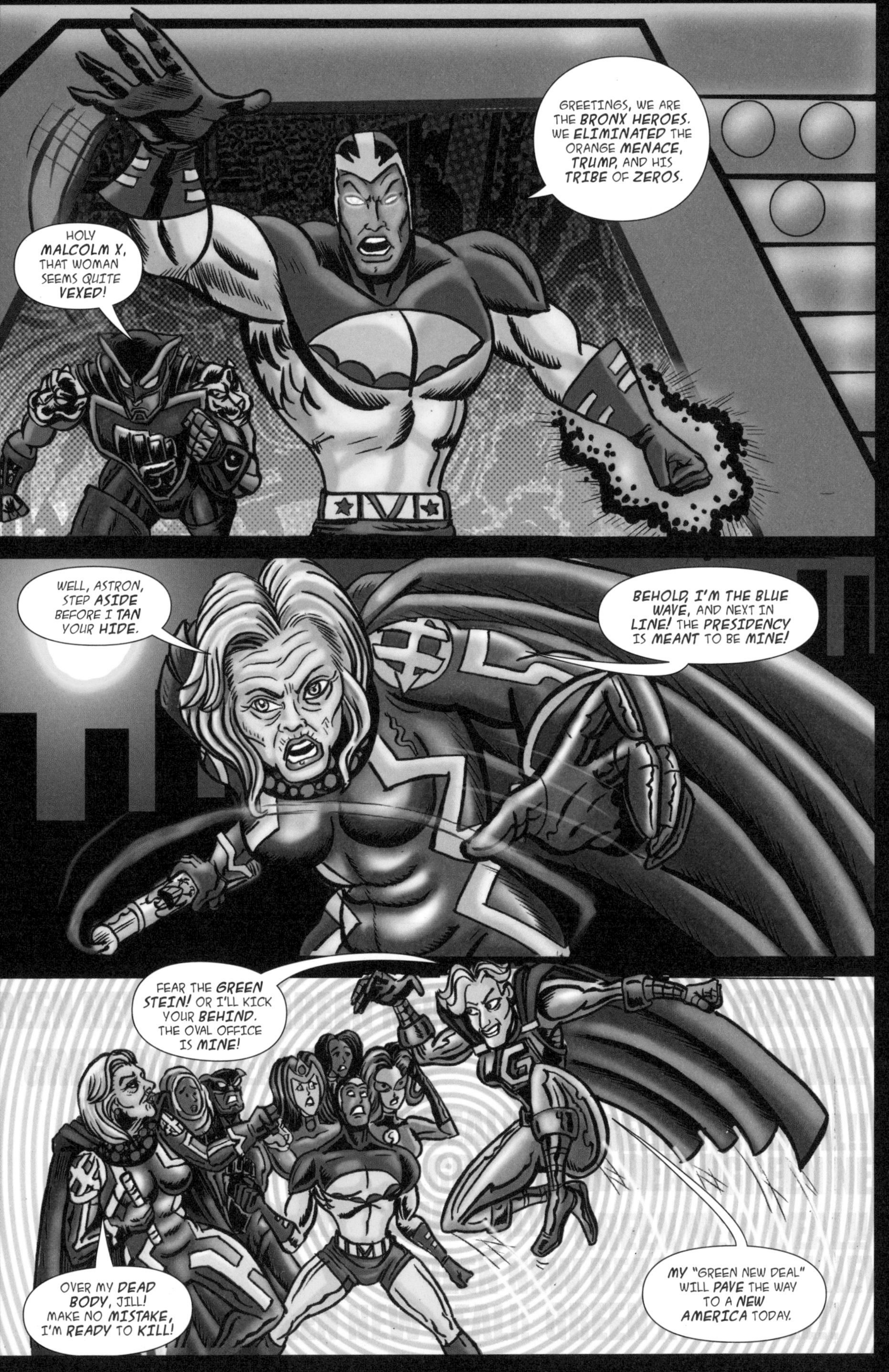
GREETINGS, WE ARE THE BRONX HEROES. WE ELIMINATED THE ORANGE MENACE, TRUMP, AND HIS TRIBE OF ZEROS.
HOLY MALCOLM X, THAT WOMAN SEEMS QUITE VEXED!
WELL, ASTRON, STEP ASIDE BEFORE I TAN YOUR HIDE.
BEHOLD, I'M THE BLUE WAVE, AND NEXT IN LINE! THE PRESIDENCY IS MEANT TO BE MINE!
FEAR THE GREEN STEIN! OR I'LL KICK YOUR BEHIND. THE OVAL OFFICE IS MINE!
OVER MY DEAD BODY, JILL! MAKE NO MISTAKE, I'M READY TO KILL!
MY "GREEN NEW DEAL" WILL PAVE THE WAY TO A NEW AMERICA TODAY.

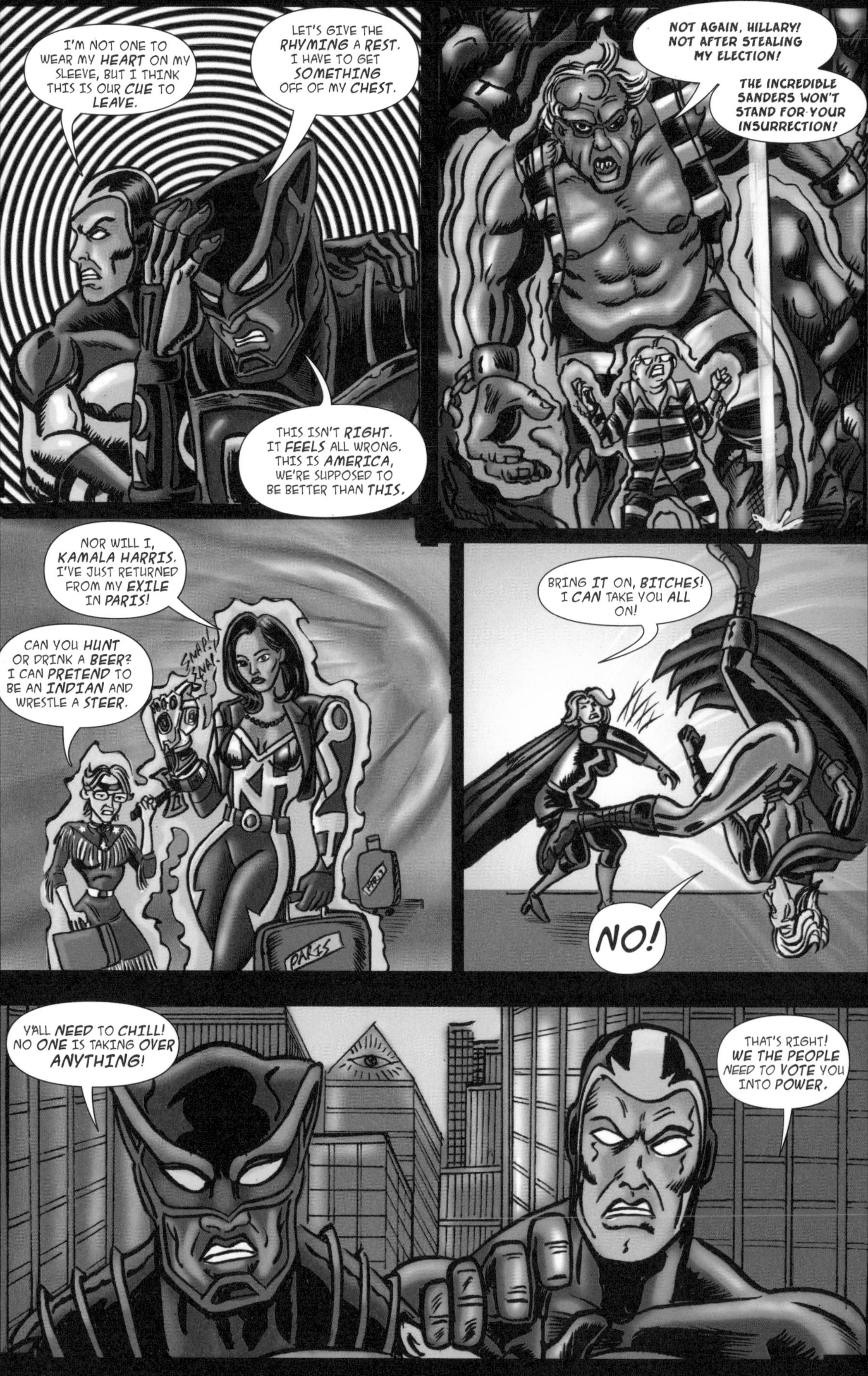
I'M NOT ONE TO WEAR MY HEART ON MY SLEEVE, BUT I THINK THIS IS OUR CUE TO LEAVE.
LET'S GIVE THE RHYMING A REST. I HAVE TO GET SOMETHING OFF OF MY CHEST.
THIS ISN'T RIGHT. IT FEELS ALL WRONG. THIS IS AMERICA, WE'RE SUPPOSED TO BE BETTER THAN THIS.
NOT AGAIN, HILLARY! NOT AFTER STEALING MY ELECTION!
THE INCREDIBLE SANDERS WON'T STAND FOR YOUR INSURRECTION!
NOR WILL I, KAMALA HARRIS. I'VE JUST RETURNED FROM MY EXILE IN PARIS!
SNAP! SNAP!
CAN YOU HUNT OR DRINK A BEER? I CAN PRETEND TO BE AN INDIAN AND WRESTLE A STEER.
PARIS
BRING IT ON, BITCHES! I CAN TAKE YOU ALL ON!
NO!
Y'ALL NEED TO CHILL! NO ONE IS TAKING OVER ANYTHING!
THAT'S RIGHT! WE THE PEOPLE NEED TO VOTE YOU INTO POWER.

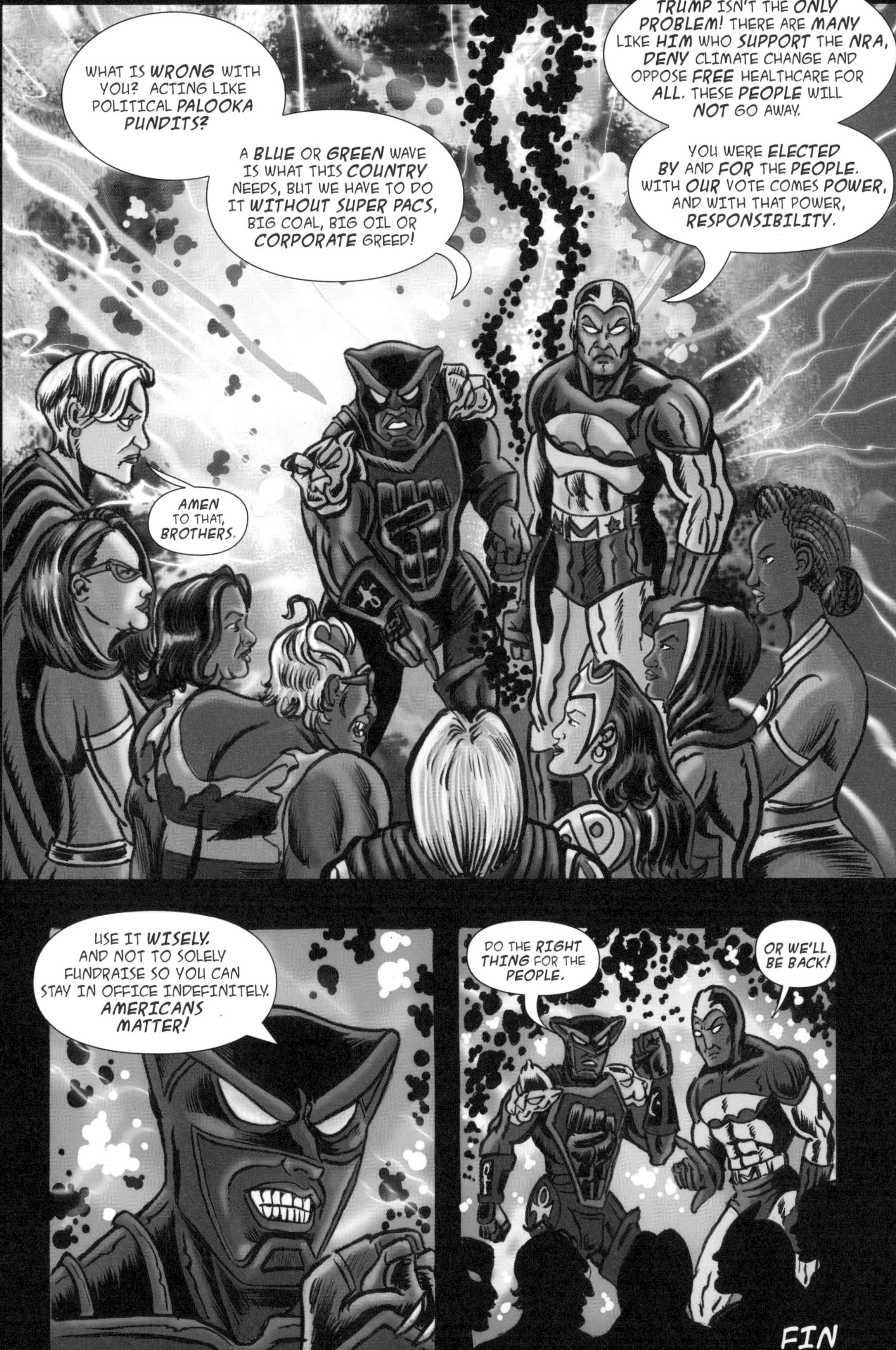
WHAT IS WRONG WITH YOU? ACTING LIKE POLITICAL PALOOKA PUNDITS?
A BLUE OR GREEN WAVE IS WHAT THIS COUNTRY NEEDS, BUT WE HAVE TO DO IT WITHOUT SUPER PACS, BIG COAL, BIG OIL OR CORPORATE GREED!
TRUMP ISN'T THE ONLY PROBLEM! THERE ARE MANY LIKE HIM WHO SUPPORT THE NRA, DENY CLIMATE CHANGE AND OPPOSE FREE HEALTHCARE FOR ALL. THESE PEOPLE WILL NOT GO AWAY.
YOU WERE ELECTED BY AND FOR THE PEOPLE. WITH OUR VOTE COMES POWER, AND WITH THAT POWER, RESPONSIBILITY.
AMEN TO THAT, BROTHERS.
USE IT WISELY. AND NOT TO SOLELY FUNDRAISE SO YOU CAN STAY IN OFFICE INDEFINITELY. AMERICANS MATTER!
DO THE RIGHT THING FOR THE PEOPLE.
OR WE'LL BE BACK!
FIN

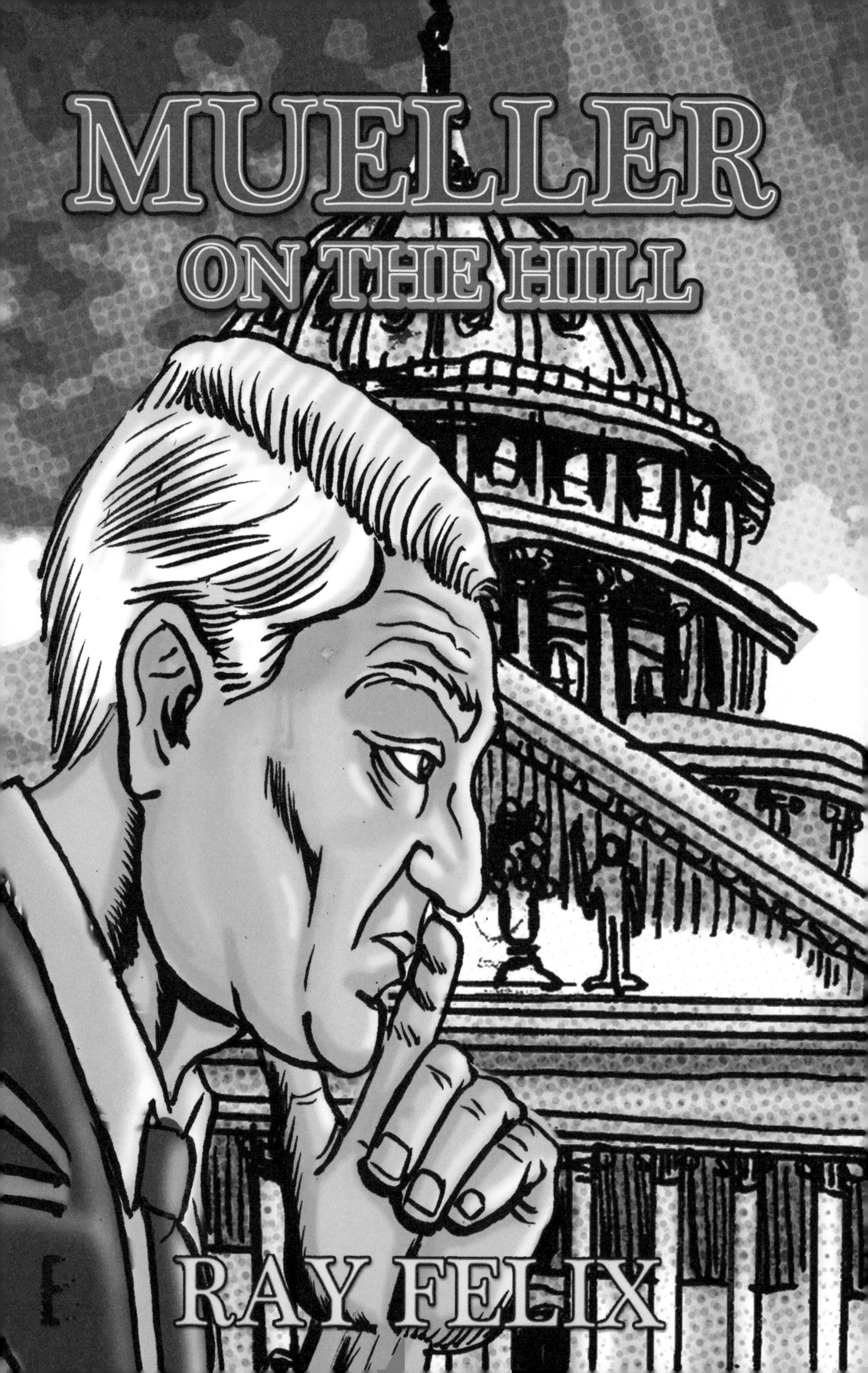
MUELLER
ON THE HILL
RAY FELIX

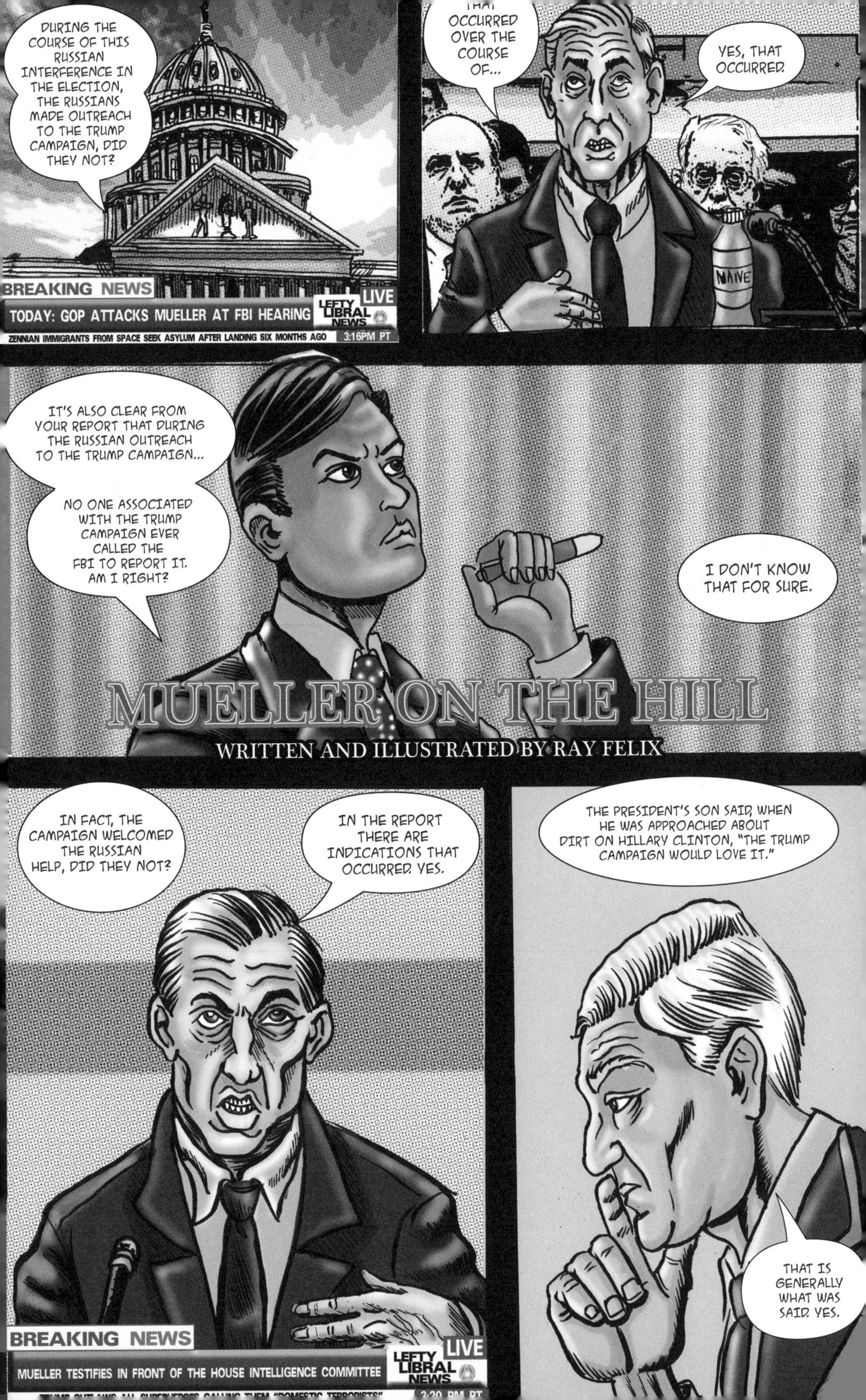
DURING THE COURSE OF THIS RUSSIAN INTERFERENCE IN THE ELECTION, THE RUSSIANS MADE OUTREACH TO THE TRUMP CAMPAIGN, DID THEY NOT?
BREAKING NEWS
TODAY: GOP ATTACKS MUELLER AT FBI HEARING
LEFTY LIBRAL NEWS
LIVE
ZENNIAN IMMIGRANTS FROM SPACE SEEK ASYLUM AFTER LANDING SIX MONTHS AGO
3:16PM PT
OCCURRED OVER THE COURSE OF...
YES, THAT OCCURRED.
NAIVE
IT'S ALSO CLEAR FROM YOUR REPORT THAT DURING THE RUSSIAN OUTREACH TO THE TRUMP CAMPAIGN...
NO ONE ASSOCIATED WITH THE TRUMP CAMPAIGN EVER CALLED THE FBI TO REPORT IT. AM I RIGHT?
I DON'T KNOW THAT FOR SURE.
MUELLER ON THE HILL
WRITTEN AND ILLUSTRATED BY RAY FELIX
IN FACT, THE CAMPAIGN WELCOMED THE RUSSIAN HELP, DID THEY NOT?
IN THE REPORT THERE ARE INDICATIONS THAT OCCURRED. YES.
BREAKING NEWS
MUELLER TESTIFIES IN FRONT OF THE HOUSE INTELLIGENCE COMMITTEE
LEFTY LIBRAL NEWS
LIVE
THE PRESIDENT'S SON SAID, WHEN HE WAS APPROACHED ABOUT DIRT ON HILLARY CLINTON, "THE TRUMP CAMPAIGN WOULD LOVE IT."
THAT IS GENERALLY WHAT WAS SAID. YES.

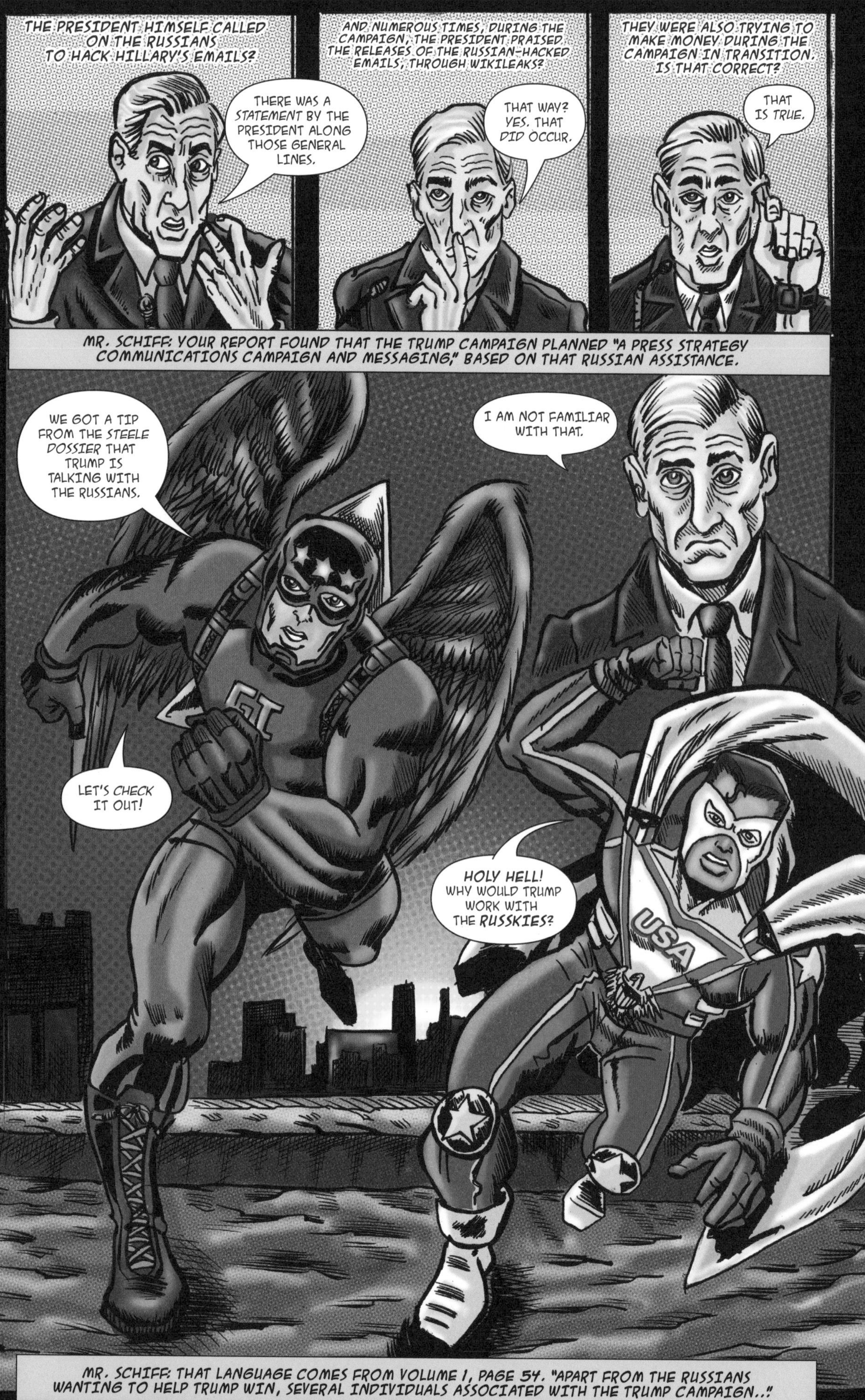
THE PRESIDENT HIMSELF CALLED ON THE RUSSIANS TO HACK HILLARY'S EMAILS?
THERE WAS A STATEMENT BY THE PRESIDENT ALONG THOSE GENERAL LINES.
AND NUMEROUS TIMES, DURING THE CAMPAIGN, THE PRESIDENT PRAISED THE RELEASES OF THE RUSSIAN-HACKED EMAILS, THROUGH WIKILEAKS?
THAT WAY? YES. THAT DID OCCUR.
THEY WERE ALSO TRYING TO MAKE MONEY DURING THE CAMPAIGN IN TRANSITION. IS THAT CORRECT?
THAT IS TRUE.
MR. SCHIFF: YOUR REPORT FOUND THAT THE TRUMP CAMPAIGN PLANNED "A PRESS STRATEGY COMMUNICATIONS CAMPAIGN AND MESSAGING," BASED ON THAT RUSSIAN ASSISTANCE.
WE GOT A TIP FROM THE STEELE DOSSIER THAT TRUMP IS TALKING WITH THE RUSSIANS.
I AM NOT FAMILIAR WITH THAT.
LET'S CHECK IT OUT!
HOLY HELL! WHY WOULD TRUMP WORK WITH THE RUSSKIES?
GI
USA
MR. SCHIFF: THAT LANGUAGE COMES FROM VOLUME 1, PAGE 54. "APART FROM THE RUSSIANS WANTING TO HELP TRUMP WIN, SEVERAL INDIVIDUALS ASSOCIATED WITH THE TRUMP CAMPAIGN..."

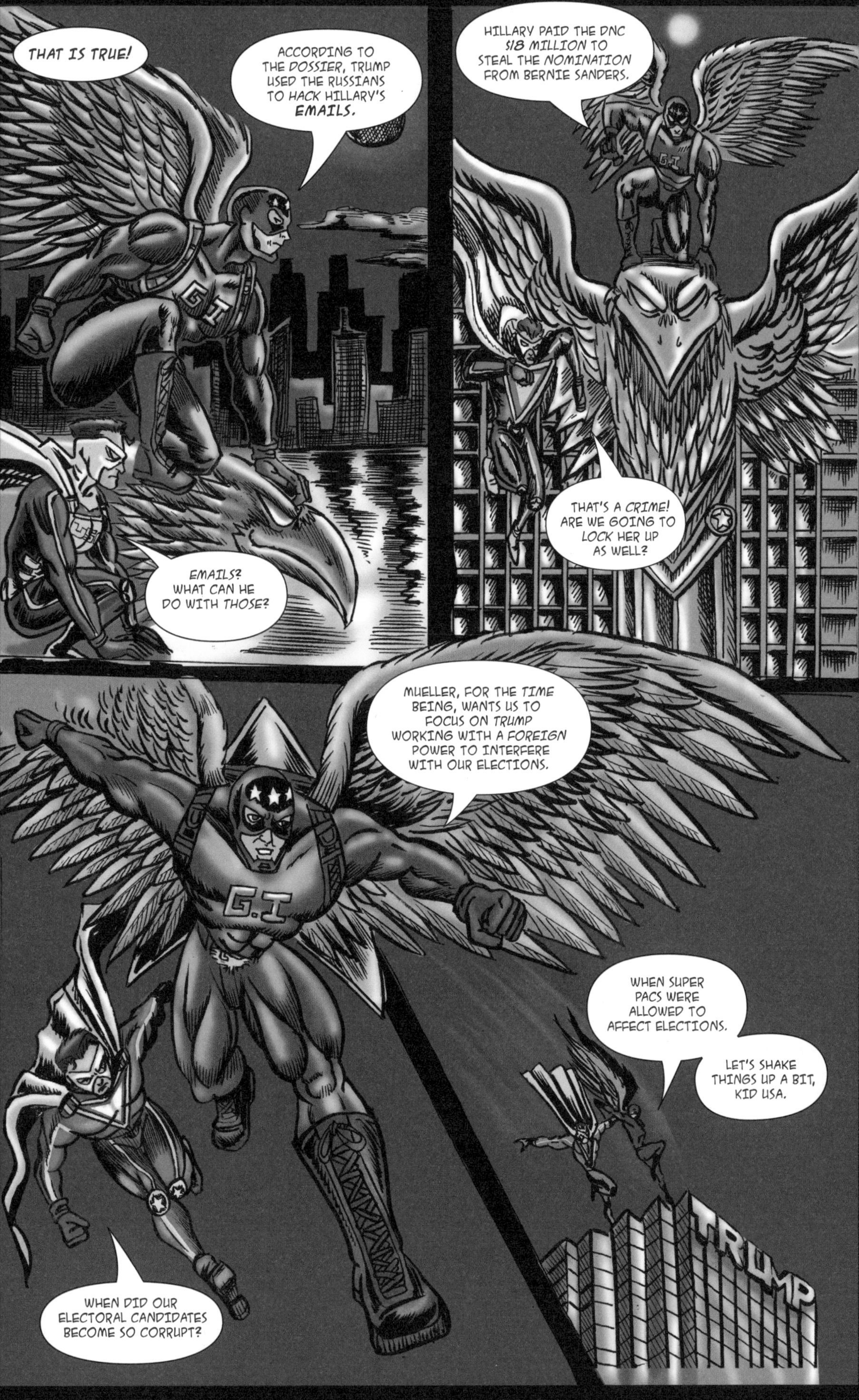

THAT IS TRUE!
ACCORDING TO THE DOSSIER, TRUMP USED THE RUSSIANS TO HACK HILLARY'S EMAILS.
EMAILS? WHAT CAN HE DO WITH THOSE?
HILLARY PAID THE DNC $18 MILLION TO STEAL THE NOMINATION FROM BERNIE SANDERS.
THAT'S A CRIME! ARE WE GOING TO LOCK HER UP AS WELL?
MUELLER, FOR THE TIME BEING, WANTS US TO FOCUS ON TRUMP WORKING WITH A FOREIGN POWER TO INTERFERE WITH OUR ELECTIONS.
WHEN DID OUR ELECTORAL CANDIDATES BECOME SO CORRUPT?
WHEN SUPER PACS WERE ALLOWED TO AFFECT ELECTIONS.
LET'S SHAKE THINGS UP A BIT, KID USA.
TRUMP

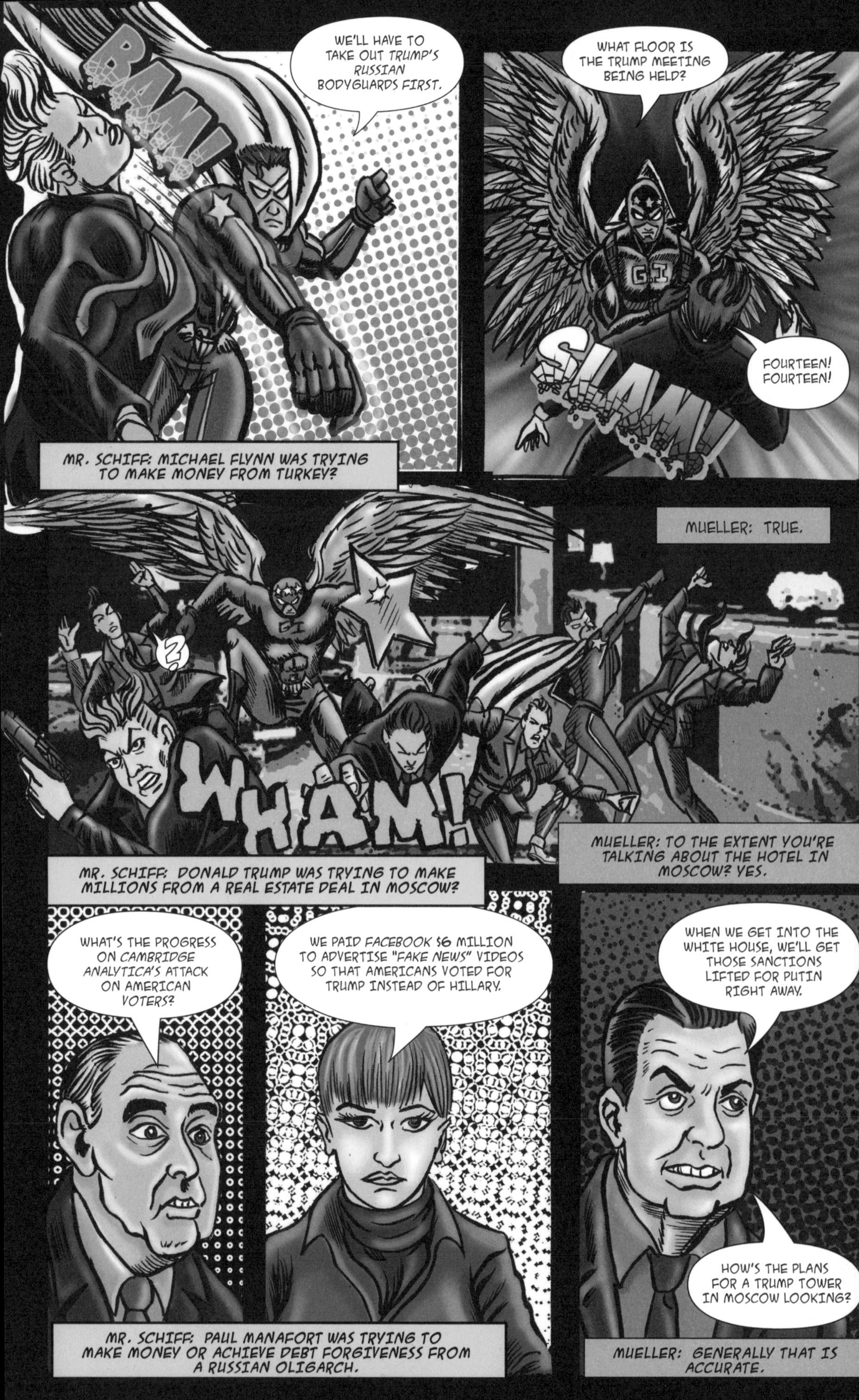
BAM!
WE'LL HAVE TO TAKE OUT TRUMP'S RUSSIAN BODYGUARDS FIRST.
MR. SCHIFF: MICHAEL FLYNN WAS TRYING TO MAKE MONEY FROM TURKEY?
WHAT FLOOR IS THE TRUMP MEETING BEING HELD?
FOURTEEN! FOURTEEN!
MUELLER: TRUE.
WHAM!
MR. SCHIFF: DONALD TRUMP WAS TRYING TO MAKE MILLIONS FROM A REAL ESTATE DEAL IN MOSCOW?
MUELLER: TO THE EXTENT YOU'RE TALKING ABOUT THE HOTEL IN MOSCOW? YES.
WHAT'S THE PROGRESS ON CAMBRIDGE ANALYTICA'S ATTACK ON AMERICAN VOTERS?
WE PAID FACEBOOK $6 MILLION TO ADVERTISE "FAKE NEWS" VIDEOS SO THAT AMERICANS VOTED FOR TRUMP INSTEAD OF HILLARY.
MR. SCHIFF: PAUL MANAFORT WAS TRYING TO MAKE MONEY OR ACHIEVE DEBT FORGIVENESS FROM A RUSSIAN OLIGARCH.
WHEN WE GET INTO THE WHITE HOUSE, WE'LL GET THOSE SANCTIONS LIFTED FOR PUTIN RIGHT AWAY.
HOW'S THE PLANS FOR A TRUMP TOWER IN MOSCOW LOOKING?
MUELLER: GENERALLY THAT IS ACCURATE.

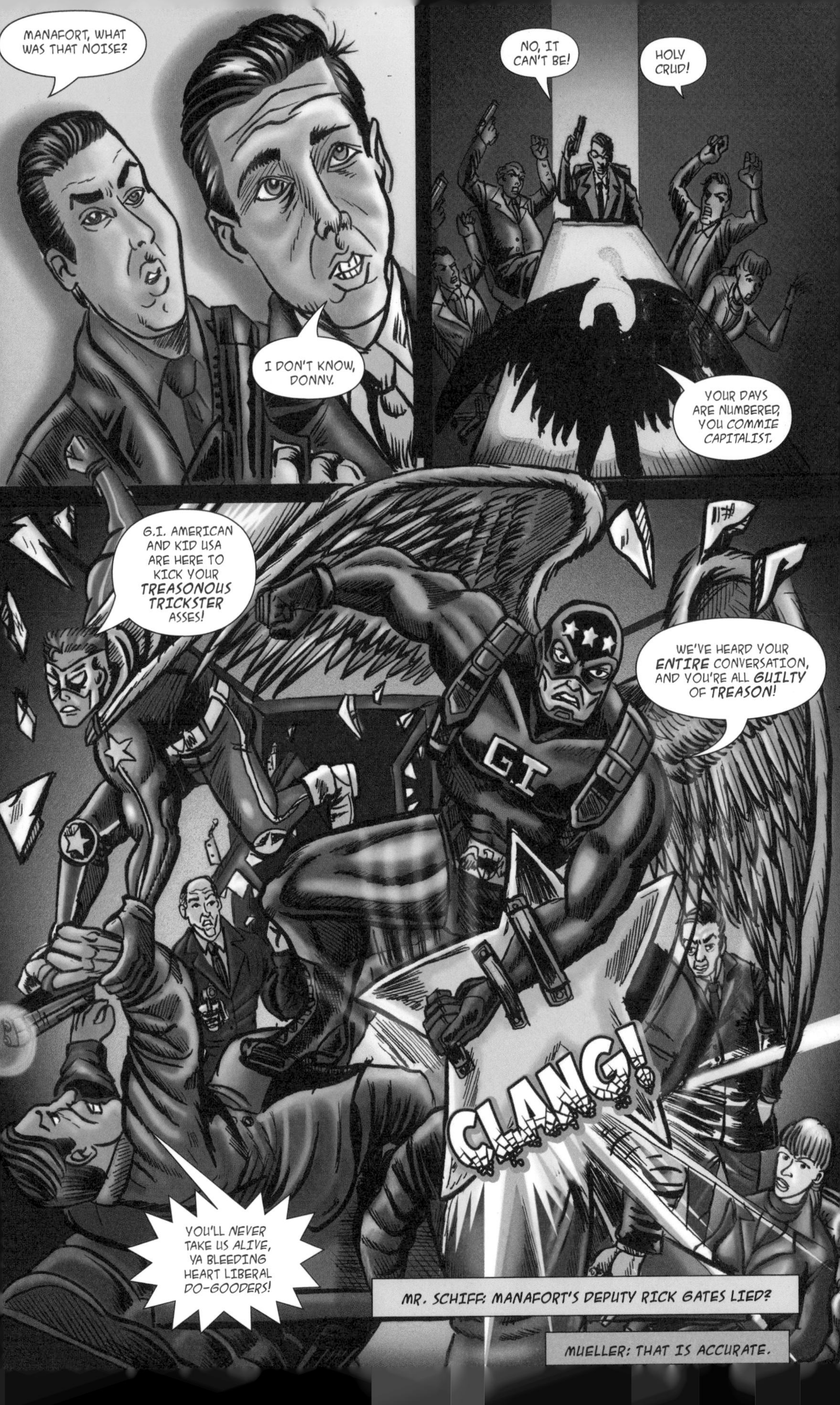
MANAFORT, WHAT WAS THAT NOISE?
I DON'T KNOW, DONNY.
NO, IT CAN'T BE!
HOLY CRUD!
YOUR DAYS ARE NUMBERED, YOU COMMIE CAPITALIST.
G.I. AMERICAN AND KID USA ARE HERE TO KICK YOUR TREASONOUS TRICKSTER ASSES!
WE'VE HEARD YOUR ENTIRE CONVERSATION, AND YOU'RE ALL GUILTY OF TREASON!
G.I.
CLANG!
YOU'LL NEVER TAKE US ALIVE, YA BLEEDING HEART LIBERAL DO-GOODERS!
MR. SCHIFF: MANAFORT'S DEPUTY RICK GATES LIED?
MUELLER: THAT IS ACCURATE.

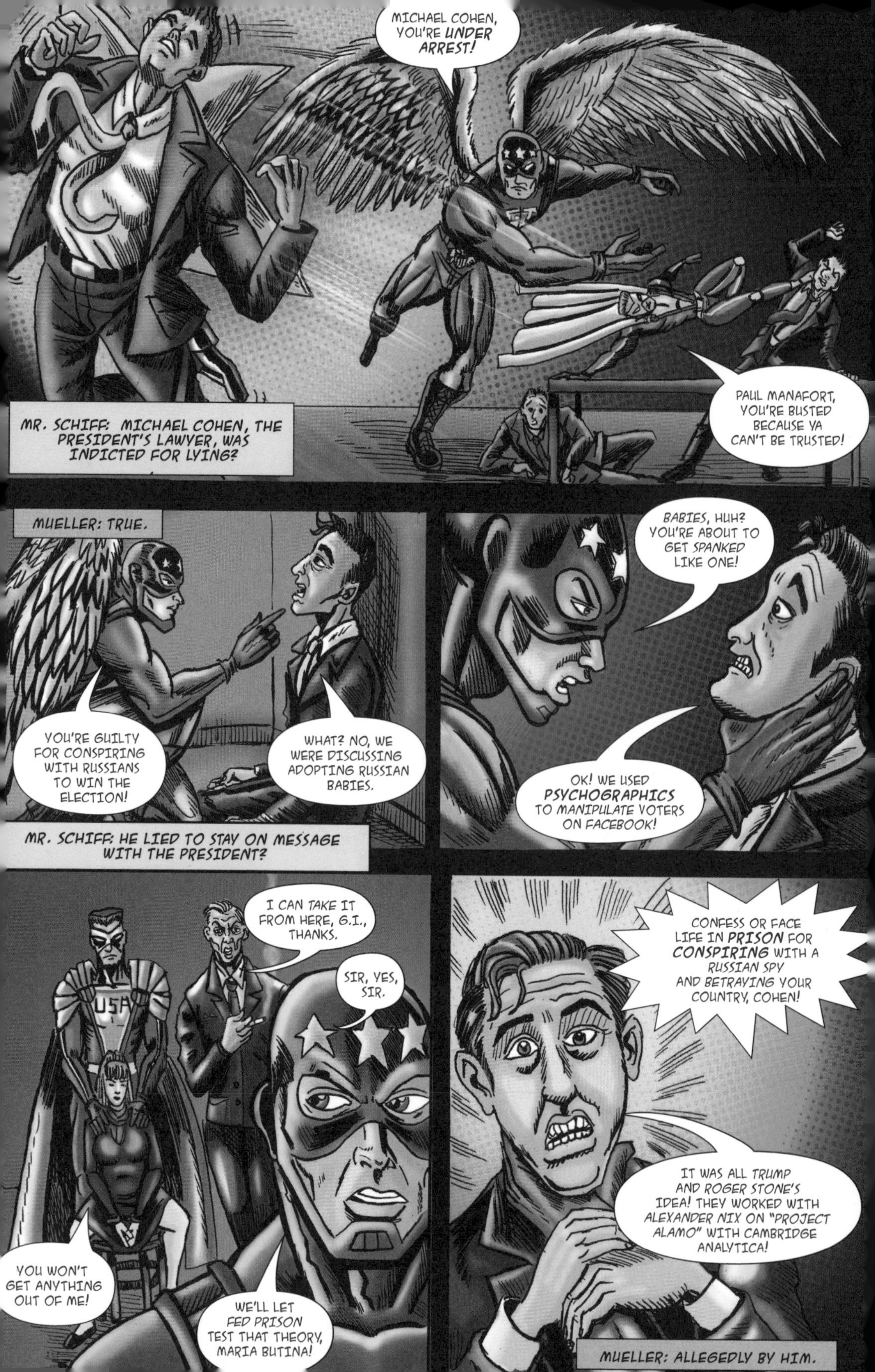
MICHAEL COHEN, YOU'RE UNDER ARREST!
PAUL MANAFORT, YOU'RE BUSTED BECAUSE YA CAN'T BE TRUSTED!
MR. SCHIFF: MICHAEL COHEN, THE PRESIDENT'S LAWYER, WAS INDICTED FOR LYING?
MUELLER: TRUE.
YOU'RE GUILTY FOR CONSPIRING WITH RUSSIANS TO WIN THE ELECTION!
WHAT? NO, WE WERE DISCUSSING ADOPTING RUSSIAN BABIES.
MR. SCHIFF: HE LIED TO STAY ON MESSAGE WITH THE PRESIDENT?
BABIES, HUH? YOU'RE ABOUT TO GET SPANKED LIKE ONE!
OK! WE USED PSYCHOGRAPHICS TO MANIPULATE VOTERS ON FACEBOOK!
I CAN TAKE IT FROM HERE, G.I., THANKS.
SIR, YES, SIR.
YOU WON'T GET ANYTHING OUT OF ME!
WE'LL LET FED PRISON TEST THAT THEORY, MARIA BUTINA!
USA
CONFESS OR FACE LIFE IN PRISON FOR CONSPIRING WITH A RUSSIAN SPY AND BETRAYING YOUR COUNTRY, COHEN!
IT WAS ALL TRUMP AND ROGER STONE'S IDEA! THEY WORKED WITH ALEXANDER NIX ON "PROJECT ALAMO" WITH CAMBRIDGE ANALYTICA!
MUELLER: ALLEGEDLY BY HIM.

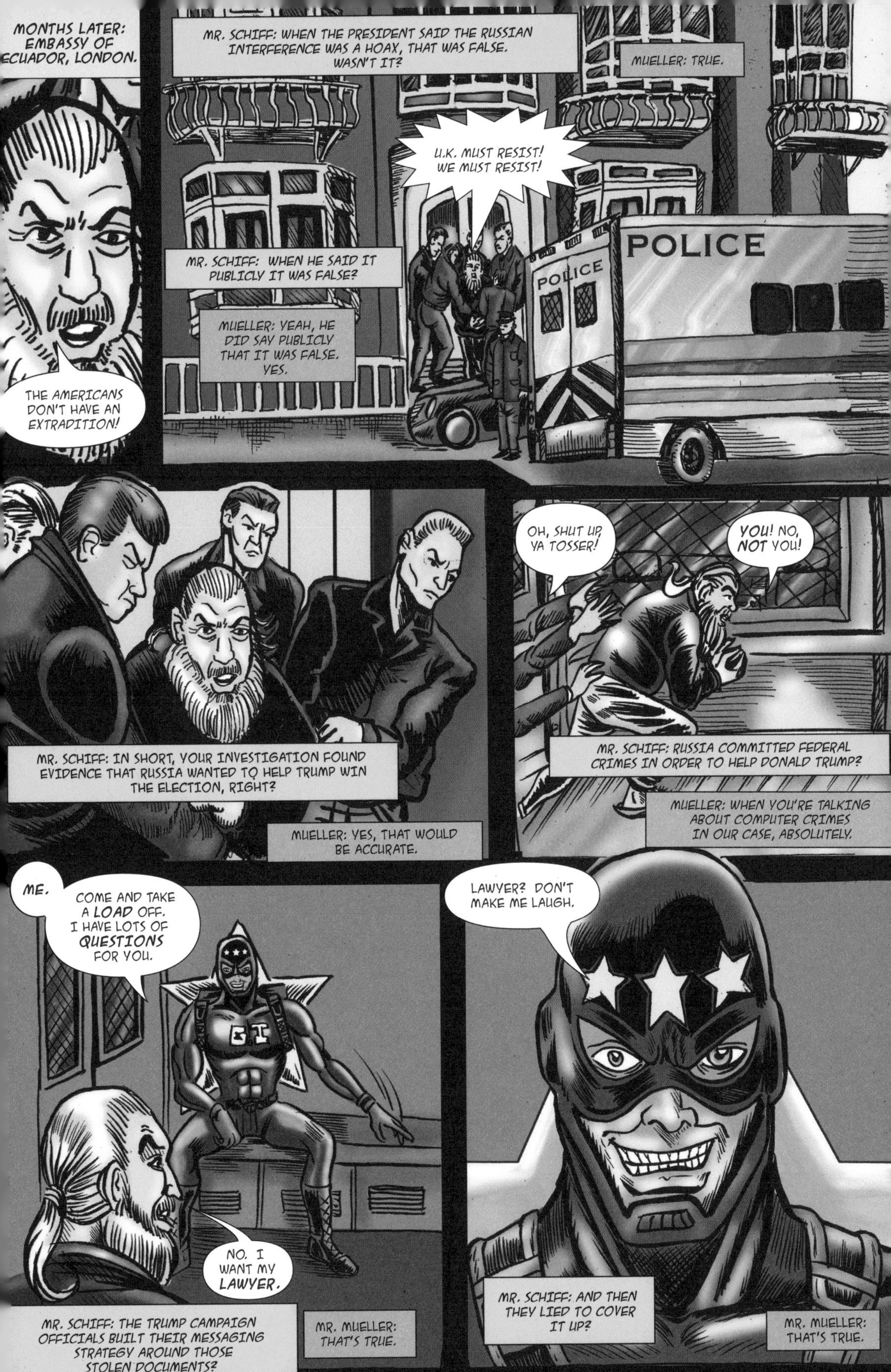
MONTHS LATER: EMBASSY OF ECUADOR, LONDON.
THE AMERICANS DON'T HAVE AN EXTRADITION!
MR. SCHIFF: WHEN THE PRESIDENT SAID THE RUSSIAN INTERFERENCE WAS A HOAX, THAT WAS FALSE. WASN'T IT?
MUELLER: TRUE.
U.K. MUST RESIST! WE MUST RESIST!
MR. SCHIFF: WHEN HE SAID IT PUBLICLY IT WAS FALSE?
MUELLER: YEAH, HE DID SAY PUBLICLY THAT IT WAS FALSE. YES.
POLICE
POLICE
MR. SCHIFF: IN SHORT, YOUR INVESTIGATION FOUND EVIDENCE THAT RUSSIA WANTED TO HELP TRUMP WIN THE ELECTION, RIGHT?
MUELLER: YES, THAT WOULD BE ACCURATE.
OH, SHUT UP, YA TOSSER!
YOU! NO, NOT YOU!
MR. SCHIFF: RUSSIA COMMITTED FEDERAL CRIMES IN ORDER TO HELP DONALD TRUMP?
MUELLER: WHEN YOU'RE TALKING ABOUT COMPUTER CRIMES IN OUR CASE, ABSOLUTELY.
ME.
COME AND TAKE A LOAD OFF. I HAVE LOTS OF QUESTIONS FOR YOU.
NO. I WANT MY LAWYER.
MR. SCHIFF: THE TRUMP CAMPAIGN OFFICIALS BUILT THEIR MESSAGING STRATEGY AROUND THOSE STOLEN DOCUMENTS?
MR. MUELLER: THAT'S TRUE.
LAWYER? DON'T MAKE ME LAUGH.
MR. SCHIFF: AND THEN THEY LIED TO COVER IT UP?
MR. MUELLER: THAT'S TRUE.

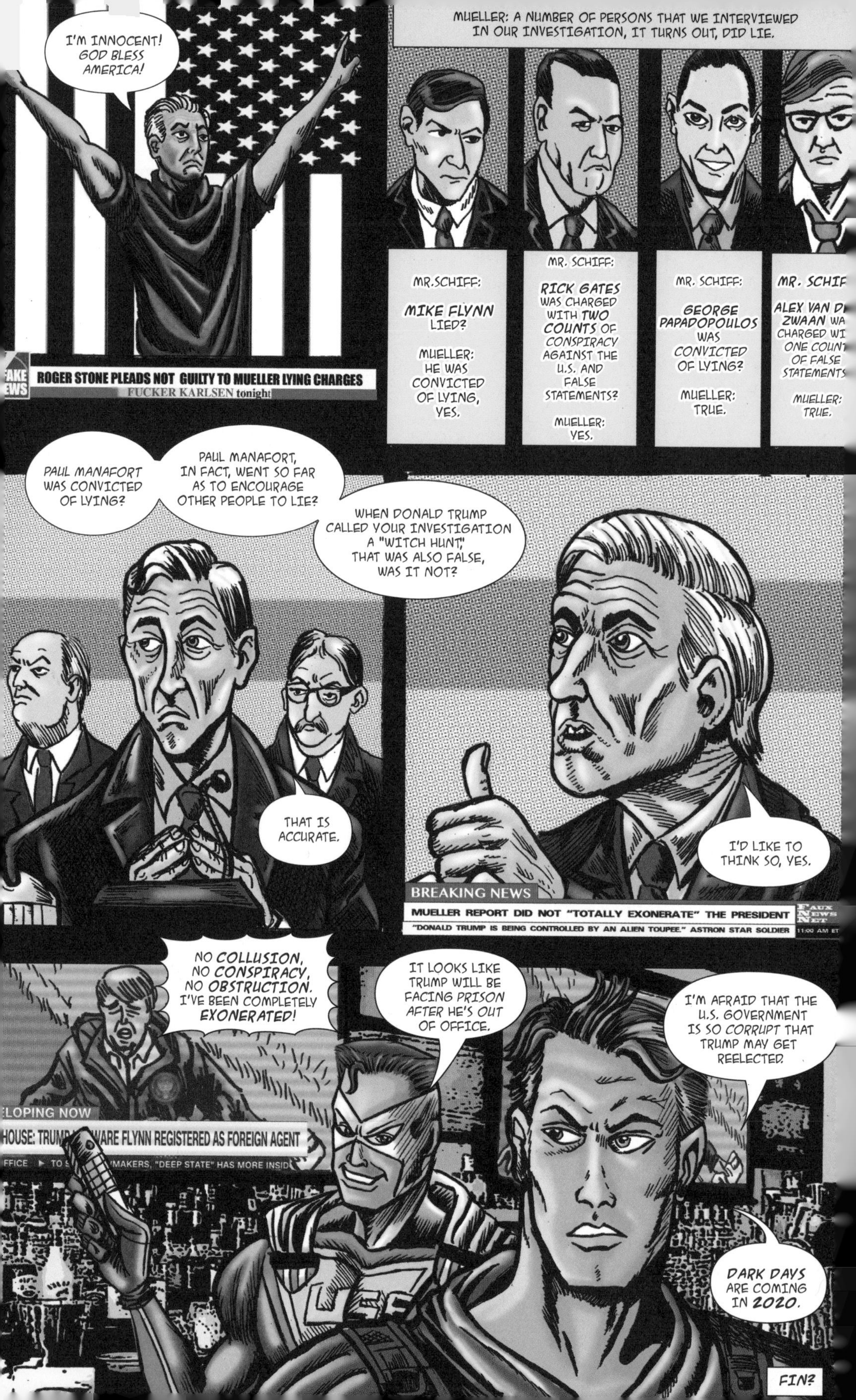
I'M INNOCENT! GOD BLESS AMERICA!
FAKE NEWS
ROGER STONE PLEADS NOT GUILTY TO MUELLER LYING CHARGES
FUCKER KARLSEN tonight
MUELLER: A NUMBER OF PERSONS THAT WE INTERVIEWED IN OUR INVESTIGATION, IT TURNS OUT, DID LIE.
MR. SCHIFF: MIKE FLYNN LIED? MUELLER: HE WAS CONVICTED OF LYING, YES.
MR. SCHIFF: RICK GATES WAS CHARGED WITH TWO COUNTS OF CONSPIRACY AGAINST THE U.S. AND FALSE STATEMENTS? MUELLER: YES.
MR. SCHIFF: GEORGE PAPADOPOULOS WAS CONVICTED OF LYING? MUELLER: TRUE.
MR. SCHIF ALEX VAN D ZWAAN WA CHARGED WI ONE COUNT OF FALSE STATEMENTS MUELLER: TRUE.
PAUL MANAFORT WAS CONVICTED OF LYING?
PAUL MANAFORT, IN FACT, WENT SO FAR AS TO ENCOURAGE OTHER PEOPLE TO LIE?
WHEN DONALD TRUMP CALLED YOUR INVESTIGATION A "WITCH HUNT," THAT WAS ALSO FALSE, WAS IT NOT?
THAT IS ACCURATE.
I'D LIKE TO THINK SO, YES.
BREAKING NEWS
MUELLER REPORT DID NOT "TOTALLY EXONERATE" THE PRESIDENT
FAUX NEWS NET
"DONALD TRUMP IS BEING CONTROLLED BY AN ALIEN TOUPEE." ASTRON STAR SOLDIER
11:00 AM ET
NO COLLUSION, NO CONSPIRACY, NO OBSTRUCTION. I'VE BEEN COMPLETELY EXONERATED!
ELOPING NOW
HOUSE: TRUMP WARE FLYNN REGISTERED AS FOREIGN AGENT
FFICE ▶ TO S MAKERS, "DEEP STATE" HAS MORE INSID
IT LOOKS LIKE TRUMP WILL BE FACING PRISON AFTER HE'S OUT OF OFFICE.
I'M AFRAID THAT THE U.S. GOVERNMENT IS SO CORRUPT THAT TRUMP MAY GET REELECTED.
DARK DAYS ARE COMING IN 2020.
FIN?

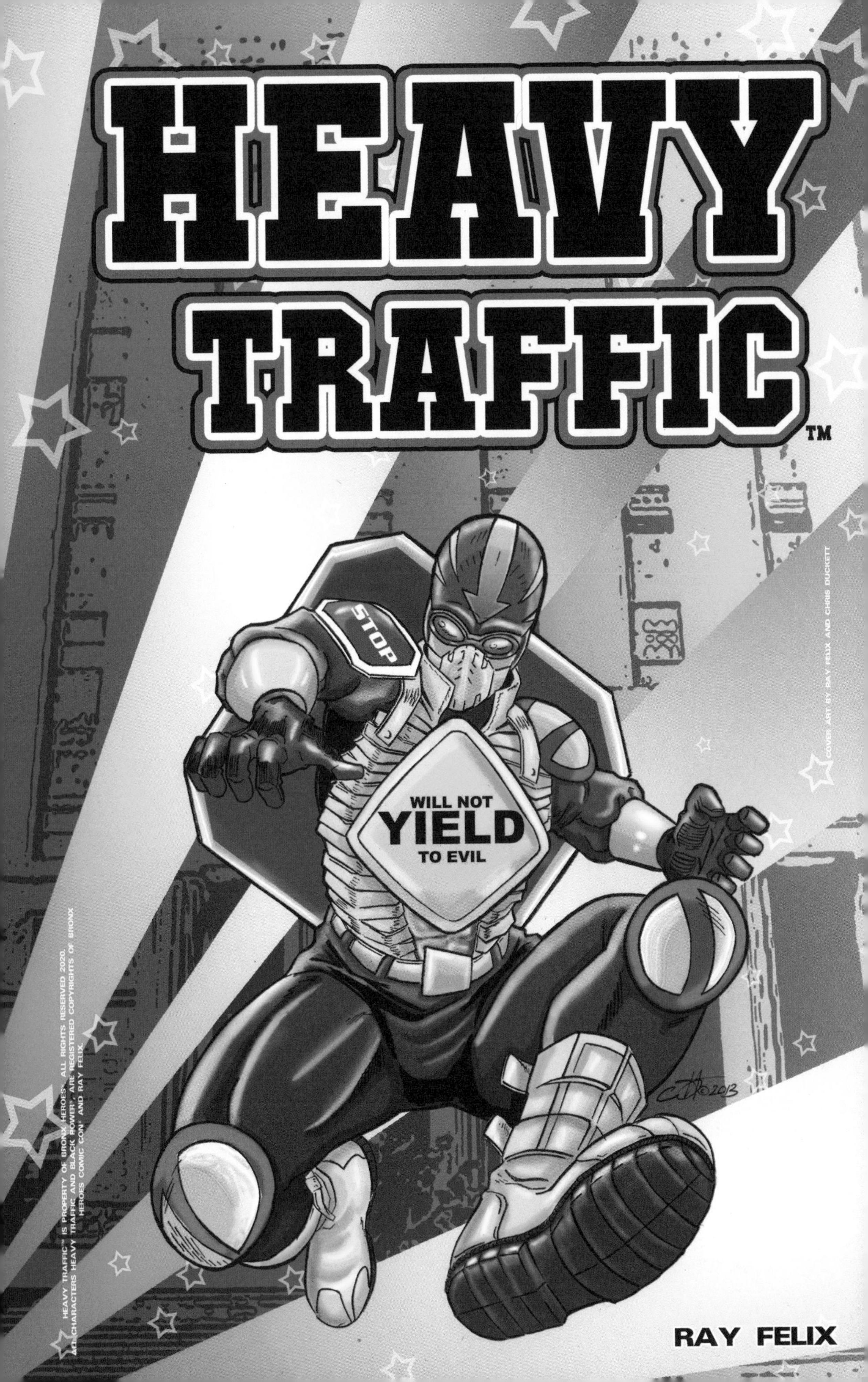
HEAVY TRAFFIC™
STOP
WILL NOT YIELD TO EVIL
COVER ART BY RAY FELIX AND CHRIS DUCKETT
RAY FELIX

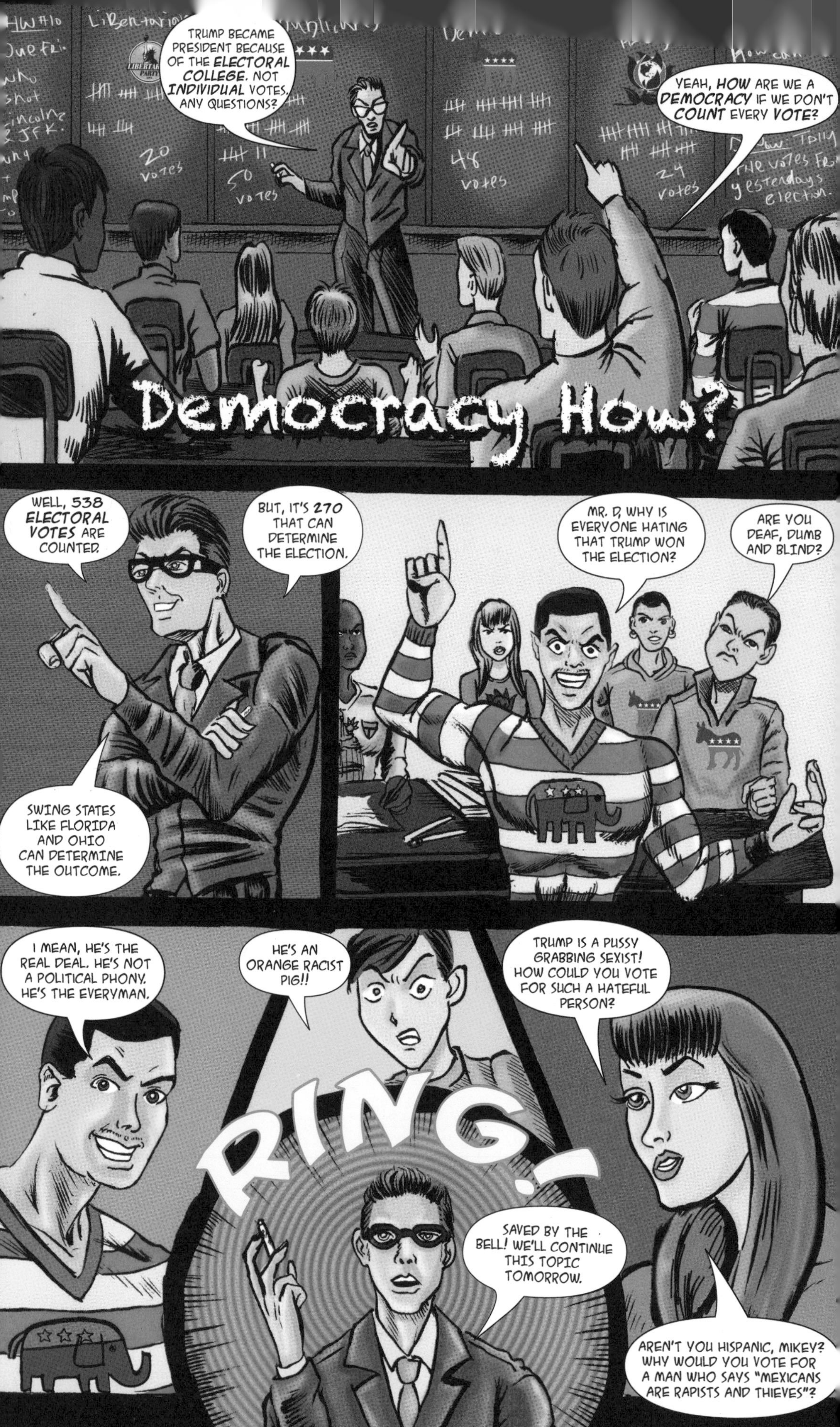
TRUMP BECAME PRESIDENT BECAUSE OF THE ELECTORAL COLLEGE. NOT INDIVIDUAL VOTES. ANY QUESTIONS?
YEAH, HOW ARE WE A DEMOCRACY IF WE DON'T COUNT EVERY VOTE?
20 votes
50 votes
48 votes
24 votes
Democracy How?
WELL, 538 ELECTORAL VOTES ARE COUNTED.
BUT, IT'S 270 THAT CAN DETERMINE THE ELECTION.
SWING STATES LIKE FLORIDA AND OHIO CAN DETERMINE THE OUTCOME.
MR. D, WHY IS EVERYONE HATING THAT TRUMP WON THE ELECTION?
ARE YOU DEAF, DUMB AND BLIND?
I MEAN, HE'S THE REAL DEAL. HE'S NOT A POLITICAL PHONY. HE'S THE EVERYMAN.
HE'S AN ORANGE RACIST PIG!!
TRUMP IS A PUSSY GRABBING SEXIST! HOW COULD YOU VOTE FOR SUCH A HATEFUL PERSON?
RING!
SAVED BY THE BELL! WE'LL CONTINUE THIS TOPIC TOMORROW.
AREN'T YOU HISPANIC, MIKEY? WHY WOULD YOU VOTE FOR A MAN WHO SAYS "MEXICANS ARE RAPISTS AND THIEVES"?

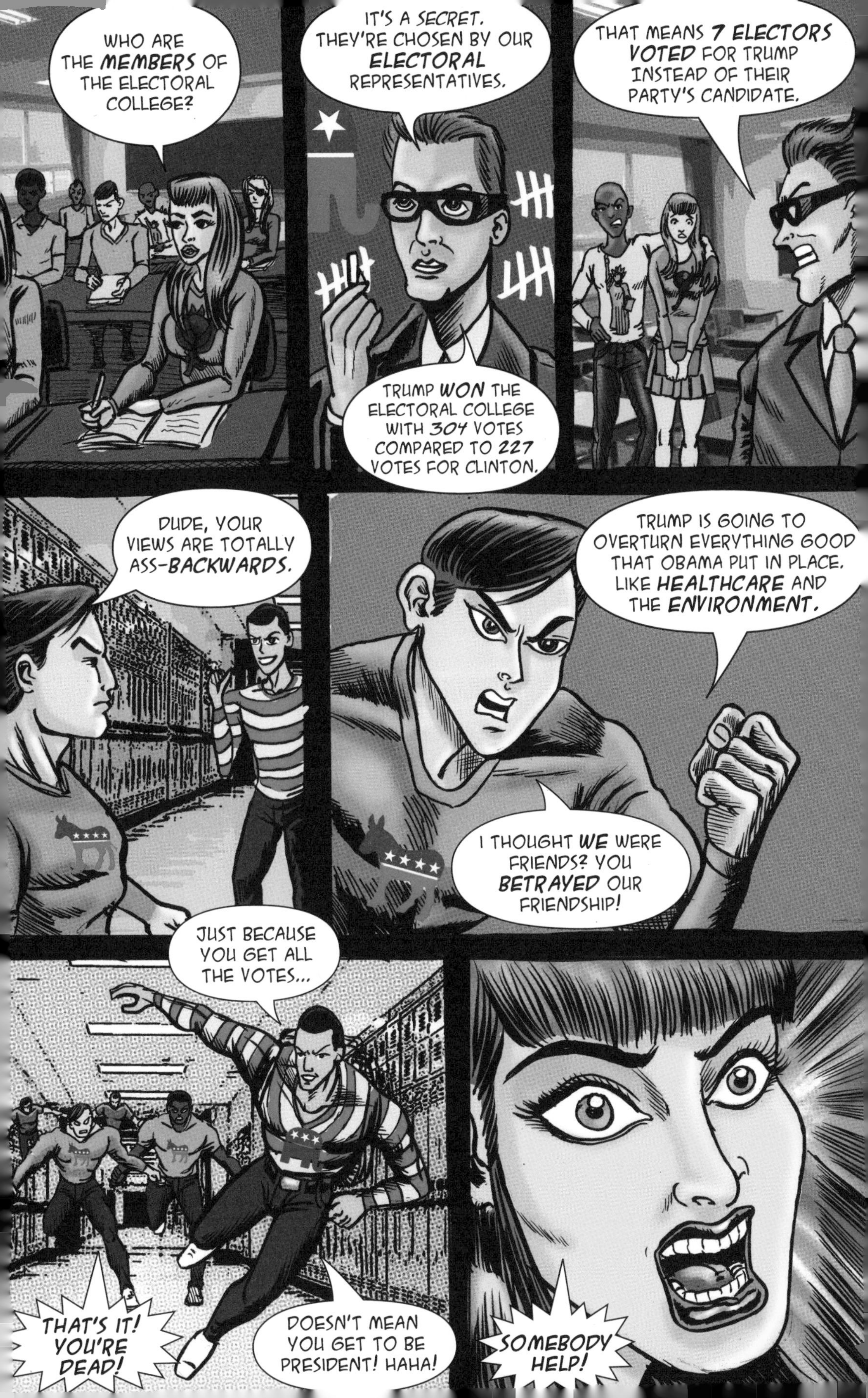
WHO ARE THE MEMBERS OF THE ELECTORAL COLLEGE?
IT'S A SECRET. THEY'RE CHOSEN BY OUR ELECTORAL REPRESENTATIVES.
TRUMP WON THE ELECTORAL COLLEGE WITH 304 VOTES COMPARED TO 227 VOTES FOR CLINTON.
THAT MEANS 7 ELECTORS VOTED FOR TRUMP INSTEAD OF THEIR PARTY'S CANDIDATE.
DUDE, YOUR VIEWS ARE TOTALLY ASS-BACKWARDS.
TRUMP IS GOING TO OVERTURN EVERYTHING GOOD THAT OBAMA PUT IN PLACE. LIKE HEALTHCARE AND THE ENVIRONMENT.
I THOUGHT WE WERE FRIENDS? YOU BETRAYED OUR FRIENDSHIP!
JUST BECAUSE YOU GET ALL THE VOTES...
DOESN'T MEAN YOU GET TO BE PRESIDENT! HAHA!
THAT'S IT! YOU'RE DEAD!
SOMEBODY HELP!

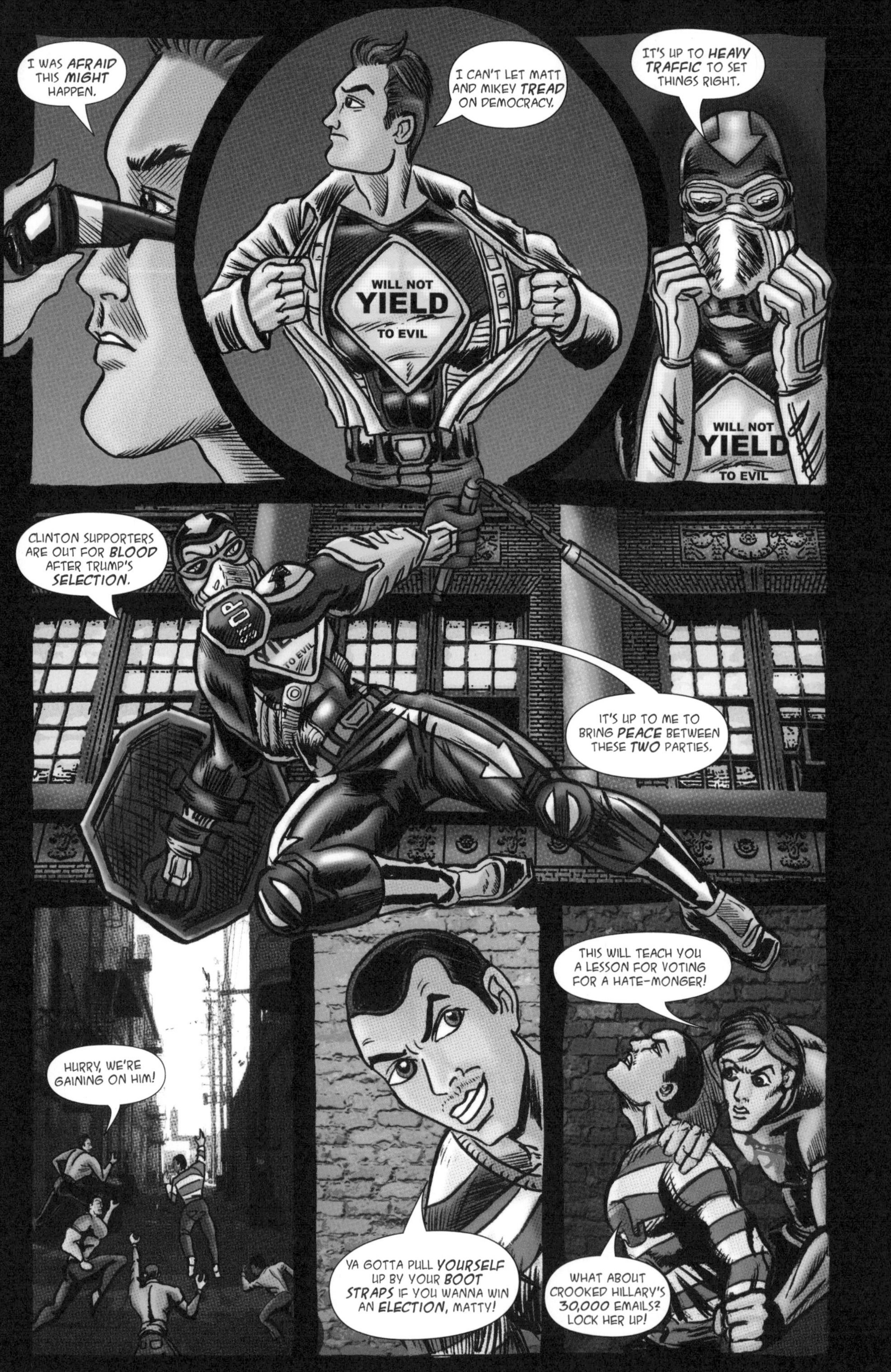
I WAS AFRAID THIS MIGHT HAPPEN.
I CAN'T LET MATT AND MIKEY TREAD ON DEMOCRACY.
WILL NOT YIELD TO EVIL
IT'S UP TO HEAVY TRAFFIC TO SET THINGS RIGHT.
WILL NOT YIELD TO EVIL
CLINTON SUPPORTERS ARE OUT FOR BLOOD AFTER TRUMP'S SELECTION.
IT'S UP TO ME TO BRING PEACE BETWEEN THESE TWO PARTIES.
HURRY, WE'RE GAINING ON HIM!
YA GOTTA PULL YOURSELF UP BY YOUR BOOT STRAPS IF YOU WANNA WIN AN ELECTION, MATTY!
THIS WILL TEACH YOU A LESSON FOR VOTING FOR A HATE-MONGER!
WHAT ABOUT CROOKED HILLARY'S 30,000 EMAILS? LOCK HER UP!

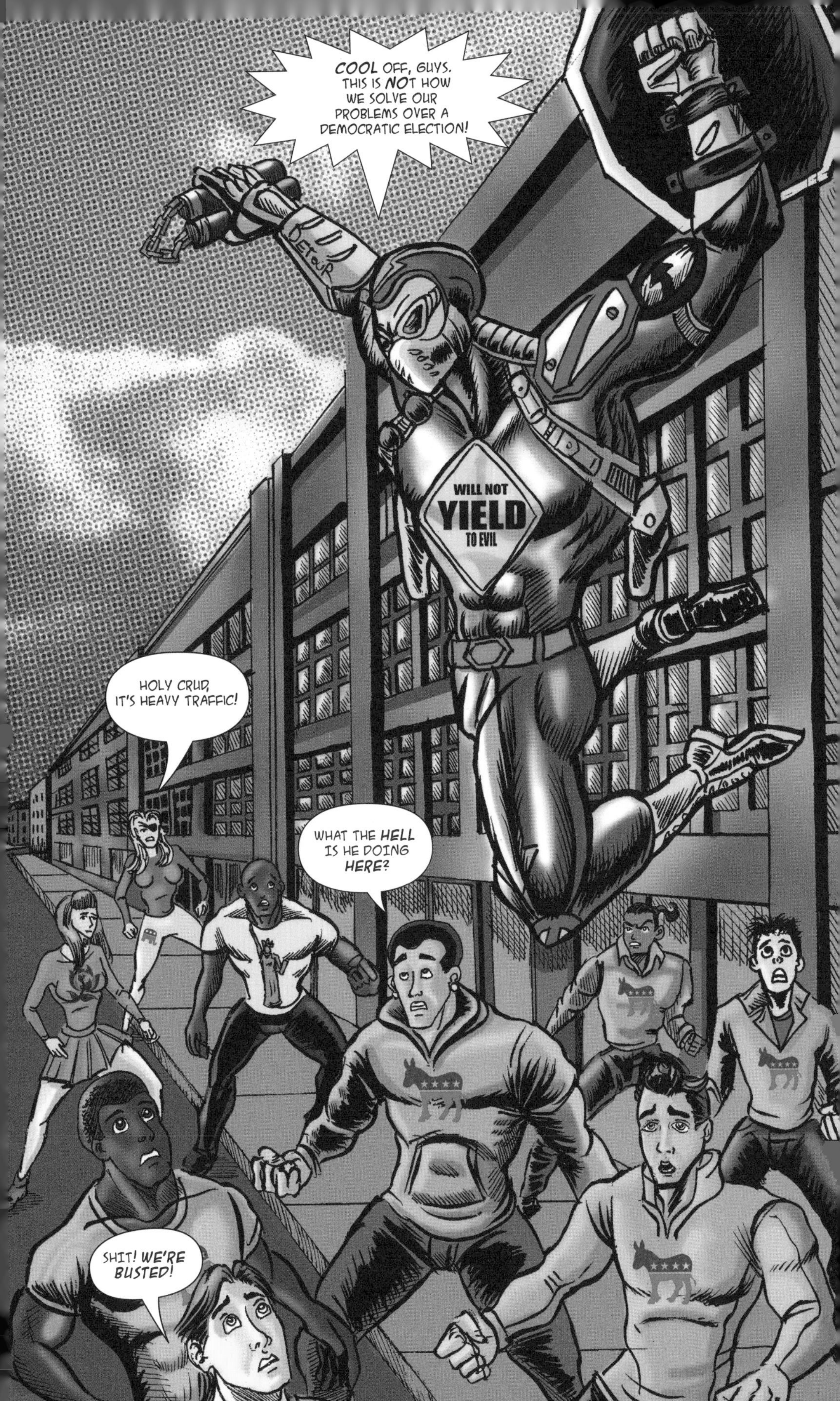
COOL OFF, GUYS. THIS IS NOT HOW WE SOLVE OUR PROBLEMS OVER A DEMOCRATIC ELECTION!
DETOUR
WILL NOT YIELD TO EVIL
HOLY CRUD, IT'S HEAVY TRAFFIC!
WHAT THE HELL IS HE DOING HERE?
SHIT! WE'RE BUSTED!

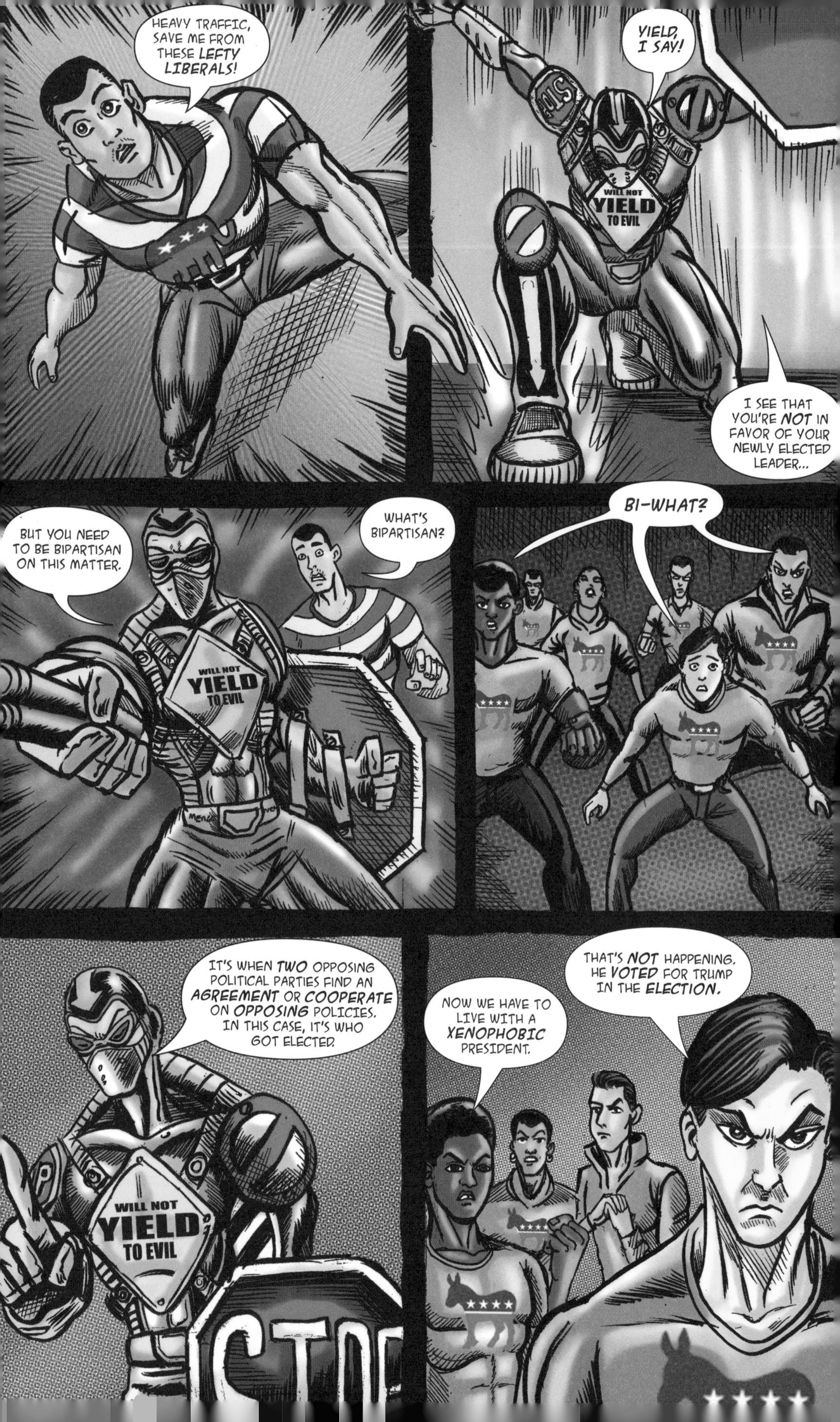

HEAVY TRAFFIC, SAVE ME FROM THESE LEFTY LIBERALS!
YIELD, I SAY!
WILL NOT YIELD TO EVIL
I SEE THAT YOU'RE NOT IN FAVOR OF YOUR NEWLY ELECTED LEADER...
BUT YOU NEED TO BE BIPARTISAN ON THIS MATTER.
WHAT'S BIPARTISAN?
WILL NOT YIELD TO EVIL
BI-WHAT?
IT'S WHEN TWO OPPOSING POLITICAL PARTIES FIND AN AGREEMENT OR COOPERATE ON OPPOSING POLICIES. IN THIS CASE, IT'S WHO GOT ELECTED.
WILL NOT YIELD TO EVIL
NOW WE HAVE TO LIVE WITH A XENOPHOBIC PRESIDENT.
THAT'S NOT HAPPENING. HE VOTED FOR TRUMP IN THE ELECTION.

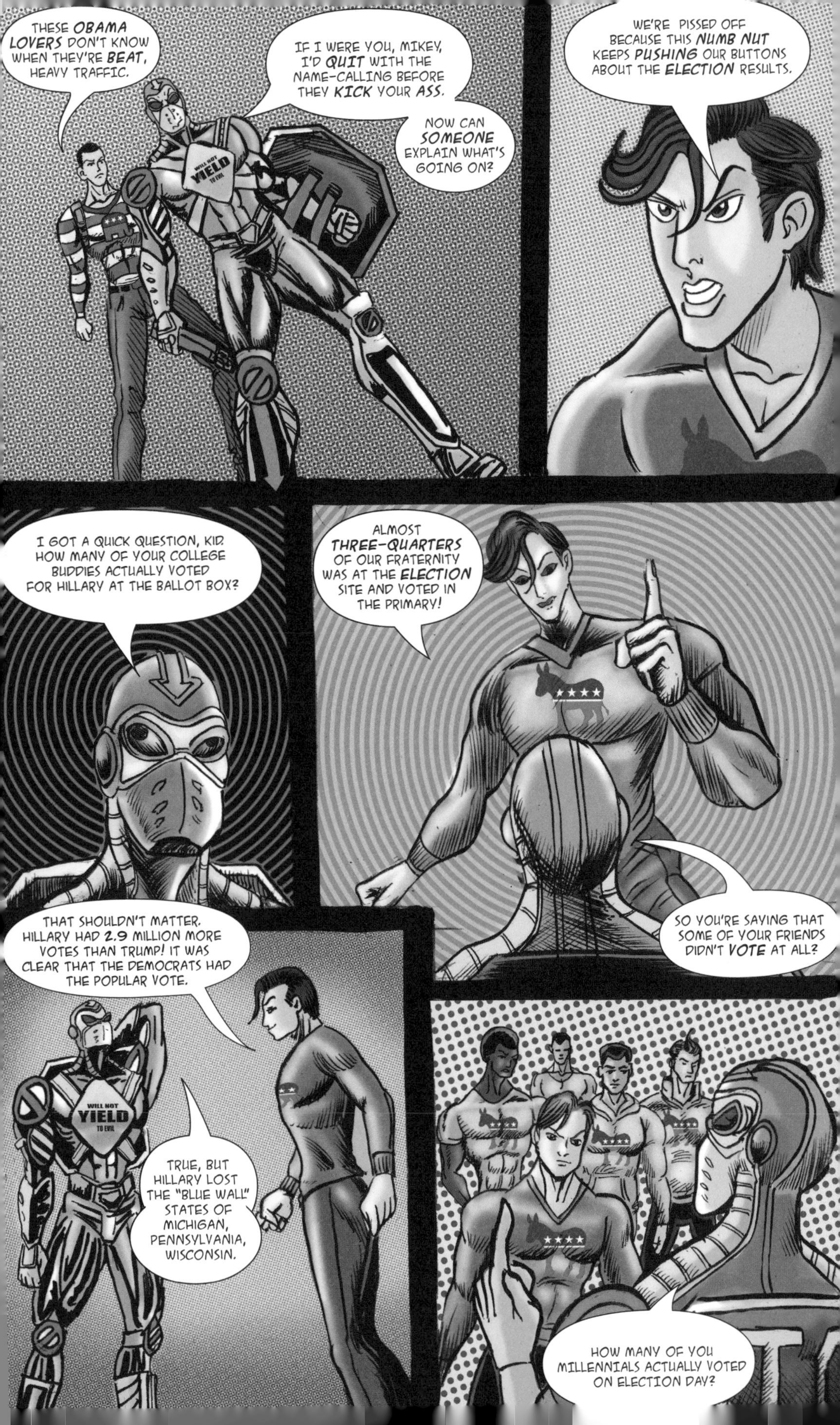
THESE OBAMA LOVERS DON'T KNOW WHEN THEY'RE BEAT, HEAVY TRAFFIC.
IF I WERE YOU, MIKEY, I'D QUIT WITH THE NAME-CALLING BEFORE THEY KICK YOUR ASS.
NOW CAN SOMEONE EXPLAIN WHAT'S GOING ON?
WILL NOT YIELD TO EVIL
WE'RE PISSED OFF BECAUSE THIS NUMB NUT KEEPS PUSHING OUR BUTTONS ABOUT THE ELECTION RESULTS.
I GOT A QUICK QUESTION, KID. HOW MANY OF YOUR COLLEGE BUDDIES ACTUALLY VOTED FOR HILLARY AT THE BALLOT BOX?
ALMOST THREE-QUARTERS OF OUR FRATERNITY WAS AT THE ELECTION SITE AND VOTED IN THE PRIMARY!
SO YOU'RE SAYING THAT SOME OF YOUR FRIENDS DIDN'T VOTE AT ALL?
THAT SHOULDN'T MATTER. HILLARY HAD 2.9 MILLION MORE VOTES THAN TRUMP! IT WAS CLEAR THAT THE DEMOCRATS HAD THE POPULAR VOTE.
WILL NOT YIELD TO EVIL
TRUE, BUT HILLARY LOST THE "BLUE WALL" STATES OF MICHIGAN, PENNSYLVANIA, WISCONSIN.
HOW MANY OF YOU MILLENNIALS ACTUALLY VOTED ON ELECTION DAY?

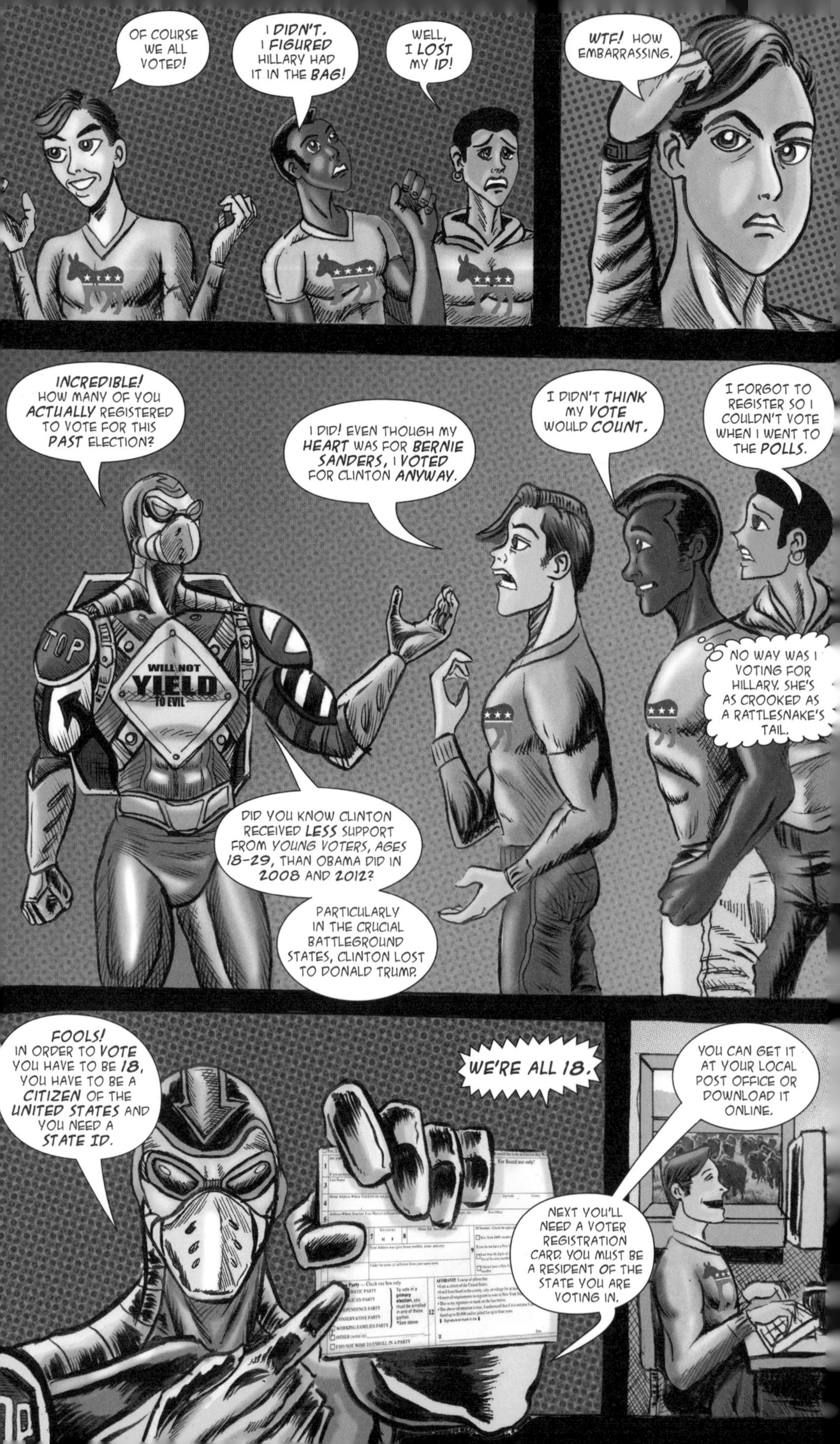
OF COURSE WE ALL VOTED!
I DIDN'T. I FIGURED HILLARY HAD IT IN THE BAG!
WELL, I LOST MY ID!
WTF! HOW EMBARRASSING.
INCREDIBLE! HOW MANY OF YOU ACTUALLY REGISTERED TO VOTE FOR THIS PAST ELECTION?
I DID! EVEN THOUGH MY HEART WAS FOR BERNIE SANDERS, I VOTED FOR CLINTON ANYWAY.
I DIDN'T THINK MY VOTE WOULD COUNT.
I FORGOT TO REGISTER SO I COULDN'T VOTE WHEN I WENT TO THE POLLS.
NO WAY WAS I VOTING FOR HILLARY. SHE'S AS CROOKED AS A RATTLESNAKE'S TAIL.
WILL NOT YIELD TO EVIL
DID YOU KNOW CLINTON RECEIVED LESS SUPPORT FROM YOUNG VOTERS, AGES 18–29, THAN OBAMA DID IN 2008 AND 2012?
PARTICULARLY IN THE CRUCIAL BATTLEGROUND STATES, CLINTON LOST TO DONALD TRUMP.
FOOLS! IN ORDER TO VOTE YOU HAVE TO BE 18, YOU HAVE TO BE A CITIZEN OF THE UNITED STATES AND YOU NEED A STATE ID.
WE'RE ALL 18.
NEXT YOU'LL NEED A VOTER REGISTRATION CARD. YOU MUST BE A RESIDENT OF THE STATE YOU ARE VOTING IN.
YOU CAN GET IT AT YOUR LOCAL POST OFFICE OR DOWNLOAD IT ONLINE.

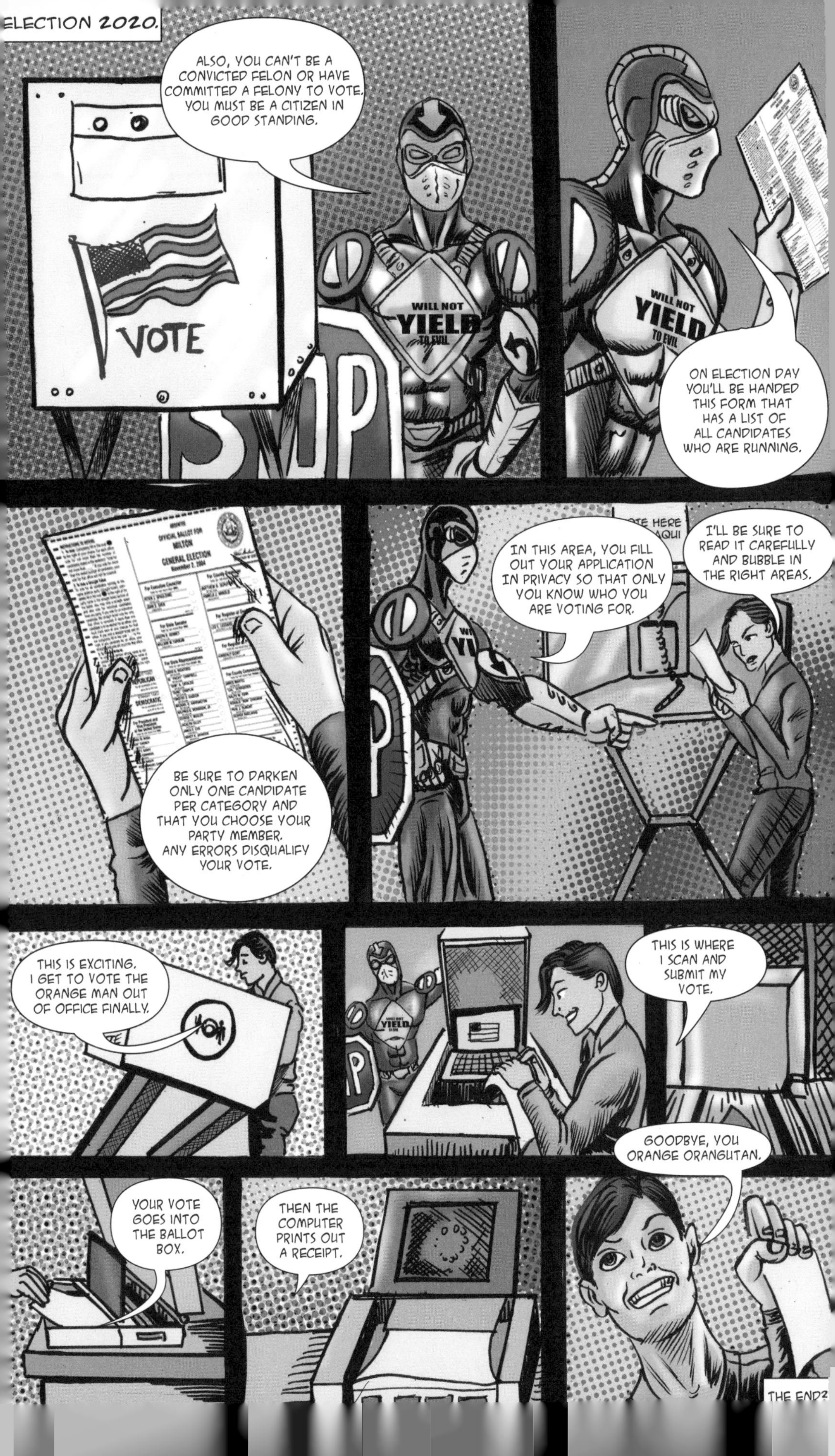
ELECTION 2020.
ALSO, YOU CAN'T BE A CONVICTED FELON OR HAVE COMMITTED A FELONY TO VOTE. YOU MUST BE A CITIZEN IN GOOD STANDING.
VOTE
WILL NOT YIELD TO EVIL
ON ELECTION DAY YOU'LL BE HANDED THIS FORM THAT HAS A LIST OF ALL CANDIDATES WHO ARE RUNNING.
BE SURE TO DARKEN ONLY ONE CANDIDATE PER CATEGORY AND THAT YOU CHOOSE YOUR PARTY MEMBER. ANY ERRORS DISQUALIFY YOUR VOTE.
IN THIS AREA, YOU FILL OUT YOUR APPLICATION IN PRIVACY SO THAT ONLY YOU KNOW WHO YOU ARE VOTING FOR.
I'LL BE SURE TO READ IT CAREFULLY AND BUBBLE IN THE RIGHT AREAS.
THIS IS EXCITING. I GET TO VOTE THE ORANGE MAN OUT OF OFFICE FINALLY.
THIS IS WHERE I SCAN AND SUBMIT MY VOTE.
YOUR VOTE GOES INTO THE BALLOT BOX.
THEN THE COMPUTER PRINTS OUT A RECEIPT.
GOODBYE, YOU ORANGE ORANGUTAN.
THE END?

ASTRON STAR SOLDIER

REAL NAME James Lopez-Hunt

OCCUPATION Astronaut

LEGAL STATUS Illegal alien resident from planet Zenna

OTHER ALIASES Star Soldier

PLACE OF BIRTH Earth/Zenna

FIRST APPEARANCE *Astral Comics #1*, 1977

HISTORY In the year 2000, an experimental warp-drive starship was sent on a mission to explore a new black hole that appeared outside our solar system. Piloting the craft was United Nations astronaut James Lopez-Hunt, an American scientist from the Bronx, New York City. James' ship, the *Starseeker*, was swallowed by the black hole... and collided with an alien craft also investigating the phenomenon. The other ship was piloted by Astron, a star soldier from the planet Zenna. The two life forces merged into one being, who now possessed cosmic powers. Together as one hybrid being, Astron possesses the memories and life force of earthman Hunt, and fights to save both Earth and Zenna from cosmic dangers.

HEIGHT 6'4"

EYES White

WEIGHT 250 lbs.

HAIR None

POWERS Flight, teleportation and Zeta beams

Astron Star Soldier® is owned by Tom Sciacca. Art by Ray Felix.

THE GREATEST HERO BLACK POWER

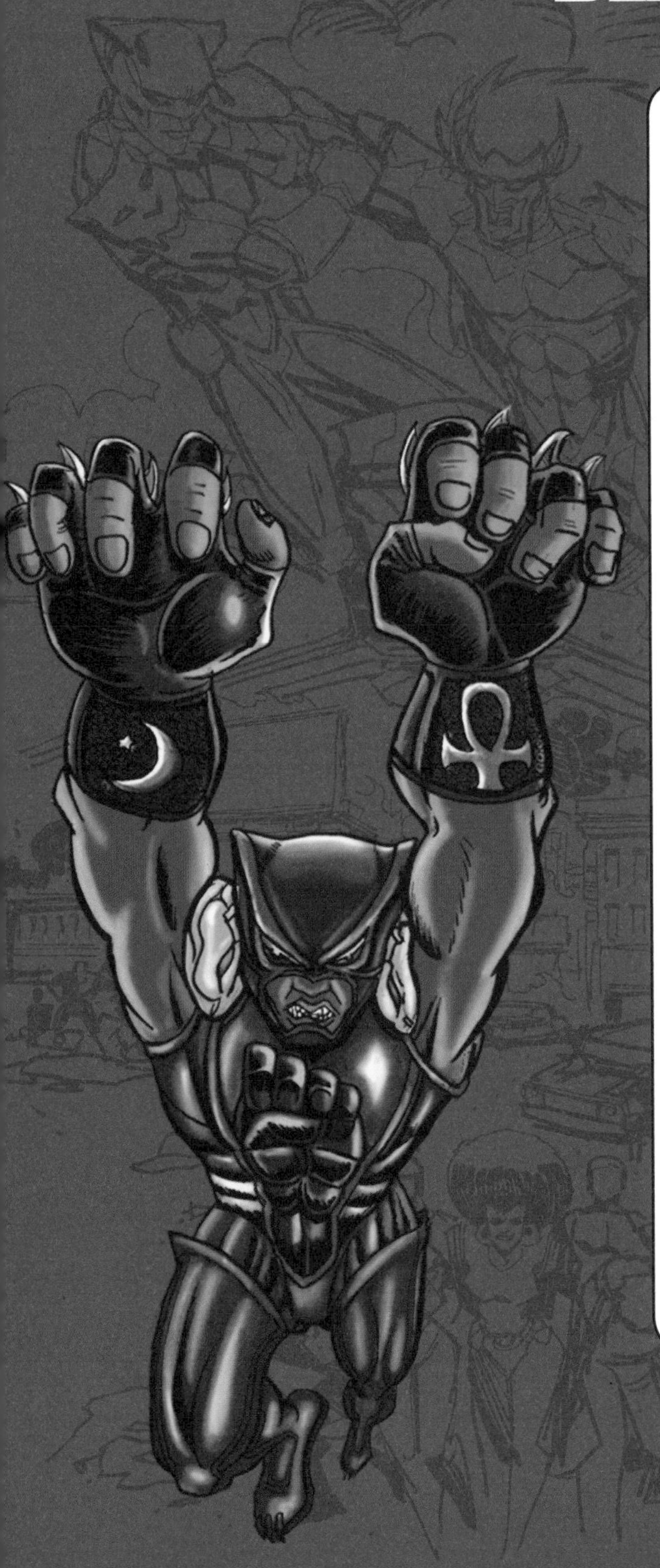

REAL NAME Muhammad X

OCCUPATION Veteran and boxer

LEGAL STATUS American citizen

OTHER ALIASES The Louisville Lip

PLACE OF BIRTH Harlem, New York

FIRST APPEARANCE *A World without Superheroes #4*, 1993

HISTORY Black Power, aka Muhammad X, was the heavyweight champion of the world when his dreams had to be put on hold as he was drafted to fight in the Vietnam War. Despite his resistance, Muhammad X was sent to Southeast Asia where he met the other members of the elite fighting force Panther X. Together they betrayed the U.S. government and switched sides to fight along the Viet Cong to help end the war in Vietnam peacefully. Upon returning to the U.S., Black Power and the members of Panther X became fugitives and went toe-to-toe with the U.S. military in Harlem.

HEIGHT 6'2"

EYES Brown

WEIGHT 210 lbs.

HAIR Black

POWERS Black Power is trained in boxing and hand-to-hand combat. His costume has magical properties which allow him to travel through time and gives him the Power of the Ebony Fist.

BRONX HEROES GALLERY

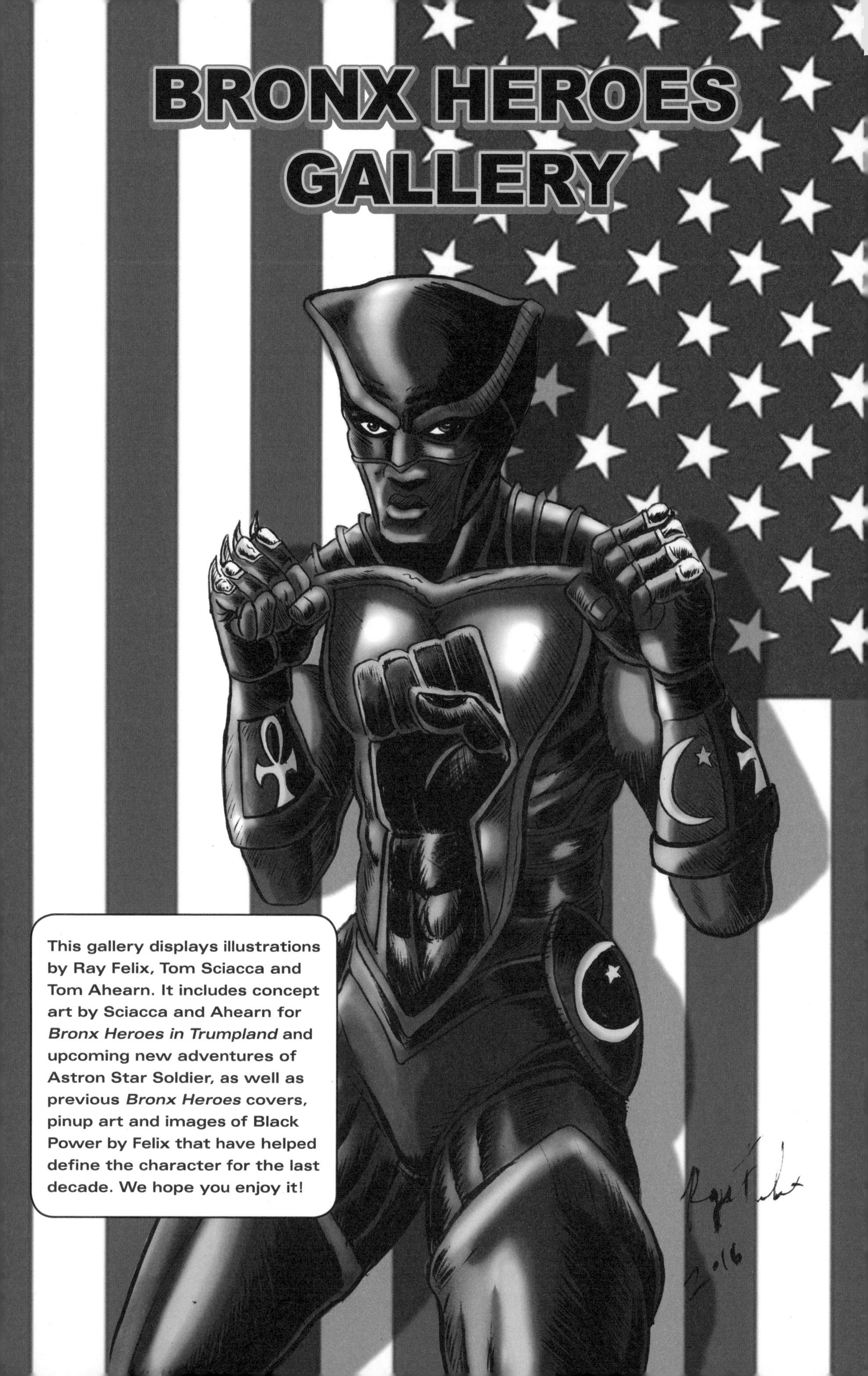

This gallery displays illustrations by Ray Felix, Tom Sciacca and Tom Ahearn. It includes concept art by Sciacca and Ahearn for *Bronx Heroes in Trumpland* and upcoming new adventures of Astron Star Soldier, as well as previous *Bronx Heroes* covers, pinup art and images of Black Power by Felix that have helped define the character for the last decade. We hope you enjoy it!

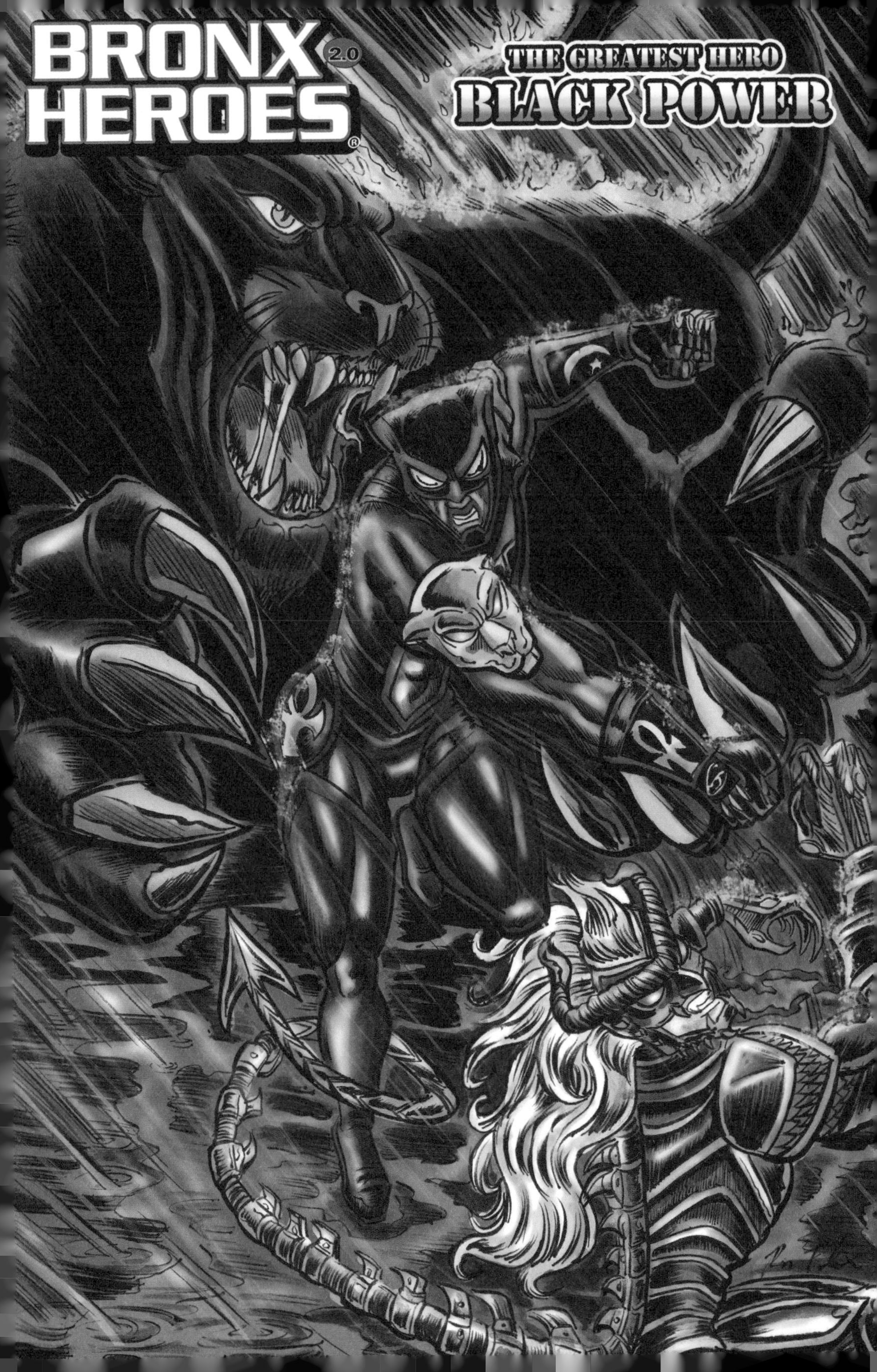
BRONX HEROES 2.0 ®
THE GREATEST HERO
BLACK POWER

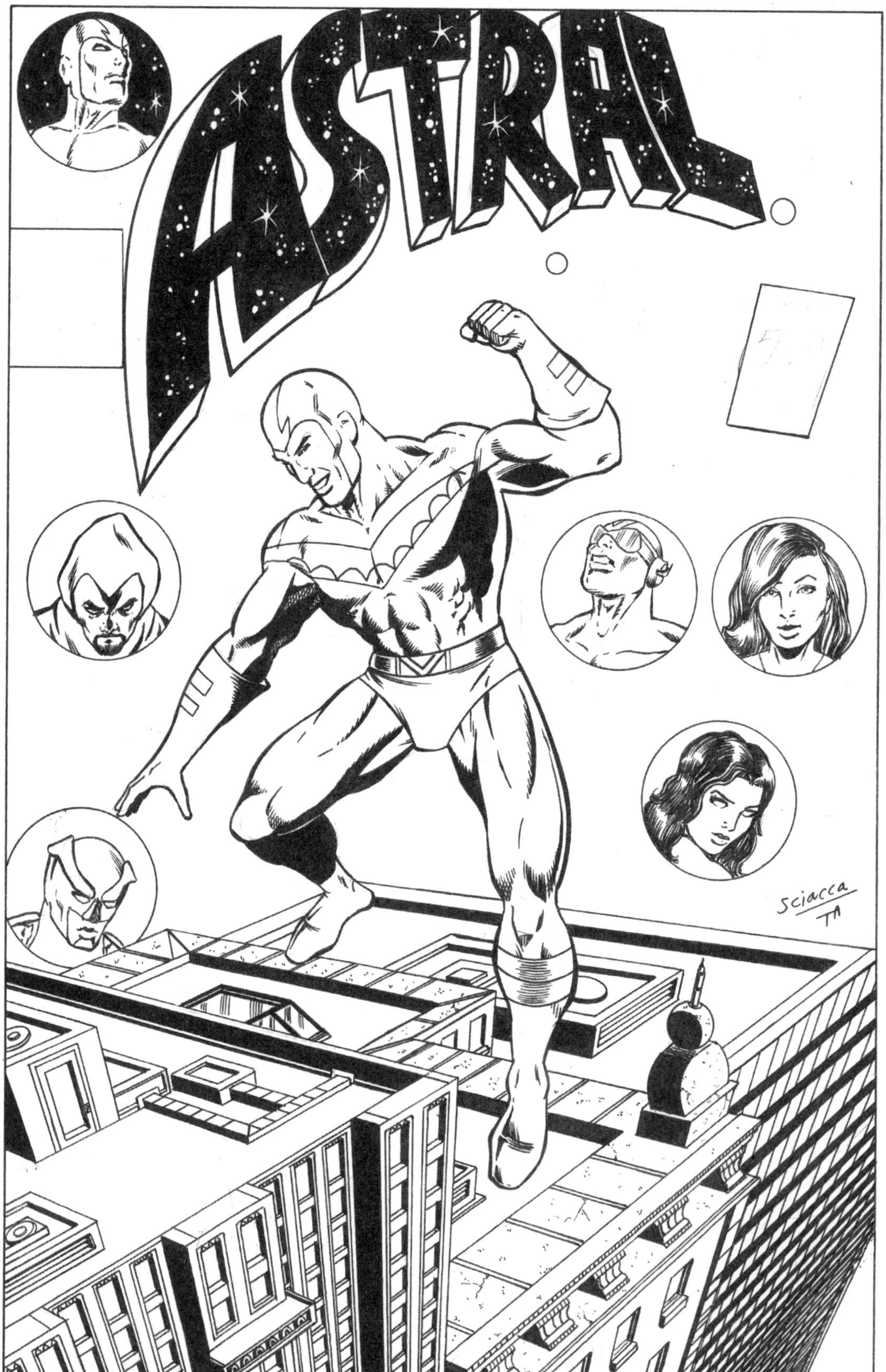
ASTRAL
sciacca
TM

The original concept pages drawn by Tom Sciacca for what was then called *Bronx Heroes Special: The Siberian Candidate,* later renamed *Bronx Heroes in Trumpland.*

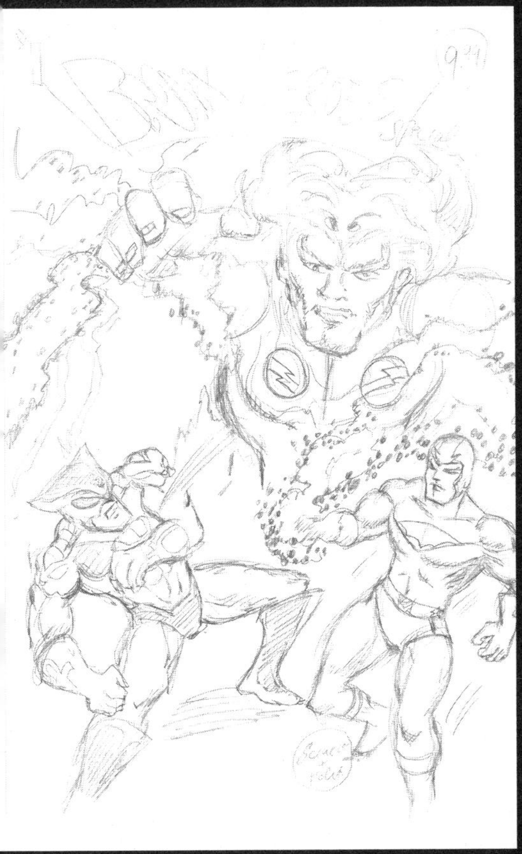

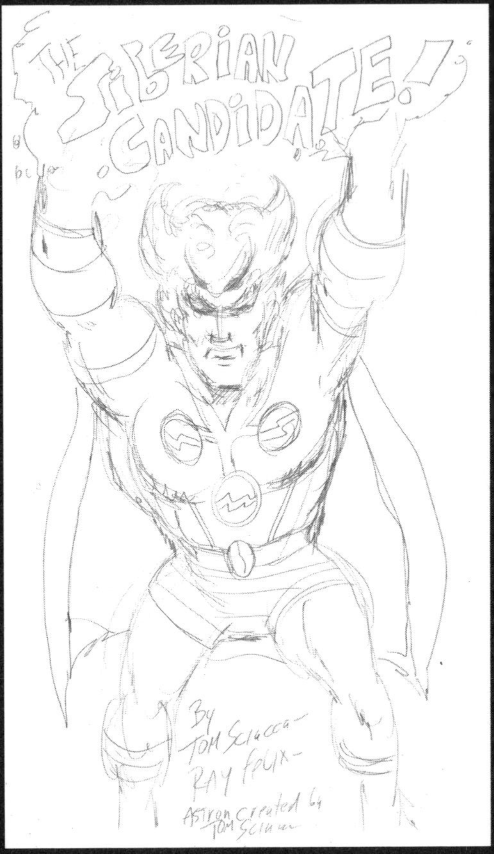
THE SIBERIAN CANDIDATE!
By TOM SCIACCA RAY FELIX
ASTRON created by TOM SCIACCA

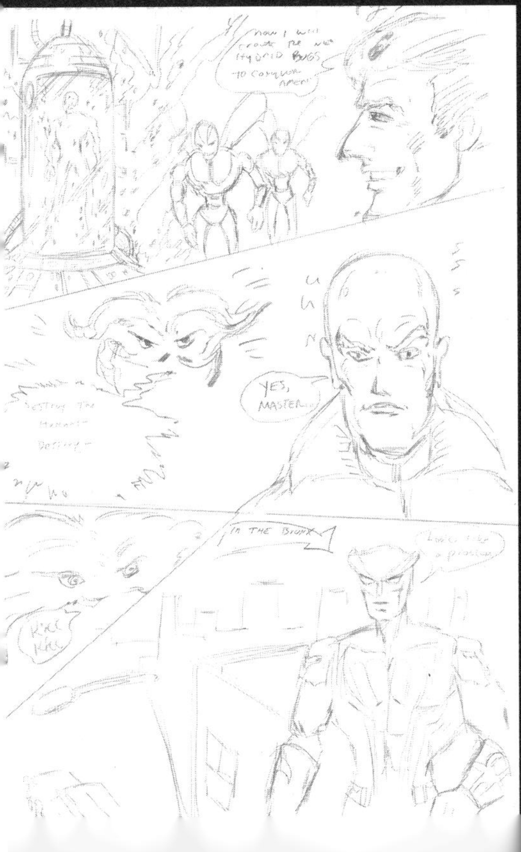
YES, MASTER...
IN THE BRONX

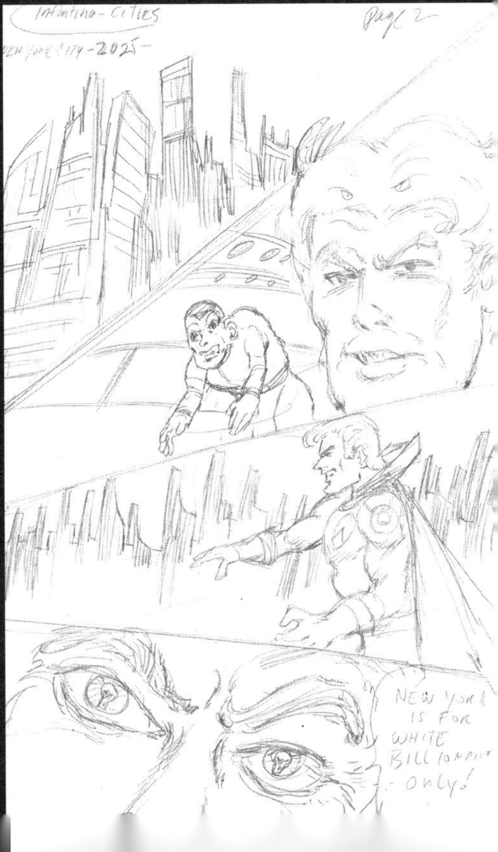
NEW YORK IS FOR WHITE BILLIONAIRES ONLY!

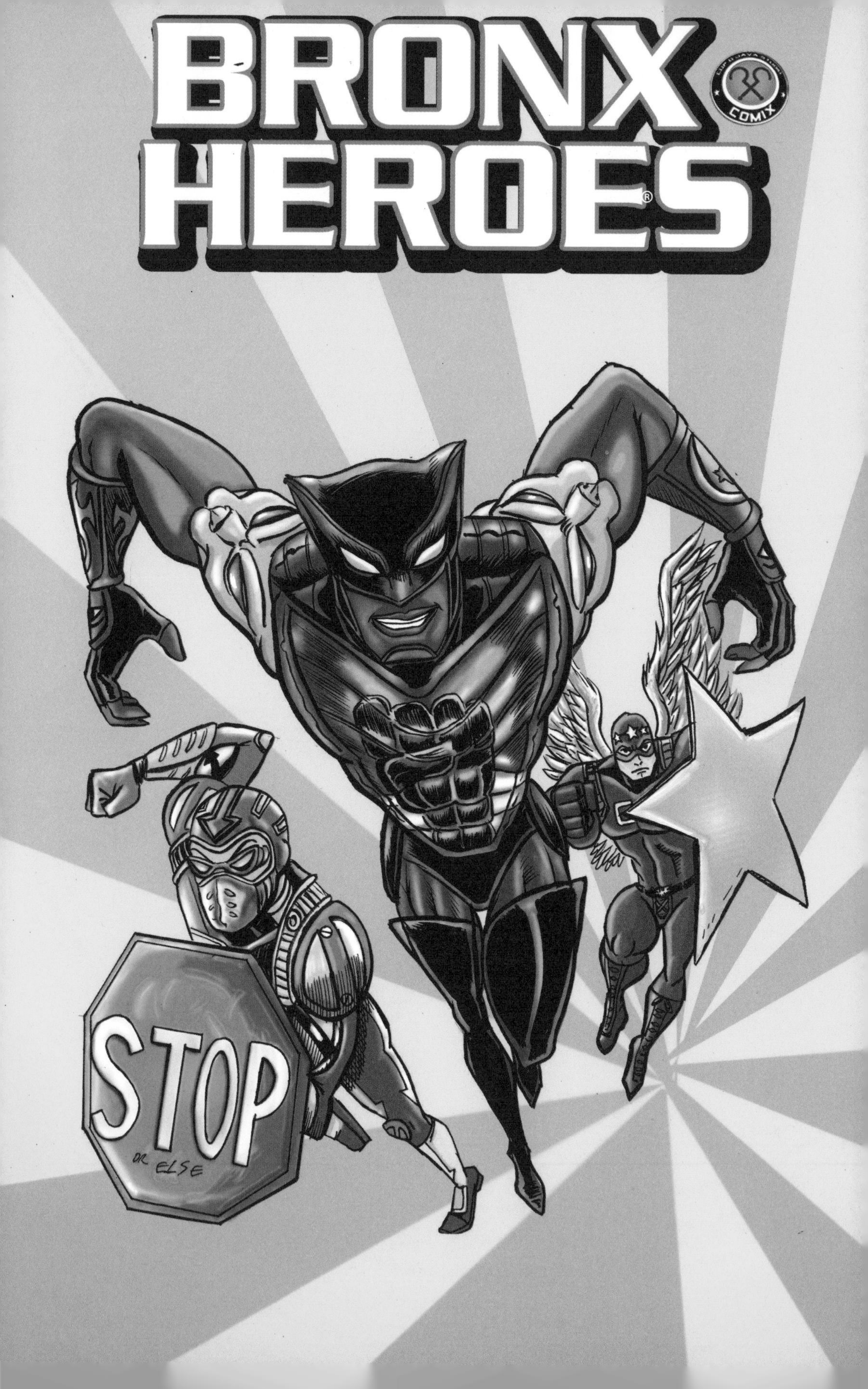
BRONX HEROES®
COMIX
STOP
OR ELSE

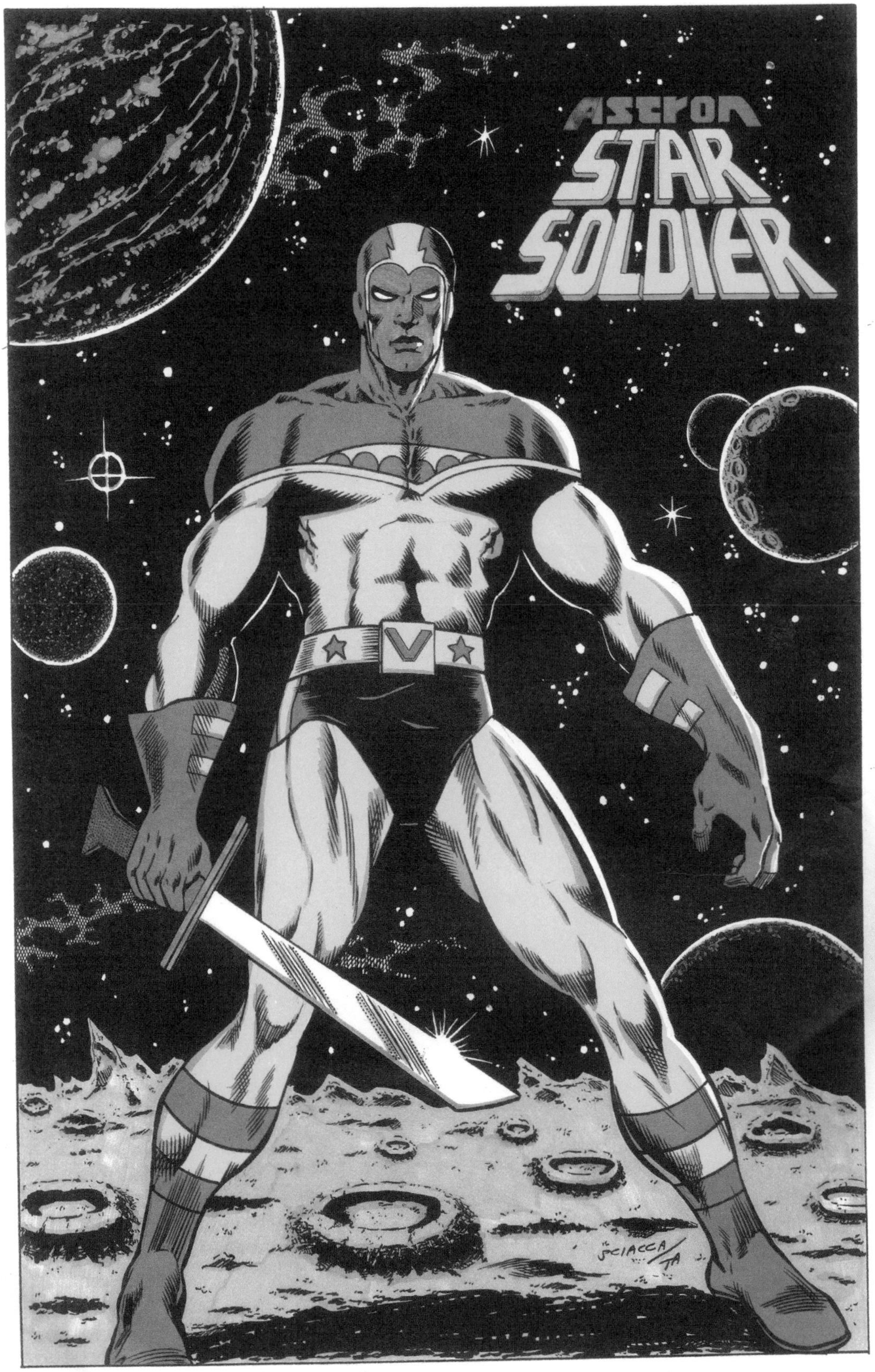
ASTRON
STAR SOLDIER
SCIACCA/TA

pin up pg 40

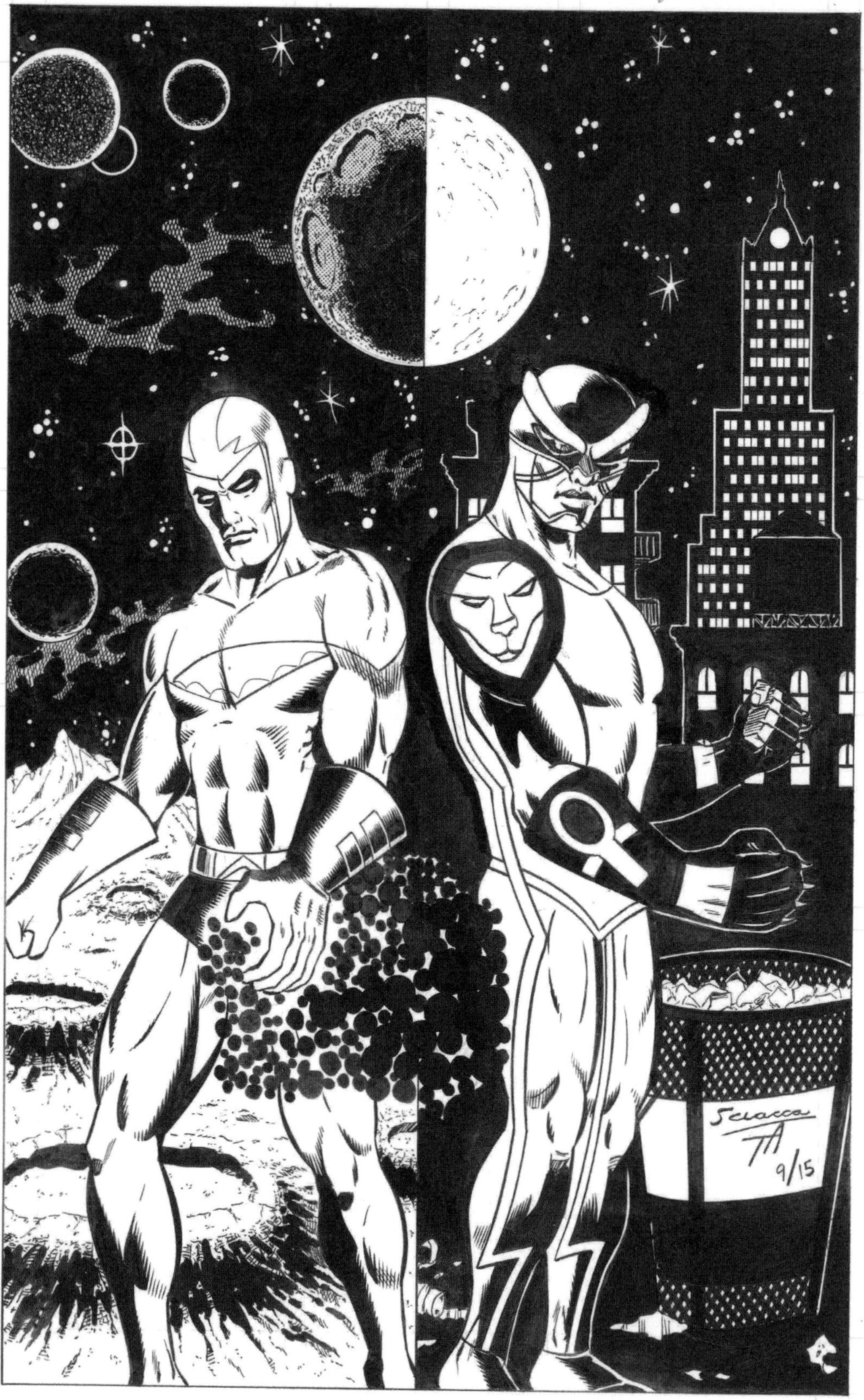
Sciacca
TA
9/15

What will Happen NEXT?

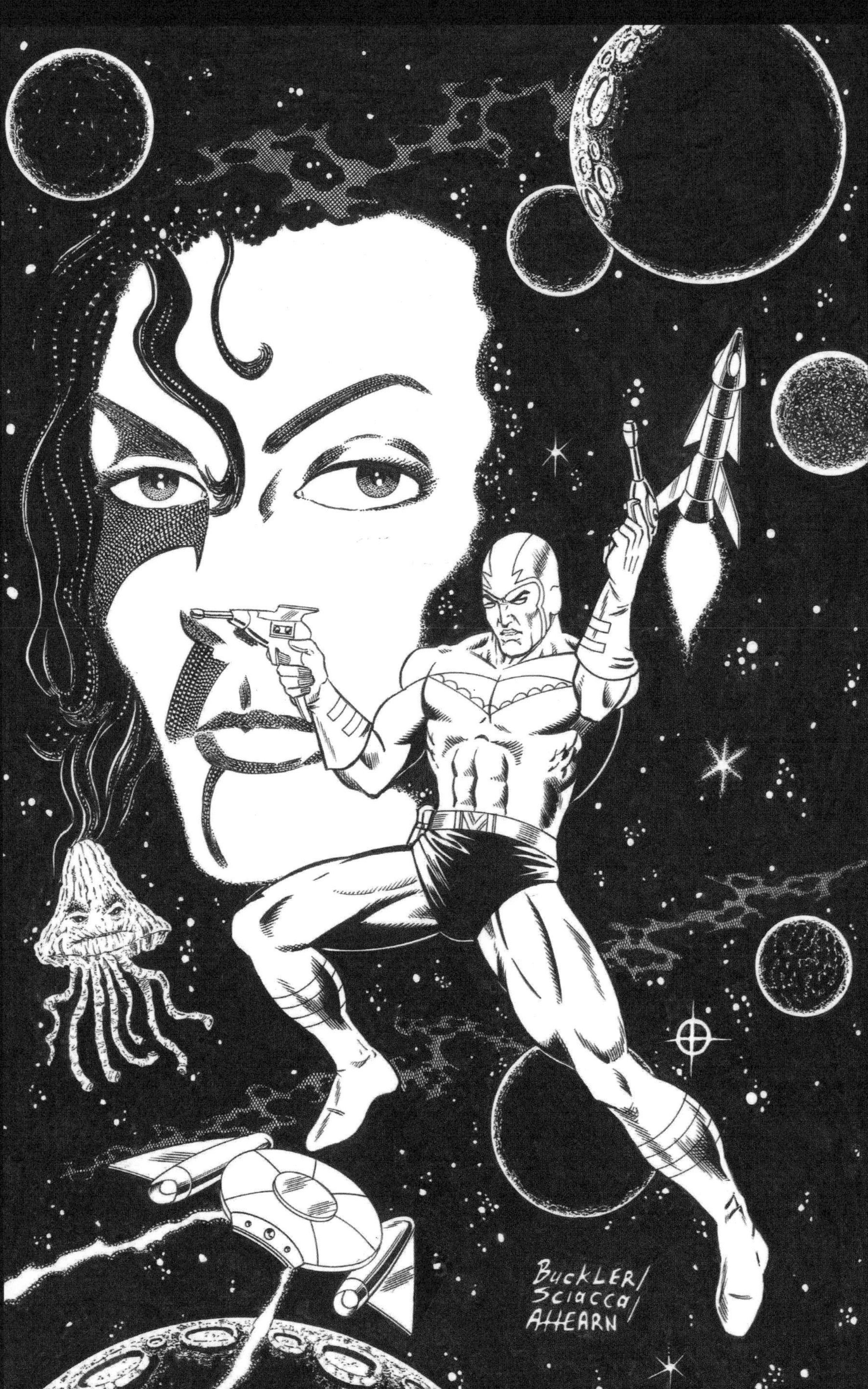
BUCKLER/
Sciacca/
AHEARN

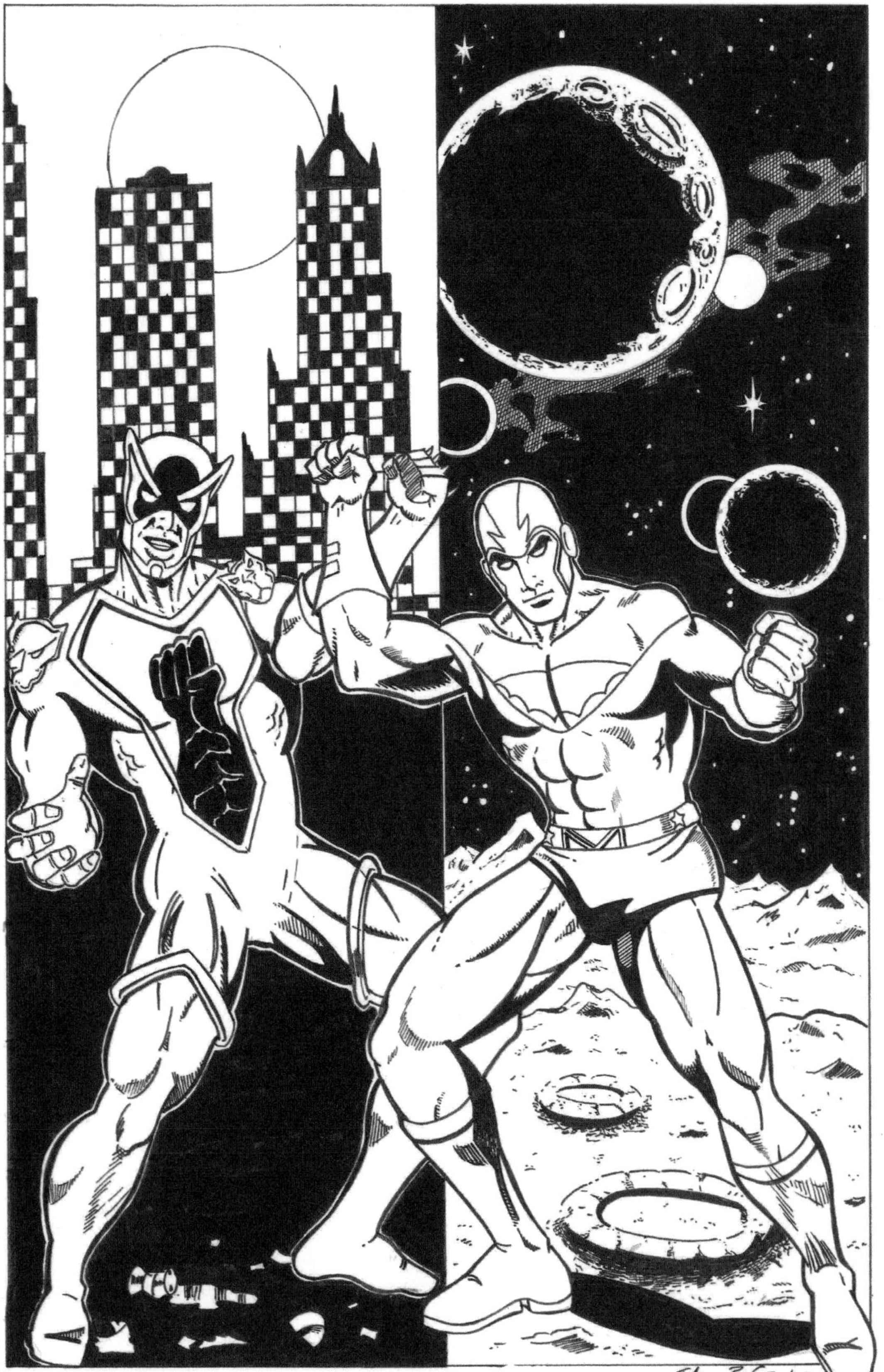
P.A. B.S. '18

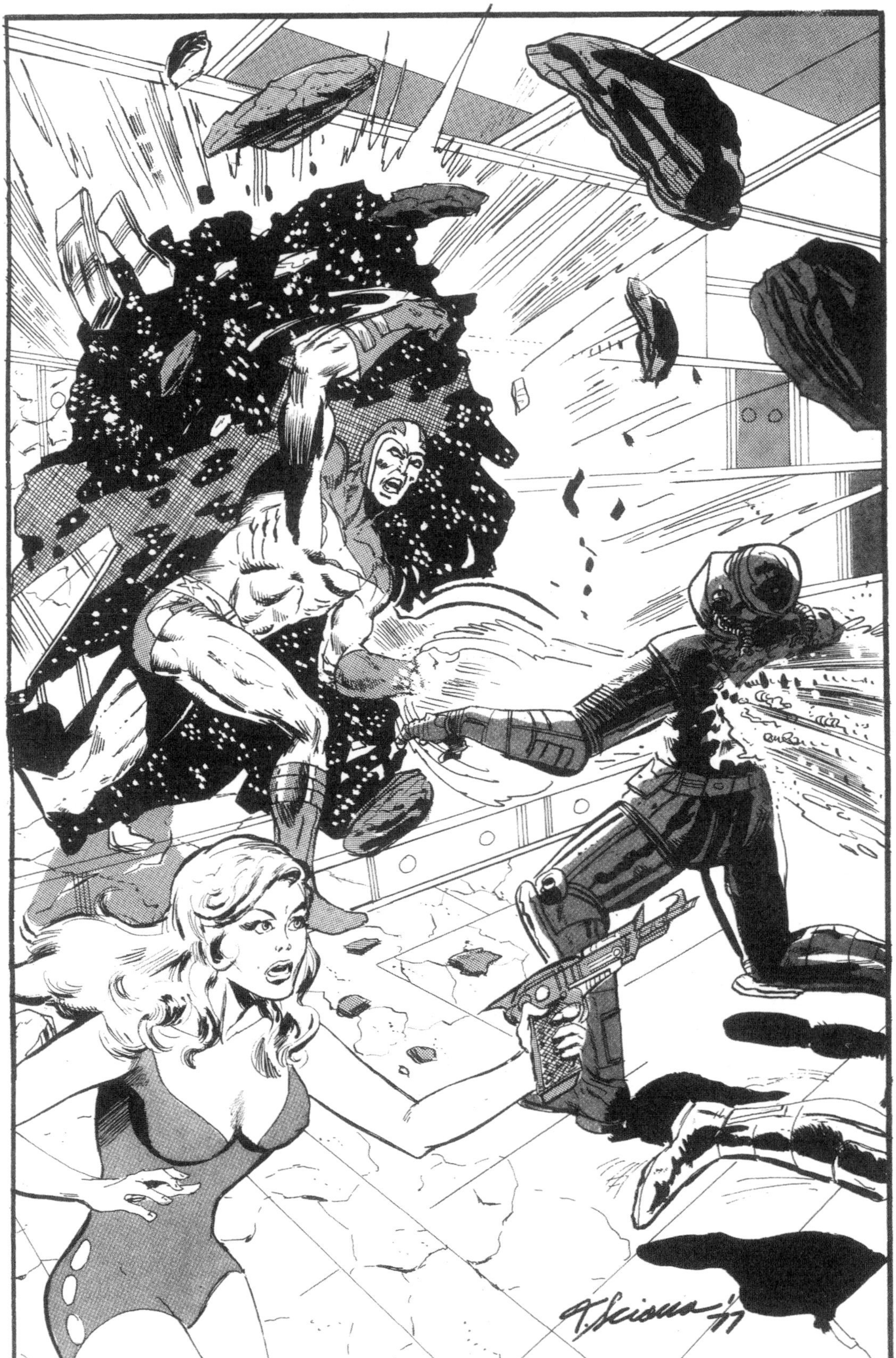

[redacted]
At some point the page was lost during the production of this book, only to be rediscovered just before the book's completion.

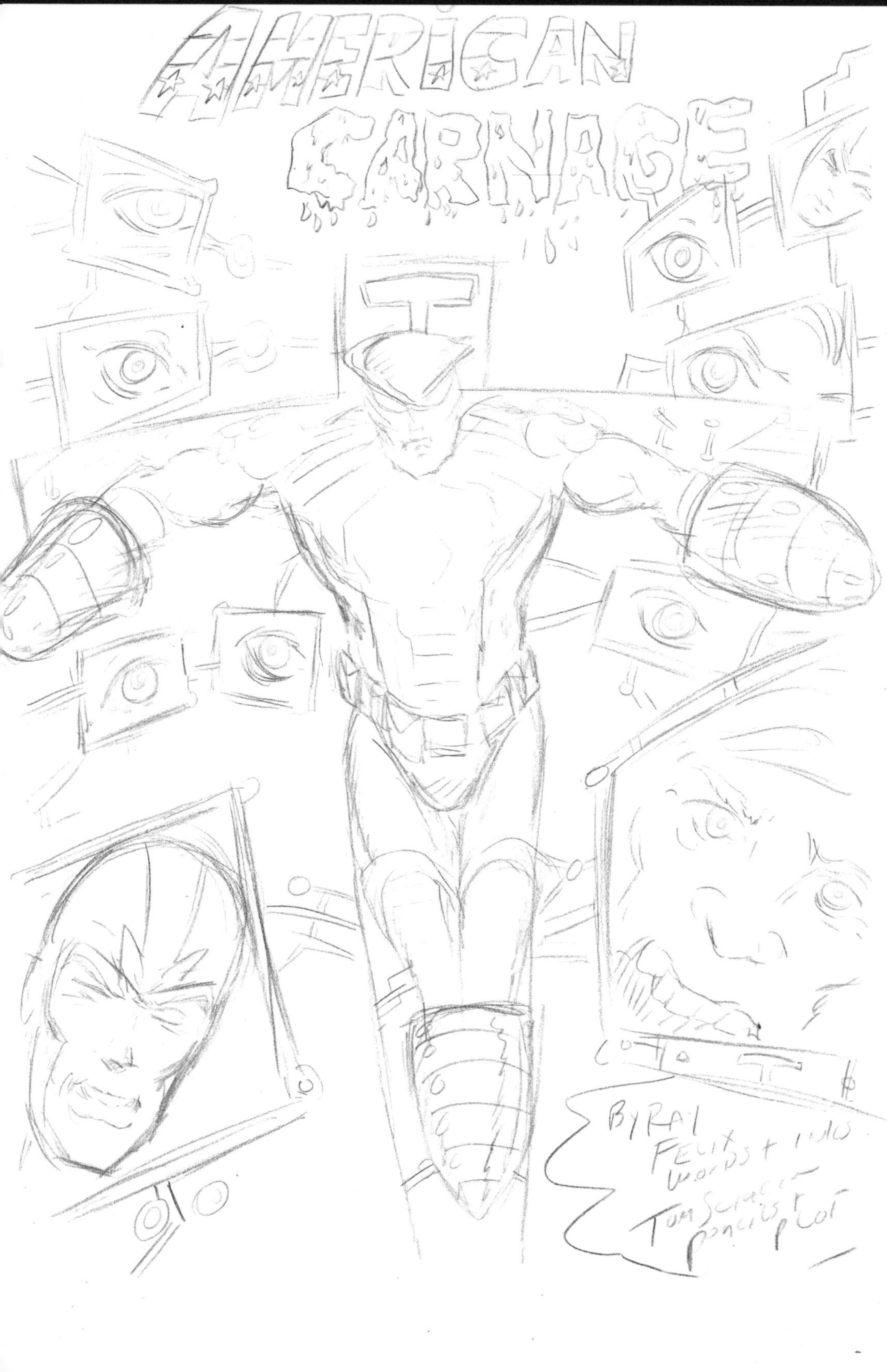
AMERICAN
CARNAGE

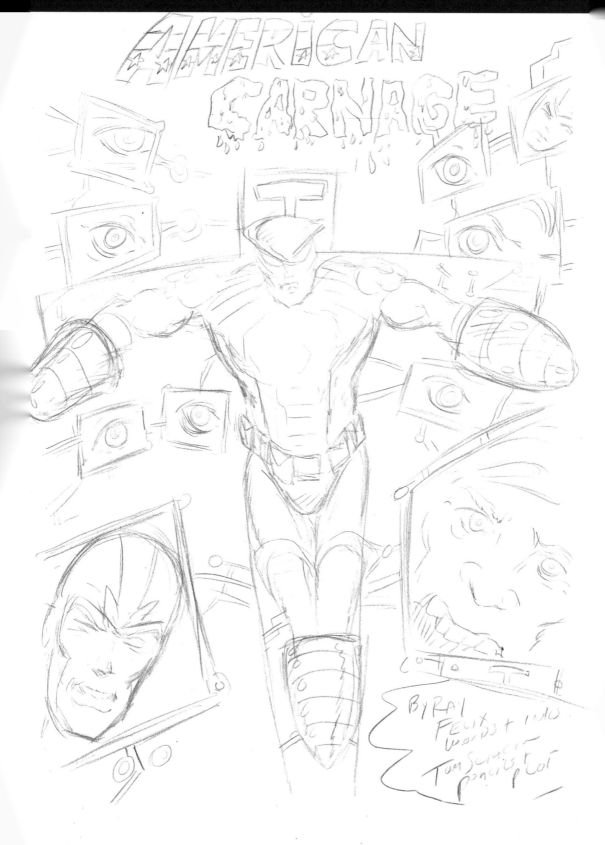

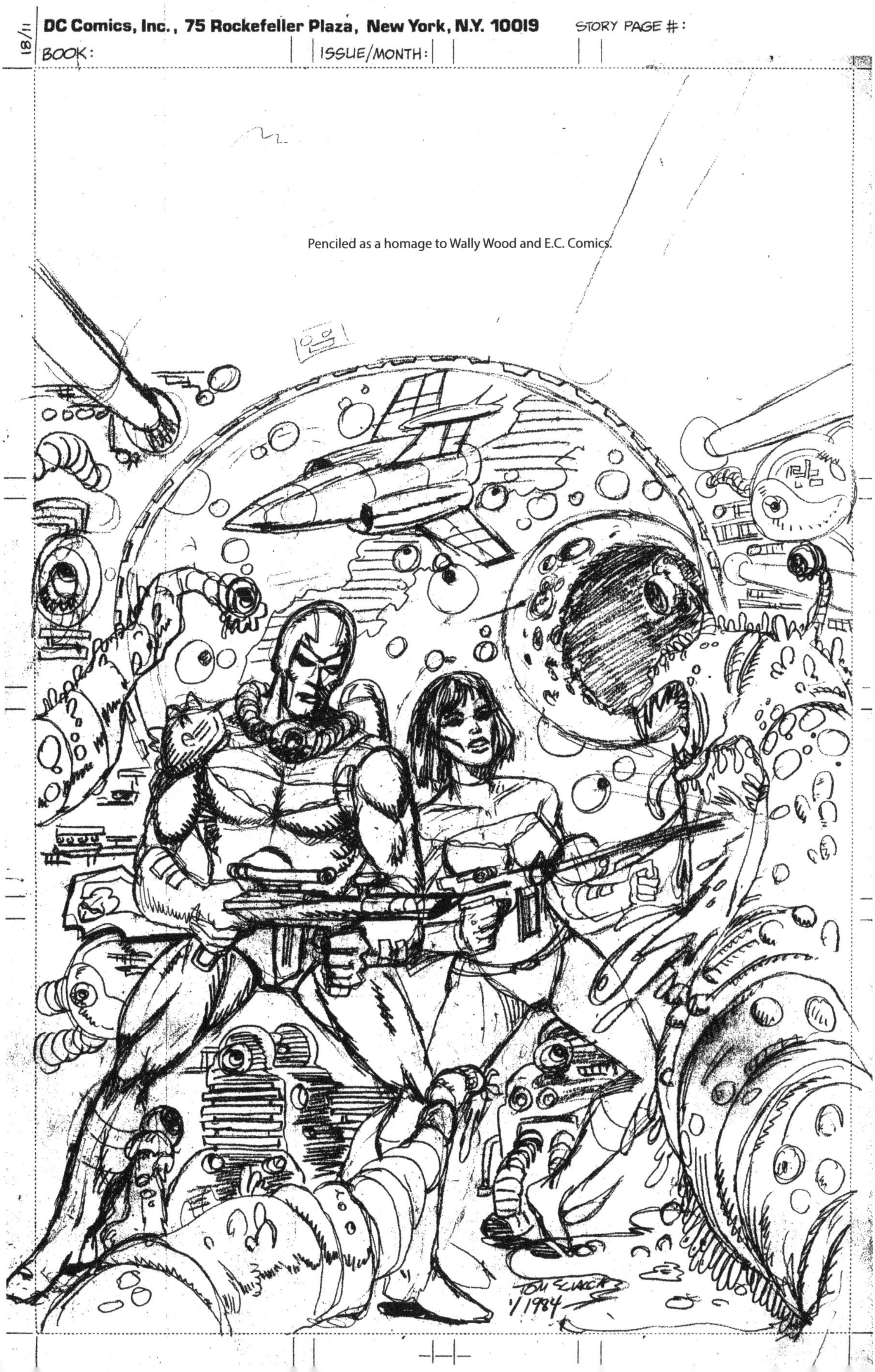
18/11
DC Comics, Inc., 75 Rockefeller Plaza, New York, N.Y. 10019
STORY PAGE #:
BOOK:
ISSUE/MONTH:
TOM SCIACCA
1/1984

Penciled as a homage to Wally Wood and E.C. Comics.

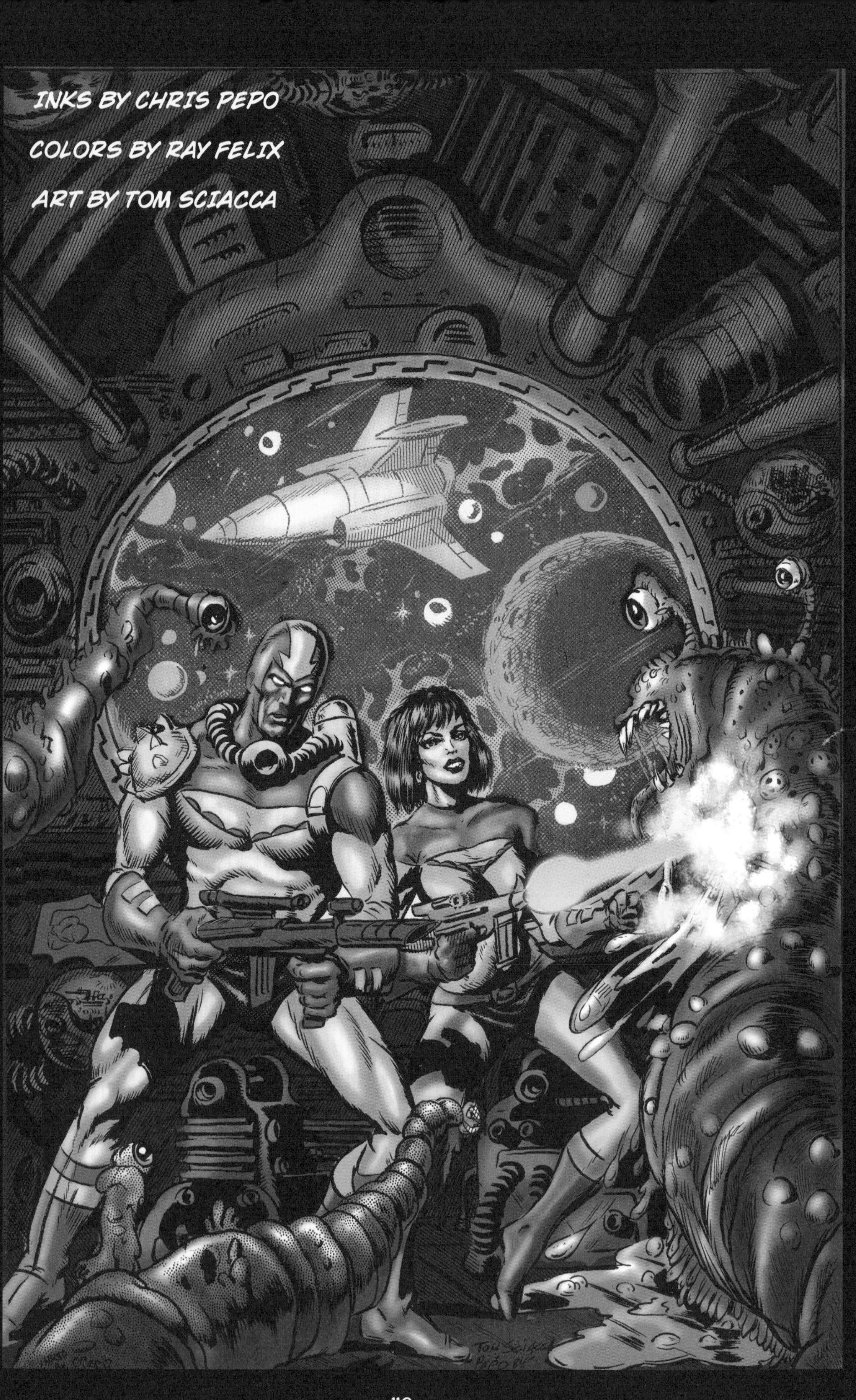
INKS BY CHRIS PEPO
COLORS BY RAY FELIX
ART BY TOM SCIACCA

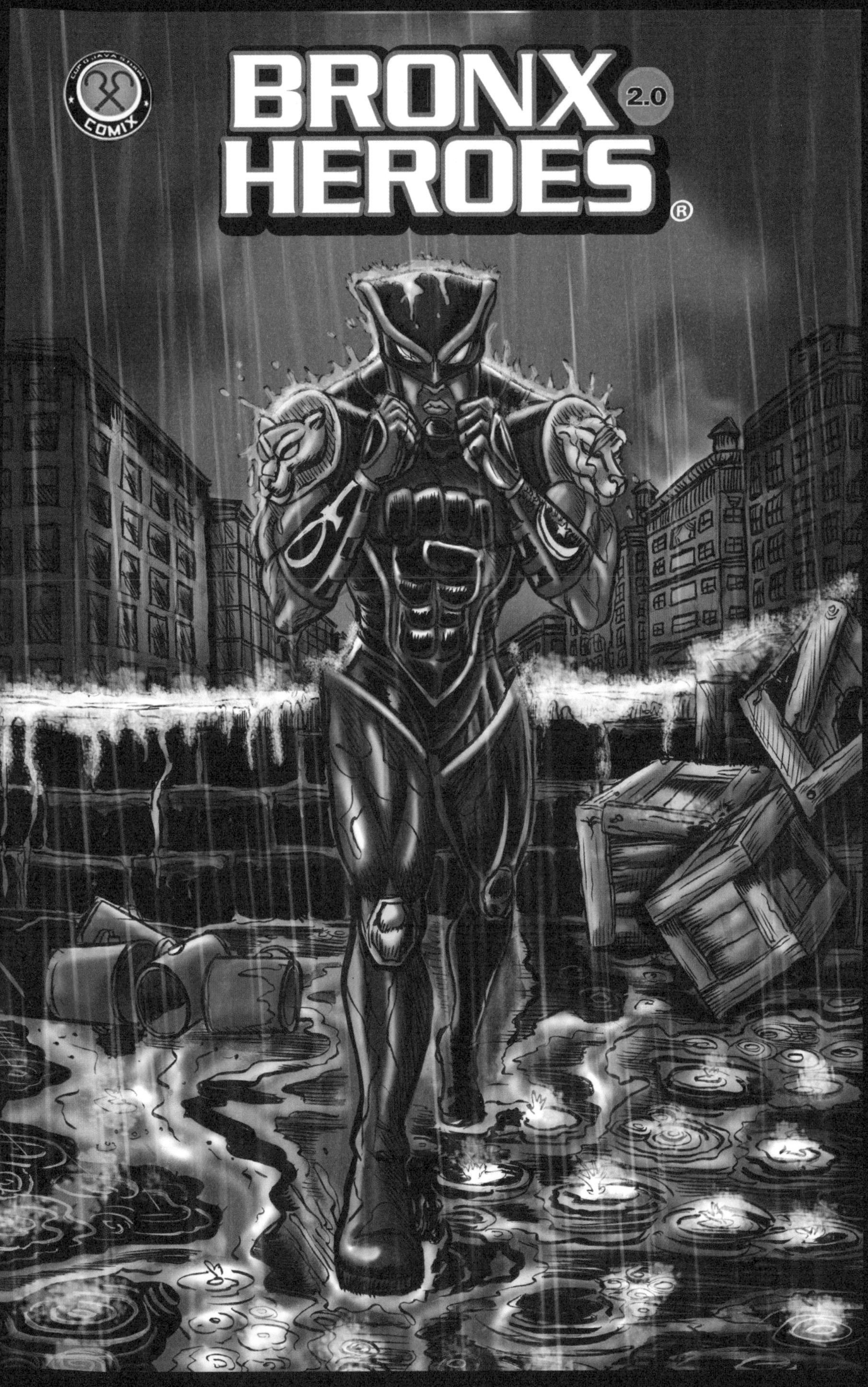
BRONX HEROES
2.0
COMIX

Photo by Frank Contreras

RAY FELIX is a Bronx native born in 1973. His comics include *Bronx Heroes 1.0: Runaway Slave*; *Bronx Heroes 2.0: The Greatest Hero Black Power*; *Heavy Traffic*; *Enter: The Roach*; and *A World without Superheroes*. Ray is also the founder of the community-based organization Bronx Heroes Comic Con and cofounder of Women in Comics Con, both of which promote literacy and education through reading and creating comics. He has been the recipient of numerous awards and grants, including those from New York State Council on the Arts in 2011–2016, the National Endowment for the Arts and Bloomberg Philanthropies. He was also awarded a Citation of Merit from the Borough of the Bronx for his community-based work and teaching at-risk LGBTQ youth.

Photo by Momo Felix

TOM SCIACCA is a Bronx-born artist, writer, journalist and filmmaker. In high school, he met future Marvel superstar George Pérez, and the two bonded over their mutual love of comics. The duo started working on various fanzines in the 1970s and, in 1974, finally broke into Marvel Comics, where Tom worked as assistant to Stan Lee. He was later assistant to Vince Colletta, art director at DC Comics, where Tom worked on projects such as the 1978 film *Superman* and the comic book *Superman vs. Muhammad Ali*. Tom was also one of the first indie comic publishers, in the 1970s and early '80s with Astral Comics, which he recently revived with Ray Felix as art director.

Photo by Tom Sciacca

TOM AHEARN is an inker, artist and tattoo designer, who worked for years with Golden and Silver Age inker Sal Trapani on such classics at Marvel as *The Defenders*, *Master of Kung Fu*, *The Incredible Hulk* and *Howard the Duck*, and at DC, *Green Lantern* and the *Superman* newspaper strip, among many others. Tom is working on the new Heavy Traffic book and the upcoming Astron Star Soldier graphic novel.